Word for WINDOWS 95 FOR BUSY PEOPLE

Christian Crumlish

Osborne/**McGraw-Hill**

Berkeley / New York / St. Louis / San Francisco / Auckland / Bogotá
Hamburg / London / Madrid / Mexico City / Milan / Montreal / New Delhi
Panama City / Paris / São Paulo / Singapore / Sydney / Tokyo / Toronto

Osborne/**McGraw-Hill**
2600 Tenth Street
Berkeley, California 94710
U.S.A.

For information on translations or book distributors outside the U.S.A., or to arrange bulk purchase discounts for sales promotions, premiums, or fundraisers, please contact Osborne/**McGraw-Hill** at the above address.

Word for Windows 95 For Busy People

1234567890 DOC 99876

ISBN 0-07-882109-6

Publisher: Lawrence Levitsky
Acquisitions Editor: Joanne Cuthbertson
Project Editor: Janet Walden
Copy Editor: Katherine A. Krause
Proofreader: Stefany Otis
Indexer: David Heiret
Graphic Artist: Marla J. Shelasky
Computer Designers: Roberta Steele, Leslee Bassin
Quality Control: Joe Scuderi
Series and Cover Design: Ted Mader Associates
Series Illustration: Daniel Barbeau

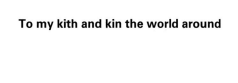

To my kith and kin the world around

About the Author...

Christian Crumlish is a writer of computer books, stories, and hyperfiction. He is the author of *The Internet for Busy People, A Guided Tour of the Internet, and The Internet Dictionary.* He is the publisher of *Enterzone*, a multimedia magazine on the World Wide Web. When he can find the time, he also paints in acrylics and visits New Orleans to hear the jazz.

Contents at a glance

Contents

ACKNOWLEDGMENTS

Never have I worked on a book project with such an amazing level of cooperation, sympathy, and communication. Larry Levitsky painted me a picture of a book for busy people, a book you could read in an evening, a book with the spirit of that famous New York radio station, 1010 WINS, whose motto—"Give us 22 minutes, we'll give you the world"—says it all. Joanne Cuthbertson recruited me and fellow series author Ron Mansfield and gave us unprecedented guidance in the early thematic, conceptual design stages of the books. Without her continuing insight and influence, these books could never have been made.

Right down the line, the Osborne team pulled out all the stops for this book and I'm heartily grateful (executive editor Scott Rogers, marketing director Kendal Andersen, and acquisitions assistant Heidi Poulin, thank you!). Before I had written a word (well, maybe a sample chapter or two), Ted Mader's witty sophisticated design, built around Dan Barbeau's frazzled, contemporary people-oids, set the tone for the project and kept my mind on you, the kind of person who needs a book like this.

As anyone who's ever been around a publishing house can tell you, it's one thing to plan a beautiful design but it's another thing entirely, an aesthetic and architectural challenge, to actually implement a design and make it look as good—or better—than the sample pages. The art and production team, headed by Marla Shelasky and including Roberta Steele, Leslee Bassin, Lance Ravella, Peter H. Hancik, Richard Whitaker, and quality control specialist Joe Scuderi, has raised my standards for design, layout, and typesetting.

I felt that my words had the full attention of technical editor Heidi Steele who fell quite gracefully into the style and feel I was shooting for, but held my feet to the fire when my explanations were overly glib or underly articulate, shall we say? Long after she was off the hook, she was calling me up with afterthoughts, sudden insights, break-throughs—all of which helped make this book what it is.

Copyeditor Kathy Krause gave my manuscript the kind of thorough, skeptical eye a book this full of facts and assertions really needs. Her expert knowledge of Microsoft Word proved invaluable. In a sense, both my technical editor and my copyeditor did each other's jobs in addition to their own. Thanks!

Janet Walden, my project editor, held it all together. With her editorial pen layered along with the other editors I felt like the most pampered author in town (aside from the nearly impossible writing schedule). Without knowing I had someone like Janet to lean on, to make sure that all the t's got crossed and the i's got dotted, I probably could not have finished this book, as I wouldn't have been able to relax about the final details and just write.

Thanks to the little elves at Microsoft for writing software that needs some help explaining. Thanks to Briggs and all my friends who cheered me through another seemingly impossible ordeal. Thanks to my family for their love and patience.

INTRODUCTION

When Osborne/McGraw-Hill publisher Larry Levitsky described to me his idea for a new computer book series "for busy people," I knew he was onto something. As I started working on this book, it seemed like every day I was hearing some friend or acquaintance talk about how busy they'd become, how their jobs had mushroomed into sprawling layers of responsibility, how they had almost no time for anything. If I had any doubts (and my own hectic schedule was enough to convince me), I was sure that there must be many people out there with only a night or a few lunch hours to learn the new version of Word. The "digital revolution" has given with one hand, creating all kinds of efficiencies and organizational wizardry, and taken away with the other, accelerating everyone's expectations, constantly moving the goalposts. For many, life has become a treadmill with someone quickening the pace each day. How often do people say to you "Fax me that draft," or "e-mail me those statistics," or "our product release deadline's been moved up due to competitive pressures," or "it took longer than we thought—can you make up the time at your end?"

To help you meet your needs, my editor, Joanne Cuthbertson, demanded opinionated, thoughtfully organized writing with a touch of skepticism about the bounties of word processing. This is the Word book I've been dying to write for years, so it was a perfect match.

I KNOW YOU'RE IN A HURRY, SO...

If you're sitting there with an as yet uninstalled copy of Word, start off by flipping to Appendix A, where you'll be taken effortlessly through the installation process. If someone has mercifully set up Word for you already, you need not know the appendix is there. Also, if you're just getting into Windows for the first time, or if you've used Windows 3.whatever, then you may want a little hand-holding or a brush-up. Appendix B will get you over the Win 95 threshold so you can take full advantage of operating system this version of Word was written for.

So, let's agree to dispense with the traditional computer book preliminaries. You've probably used a mouse, held down two keys at once, and know (or choose not to know) the history of Microsoft. So, we'll cut to the chase. After reading the first few chapters, you'll be able to:

- Create a simple document in Word
- Format your document
- Reuse your work whenever possible, and
- Produce a simple report

Later chapters will show you how to convert other people's documents, find missing files, create forms, send out mass mailings, create your own World Wide Web page, and more. As long as you've picked up the basics of Word (and you can pick them up in the first few chapters if you need to), you shouldn't have to work your way through the book chapter by chapter. You'll also be able to skim through the book, reading only the parts you need now. Remember: just because you *can* do something with Word doesn't mean that you *should*. Simple is often best, particularly when you are busy. I'll try to remind you of that from time-to-time.

HOW WORD FOR WINDOWS 95 DIFFERS FROM EARLIER VERSIONS

Word is "Windows 95 Smart," taking advantage of the new interface and features such as the ability to handle long filenames, shortcut menus that pop up when you right-click with the mouse, and easier file management and searching. There are also a host of new automatic and interactive features, such as the Tip Wizard, and AutoCorrect and AutoFormat, which help spruce up and correct your documents while you work on them.

For example, the new spelling checker checks *as you type*—if you misspell something, a squiggly red line appears beneath the word. If you see the error, you can retype the word to eliminate the squiggly reminder. Right-clicking on the word brings up a list of suggested spellings. If you don't want to fix your typos as you go, you can wait until you've finished with the document and the spelling checker will compile a list of misspelled words for you to review at the end.

There are also some cool automatic formatting tools, For example, if you start typing a numbered or bulleted list, Word will figure out what you're doing, and when you hit ENTER it will insert the correct number, bullet, or indentation for you.

Finally, seamless OLE (object linking and embedding) allows you to insert material created in other Windows programs into your Word document, and keep a live link so that changes to the source material will be reflected in the document.

THINGS YOU MIGHT WANT TO KNOW ABOUT THIS BOOK

You can read this book more or less in any order. I suggest cruising Chapter 1 and reading Chapter 2 first, but you'll be fine no matter how you go. Use the book as a reference. When you're stuck, not sure how to do something, know there's an answer but not what it is, pick up the book, zero in on the answer to your question, and put the book down again. Besides the clear, coherent explanations of this all-over-the-map program, you'll also find some special elements to help you get the most out of Word. Here's a quick rundown of the other elements in this book.

Fast Forwards

Each chapter begins with a section called *Fast Forward*. Fast Forwards are, in effect, a book within a book—a built-in quick reference guide, summarizing the key tasks explained in each chapter. If you're a fast learner, or somewhat experienced, this may be the only material you need. Written step-by-step, point-by-point, there are also page references to guide you to the more complete information later in the chapter.

Habits & Strategies

Habits & Strategies suggest time-saving tips, techniques, and worthwhile addictions. (Look for the man at the chessboard.) Force yourself to develop some good habits now, when it's still possible! These notes also give you the big picture and help you plan ahead. From time to time, for example, I'll suggest that you save your document before performing some magical automatic transformation that you might live to regret.

Shortcuts

Shortcuts are designed for the busy person—when there's a way to do something that may not be as full-featured as the material in the text, but is *faster*, it will show up in the margin, below the businessman leaping over a fence.

Cautions

Sometimes it's too easy to plunge ahead and fall down a rabbit hole, resulting in hours of extra work just to get you back to where you were before you went astray. This hard hat will warn you before you commit time-consuming mistakes.

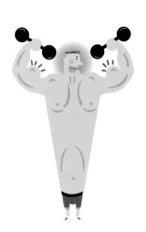

Definitions

Usually, I'll explain computer or word processing jargon in the text, wherever the technobabble first occurs. But if you encounter words you don't recognize, look for this body builder in the margin. *Definitions* point out important terms you reasonably might not know the meaning of. When necessary, they're strict and a little technical, but most of the time they're informal and conversational.

Step by Step

To help clarify some of the more complicated procedures, blue *Step by Step* boxes will walk you through the necessary steps, using helpful screenshots from the program.

Upgrade Notes

If you've used early versions of Word for Windows, such as 2.0 or 6.0, then be on the look-out for *Upgrade notes*. They will tell you when something has changed and make sure you don't miss any of the latest advances.

Throughout the book, cross-references and other minor asides appear in the margins.

LET'S DO IT!

Ready? Let's dig into Word for Windows 95 before Win 97 arrives!

Incidentally, I'm always happy to hear your reactions to this or any of my other books. You can reach me through the publisher or on the Net (*xian@pobox.com*).

CHAPTER 1

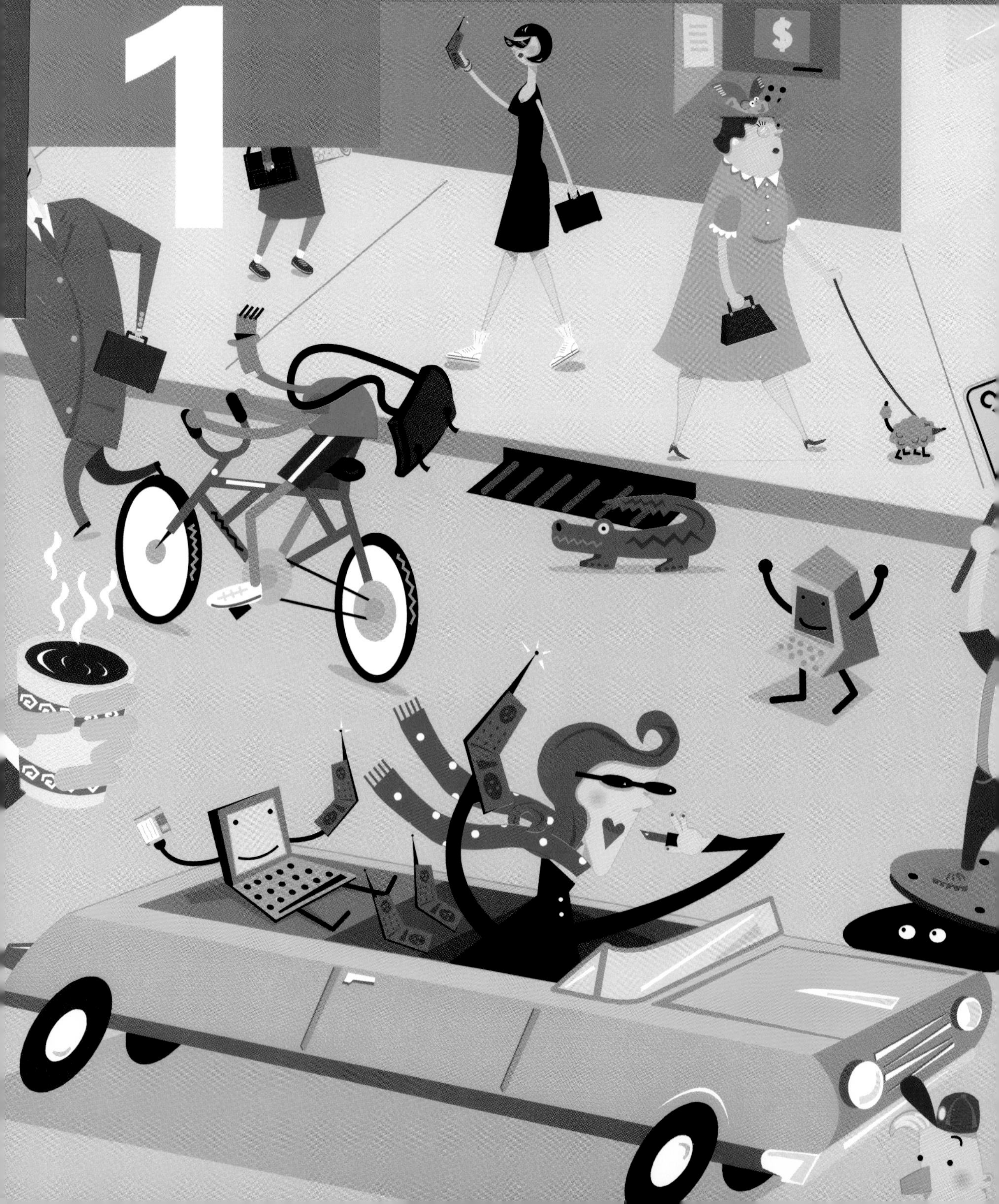

What Every Word User Needs to Know

FAST FORWARD

Herbert Stencil. I will, however, be
ctly about less pressing matters.

of Your Time in the Office.

e direct all questions during
mail every day, so feel free

START WORD ➤ *pp 4-5*

1. Click on the Start button.
2. Point to Programs.
3. Click on Microsoft Word.

TYPE A PARAGRAPH ➤ *pp 6-7*

- Let Word handle the line breaks
- Type only one space after each sentence
- Press ENTER only when you get to the end of a
  paragraph

DEAL WITH A SPELLING SUGGESTION ➤ *p 8*

1. Right-click on any word underlined with a red squiggle.
2. Make one of four choices:
- If the word is correct as is, click on Add on the menu
  that pops up.
- If the word is spelled incorrectly and the pop-up manu
  offers the correct spelling as one of the choices,
  choose the correct spelling.
- For unusual words that are spelled correctly but that you
  don't want to add to your dictionary, simply choose
  Ignore All. That word will not be queried for the rest of
  your Word session.
- If Word doesn't suggest the correct spelling but you
  know what it is, just retype the word yourself.

ERASE A CHARACTER ➤ *pp 9-10*

- To the left of the insertion point, press Backspace
- To the right of the insertion point, press DELETE

of Your Time in the Office

e direct all urgent during th
mail every day, so feel free

ERASE A WORD ➤ *pp 9-10*
- To the left of the insertion point, press CTRL-DELETE
- To the right of the insertion point, press CTRL-Backspace

UNDO A MISTAKE ➤ *p 10*
Click on the Undo button on the Standard toolbar.

SAVE YOUR WORK ➤ *pp 10-12*
Click on the Save button on the Standard toolbar. If this is the first time you're saving this document:
1. Type the filename in the Save As dialog box that appears.
2. Choose where to save the document.
3. Click on Save.

PRINT A DOCUMENT ➤ *p 13*
1. Open the document if it's not already open.
2. Click on the Print button on the Standard toolbar.

EXIT WORD ➤ *p 13*
1. Click the Close button in the upper-right corner of the Word window.
2. Click on Yes to save any unsaved work, if necessary.

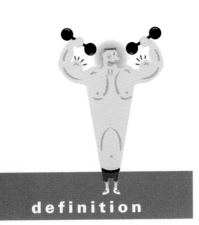

Document: A file created by a word processing program (as well as other types of programs). Any time you create anything with Word—a memo, a letter, some notes, a transcript, etc.—and save it under a filename, it's a document.

If Word for Windows 95 is not yet installed on your computer, jump now to Appendix A for basic installation instructions. Then come back here once everything's hunky dory.

If you are new to Windows 95, see Appendix B for a brief introduction.

As a busy person, you don't have a lot of time to study the niceties of whatever computer programs you have to use. You've got to be able to get the gist of them quickly and start getting work done right away. This chapter covers the things you'll do every time you use Word. If all you need to do for now is fire up Word, type a document, save it, print it, and quit, this chapter will show you how. If you already know the basics for these tasks, feel free to skip ahead to whatever chapter discusses your specific goals for today. You can always come back here if you need a refresher.

GETTING BUSY

There are a few routines that you'll follow every time you sit down at your computer to work on a writing project. As soon as you have a comfortable way of getting these things done, those steps will take up much less of your time, so the sooner we buzz through these basic routines, the better.

SKIP THIS CHAPTER IF...

You can skip this chapter if you already know how to start Word (or how to start programs in general with Windows 95), if you already know how to type words and create paragraphs, and if you already know how to correct mistakes, save, print, and exit.

Chapter 2 shows you a handful of things you can do once to customize Word and make it easier to use forever after. If you'd rather just get on with using Word the way it comes right out of the box, skip directly to Chapter 3.

STARTING WORD

Starting Word for Windows 95 is as easy as clicking on the Start button and pointing to Microsoft Word on the Programs submenu.

(If you don't have a Microsoft Word option on your Programs menu, read down the menu to see if there's a Microsoft Office submenu or another option that might lead to Word. If you still can't find it, go get whoever installed Word for you and make them show you where it is!) You also can make a shortcut (an icon on your desktop) for Word or add Word to the main Start menu. For more on these two options, see Chapter 2.

When Word starts, it comes up with a blank document. If the Word window does not fill up the whole screen, click on the Maximize button:

TAKING A LOOK AROUND

Let's take a look at the basic Word screen (see Figure 1.1). You can see the normal elements typical of every program that runs under Windows 95 on the screen, such as the Taskbar at the bottom of the screen and the title bar and menu bar at the top. In addition, you'll see many specific Word elements, which are there either to give you information or to make certain procedures automatic.

- The Standard and Formatting toolbars help you create, edit, and format your documents.
- The Tip Wizard volunteers information and advice about Word.
- The Ruler helps you set margins and indents.
- The typing area is where you do (and see) all your work. The more room you have there the better.
- The insertion point shows you where the next character you type will appear.

habits & strategies

To reopen a Word document you worked on recently, select Start / Documents and choose the document from the menu that pops up. You can also click on the My Computer icon, work your way through the folders, and double-click on the Word icon next to the name of your document.

- The end-of-document marker marks (surprise!) the end of the document. It moves down as you type.
- The I-beam pointer can be used to move the insertion point and make selections.
- The scroll bars, as in all Windows programs, enable you to get to parts of the document that are temporarily off the screen.
- The status bar tells you useful information about your document, such as what page you're on or whether you're in Insert or Overtype mode (more on this in Chapter 2).

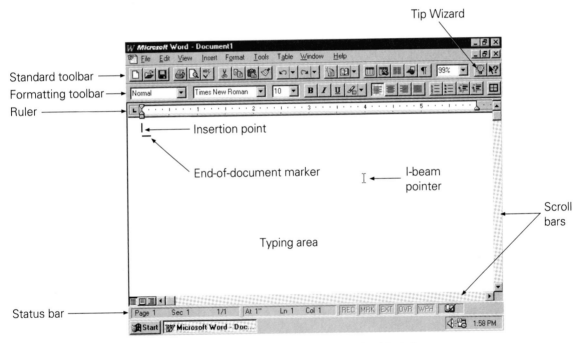

Figure 1.1 The Word for Windows 95 screen with a blank document

THAT'S NOT WRITING— THAT'S TYPING

The crux of the matter, of course, is typing. The whole purpose of having a program such as Word on your computer is to make it possible and, ideally, easy for you to type and print documents. You have probably typed before, so there most likely won't be any surprises here for you.

Word's AutoFormat as You Type automatically changes a typed tab at the beginning of a paragraph into a first-line indent.

While typing, don't press ENTER when you get near the end of a line (as you would with a typewriter). Let Word handle the line breaks for you. That way, when you make changes, you won't have to redo the line breaks yourself. Similarly, don't line up columns of text by inserting spaces. Instead, use tabs, tables, or columns, depending on the text involved. Some people go so far as to eschew typing a tab at the beginning of each paragraph—they use the indent markers on the Ruler to create first-line indents—but that's probably a little hard-core computery for most people. Oh, one other difference from old typewriter-based touch-typing is that you don't add two spaces after the end of a sentence.

Type up the beginning of a short sample memo (if you want to follow along):

To:	All Staff
From:	Debussy Fields
Date:	June 3, 1996
Re:	My schedule

Press TAB after each colon and press ENTER at the end of each line. Press ENTER again to add a blank line (see Figure 1.2).

habits & strategies

One of the most important rules of thumb in word processing is that you shouldn't do anything that the computer can do for you. This is not simply to make your life easier, but also because the computer can often do a better job of keeping things consistent.

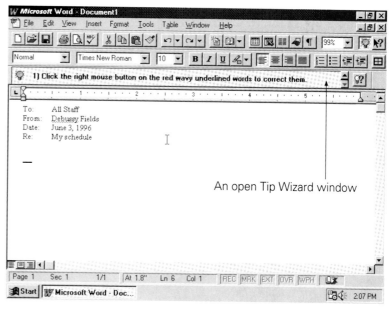

An open Tip Wizard window

Figure 1.2 The beginning of a memo, showing items lined up with tabs

Background Spell Checking

What's that squiggly red line under the name "Debussy"? you might be wondering. It indicates a word that Word's new automatic background spell checking does not recognize.

In Chapter 2, I'll show you how to turn off background spell checking when you don't want to deal with it.

You may regard background spell checking as a godsend or as a royal pain. When you're in a hurry and you don't have time for a conventional spell checking session, the automatic checker finds your typos and allows you to correct them on the fly. For more involved documents, however, you may find the constant queries distracting and you might prefer to do all your spell checking at once, when you've completed an entire draft. While I would normally recommend that you do your writing in one session and your editing and proofreading in another, the decision here is a matter of personal preference.

For now, I'll show you how to respond to a spelling query from the background spell checker. When you notice that Word has used its squiggly underline to call your attention to a suspect word, either edit (or retype) it yourself manually or right-click on the word. A menu will pop up, offering suggested spellings, along with the options to ignore the unusually spelled word or add it to the dictionary.

definition

Right-click: *To place the mouse pointer on an object on screen and click the right mouse button. A menu will pop up from which the user can choose a command.*

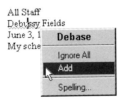

For a proper name, such as Debussy, choose Add so that you won't have to explain the word to Word again.

Creating a Paragraph

Now continue the memo by typing the following:

> I'll be out of the office next week from Tuesday to
> Thursday, attending a conference on How to Make the
> Most of Your Time in the Office.

Remember, don't press ENTER until you get to the end of the paragraph. Then press ENTER again to skip a line and type this last paragraph:

> Please direct all urgent questions during that period
> to my assistant, Herbert Stencil. I will, however, be
> checking my e-mail every day, so feel free to send
> me messages directly about less pressing matters.

Press ENTER when you get to the end of the second paragraph (see Figure 1.3).

For more complicated text changes and corrections, see Chapter 3.

Figure 1.3 The completed memo

Correcting Little Mistakes

Gone are the days when a single typo meant having to retype an entire document. With Word, correcting errors is a snap. If you catch a mistake immediately after typing it, the easiest way to correct it is to press the Backspace key. The Backspace key erases the character to the left of the insertion point.

If you notice a mistake later, you can either move the insertion point to the right of the error and press Backspace or move the insertion point to the left of the error and press DELETE. DELETE erases the character to the right of the insertion point.

To erase an entire word at once, you can hold down CTRL as you press the Backspace key or as you press DELETE. Here's a rundown of when to use Backspace and when to use DELETE:

To Erase	Press
A character to the left of the insertion point	Backspace
A character to the right of the insertion point	DELETE
A word (or portion of a word) to the left of the insertion point	CTRL-Backspace
A word (or portion of a word) to the right of the insertion point	CTRL-DELETE

You can always press CTRL-Z to undo your last action without having to take your hands away from the keyboard.

For more on how to use the Undo feature and how to undo several steps at once, see Chapter 3.

Undoing Big Mistakes

Another benefit you derive from writing with a computer is that you can go back and undo big mistakes. Word keeps track of the state of your document as you work on it and can restore your work to a previous state (most of the time). If you realize you've done something you really want to undo, just click on the Undo button on the Standard toolbar:

SAVING A DOCUMENT

When a document is completed, you need to save it. In fact, to be safe, you need to save your work regularly, even before it's done. The first time you save, Word will ask you to provide a filename for your document. Try this now. First, click on the Save button on the Standard toolbar:

This brings up the Save As dialog box (see Figure 1.4).

My Documents folder   Create New Folder

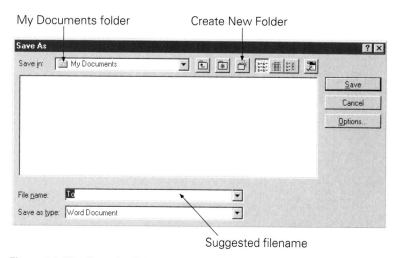

Suggested filename

Figure 1.4 The Save As dialog box, which lets you name your document and decide where to save it

The first time you save something, Word suggests saving it in the My Documents folder, which may or may not be the best place for it. You can make a new folder inside the current folder by clicking on the Create New Folder button. Word also suggests a filename, based on the first word in your document.

First, you need to name your new document. Windows 95 now allows longer, descriptive filenames, so type **Memo (June 3)**, but don't press ENTER. (Yes, you can now include spaces in a filename.) Then click on the Create New Folder button to bring up the New Folder dialog box.

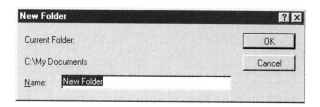

Type **Memos** and press ENTER. A Memos folder will appear in the main area of the Save As dialog box. Double-click on it and then click on Save to save your memo in the new folder (see Figure 1.5).

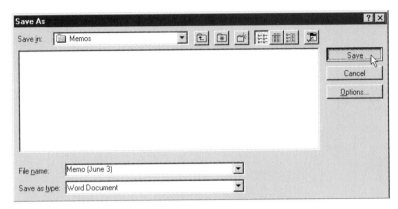

Figure 1.5 Saving Memo (June 3) in the new Memos folder

The next time you change this document, click on the Save button again. This time Word will simply update the saved document without asking you for a filename.

Here's the basic procedure for saving any document.

SAVING A DOCUMENT step by step

1. Click the Save button on the Standard toolbar. If you have saved this document before, your latest changes will be saved as well and you're done.

2. If this is the first time you've saved this document, the Save As dialog box will appear. Type a filename for the document in the File name box.

3. Change where the document will be saved with the Save in box or by clicking (or creating a new) folder.

4. Click the Save button.

SHORTCUT

Press CTRL-P and then press ENTER to print your document without lifting your fingers from the keys.

See Chapter 10 for more on sharing documents and Chapter 11 for other alternatives to printing.

PRINTING YOUR WORK

Although some documents nowadays are made and passed around from computer to computer and never committed to paper ("hard copy," in computer-geek lingo), most of us still use computers as typewriters and most documents still get printed out.

This may seem obvious, but you have to open a document before you can print it from within Word. After that, printing a document is a simple matter of clicking on a single button, the Print button:

By the way, I purposely presented the information on saving before I discussed printing, because you should get into the habit of always saving your work before printing it. You never know when something will go wrong during the printing process, and you don't want to risk losing your work because you forgot to save it.

EXITING WORD

Once you've typed something up, saved it, and printed it out (and sure, maybe made some changes, saved it again, printed it out again, made some more changes, and so on), it's time to quit Word. To do so, pull down the File menu and select Exit, or just click the Close button in the upper-right corner of the Word window.

If you try to exit Word after having made unsaved changes to a document, Word will first ask if you want to save your changes before exiting. Generally, you *will* want to save the changes, and should click on Yes. If you're not sure about saving changes, it's usually safer to click Cancel and review things instead of clicking No and possibly losing important work. No matter how busy you are, rushing and accidentally losing your work will ruin your day. Unsaved work is harder to recover than deleted work.

WHERE TO GO FROM HERE

Chapter 2 explains some simple things you can do (and you'll only have to do them this one time) to make Word easier and more comfortable to use. If you're so busy that you can't even spare a little tinkering time, you can skip ahead. Chapter 3 elaborates on how you can edit and format a Word document.

Stuff You Only Have to Do Once That Will Make Your Life a Lot Easier

FAST FORWARD

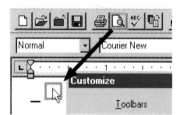

CHANGE THE TYPEFACE
WORD STARTS YOU OFF WITH ➤ *pp 19-20*

1. Select Format | Font.
2. Choose the font and size you want.
3. Click on the Default button.
4. Click on Yes.

CUSTOMIZE YOUR TOOLBARS ➤ *pp 24-27*

1. Select Tools | Customize.
2. Drag the useless buttons off the toolbars.
3. Select more useful commands and drag them onto the toolbars.
4. Choose icons for buttons that don't have them.
5. Click on OK.

RETURN A TOOLBAR TO
ITS ORIGINAL SETTINGS ➤ *p 27*

1. Right-click on any toolbar and choose Toolbars.
2. In the Toolbars dialog box that appears, select the toolbar you want to restore and click on the Reset button.
3. Click on OK in the Reset Toolbars dialog box.
4. Click on OK in the Toolbars dialog box.

CLOSE THE TIP WIZARD ➤ *pp 27-28*

Just click the Tip Wizard button in the Standard toolbar and the Tip Wizard toolbar will close. (To reopen it at any time, click the Tip Wizard button again.)

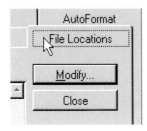

CHANGE THE SAVE FOLDER ➤ *p 31*

1. Select Tools | Options.
2. Click on the File Locations tab.
3. Click on the Modify button.
4. Select (or create) a folder, select it, and click on OK.
5. Click on Close.

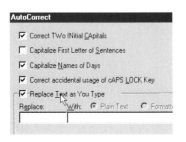

CHOOSE YOUR AUTOCORRECT PREFERENCES ➤ *pp 31-32*

1. Select Tools | AutoCorrect.
2. To prevent AutoCorrect from "fixing" instances of two capital letters at the beginnings of words, uncheck Correct TWo INitial CApitals.
3. To make AutoCorrect automatically capitalize the first letter of any new sentence, check Capitalize First Letter of Sentences.
4. Uncheck Correct accidental usage of cAPS LOCK Key if you have a need for such unusual capitalization.
5. To essentially turn AutoCorrect off, uncheck Replace Text as You Type.
6. When you've specified all your preferences, click on OK.

PUT A WORD ICON ON THE DESKTOP ➤ *pp 32-33*

1. Select Start | Find | Files or Folders.
2. Type **winword** and press ENTER.
3. Click on the Winword program icon (the blue W) and drag it onto the desktop.
4. Click on the label, type **Word**, and press ENTER.

PUT WORD ON THE START MENU ➤ *p 33*

1. Select Start | Find | Files or Folders.
2. Type **winword** and press ENTER.
3. Click on the Winword program icon (the blue W) and drag it onto the Start button.

If your idea of easy is to just accept things the way they are and make the best of them, you may want to skip over this chapter. But if you're willing to take ten minutes to make Word easier from now on and save yourself hours of "twiddling" time in the future, stay with me.

I'll take you step by step through some simple things you can do to make Word easier and more comfortable for you to use. You won't need to understand everything you do in this chapter, but you'll be happy you took the time (and you'll only have to do these things once).

START OFF WITH THE RIGHT FONT EVERY TIME

You may have noticed by now that every time you start Word or create a new document you get a standard font and font size (as well as a standard page setup, and so on). If you like the way the default typeface and font size look, and you're happy with the documents produced with them, you don't need to change the *defaults*—you can skip to the next section. If you like the defaults, just leave them alone. If you don't, you have to change them "by hand."

If you find yourself frequently changing default settings, it's time to set up new defaults. You can change any of Word's default settings from their original selection (the *default* default) to anything else, making *your* choice the default from that point forward.

Which brings us back to the default font. Out of the box, Word uses a default font and size of Times New Roman, 10 points (see Figure 2.1).

Choose a Font

Most people prefer 12 points as a basic font size. For one thing, it's easier on the eyes. For another, it's closer to the size of the characters produced by most traditional typewriters, which still seems to matter (though it probably won't to our children).

Times New Roman is an acceptable typeface for most people. It has serifs, so it's easy to read. However, some people prefer a more typewritten look, especially for first drafts, and may therefore want to use a font like Courier New. You can choose to make any available font your default, if there's one you like better. For instance, I like my

definition

Default: A preset feature. Word assigns to some of its features "factory settings" that should be generally acceptable to most users. The settings for these features can be changed, but using the defaults often saves time.

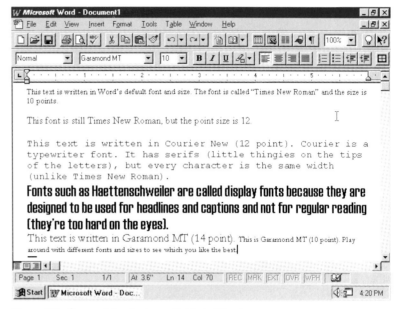

Figure 2.1 Some of the fonts available in Word

Whenever you find yourself doing the same thing repeatedly on the computer, especially in the same type of situation, look for a shortcut or a way to achieve your results automatically. Computers like doing the same thing over and over. Most people don't.

Garamond font quite a lot, but it might not translate well to another person's computer (and it doesn't look all that great on the screen). So I stick with 12-point Courier New as my default font (see Figure 2.1).

Not every computer has the same fonts installed (although Windows comes with a few standard fonts, including Times New Roman, Courier New, Wingdings, and a few others). If you open a document on a computer that doesn't have one of the document's fonts, Word will substitute a different font.

Make the Font You Choose the Default Font

Once you've decided what font you like working with, you're ready to make it the new default. It's easy. Just follow the steps listed in the box on the next page.

Once you're finished, Word will display a dialog box asking you if you're sure you want to make this change. It will also tell you that the change will affect all new documents based on the normal template, but there's no need to worry about that part. Just make sure the font and size are correct and then click on Yes. There, you've done it. That wasn't so painful, was it?

CHOOSE A DEFAULT FONT step by step

1. Start a new document by clicking on the New button (the first one on the Standard toolbar).

2. Select Format|Font.

3. Scroll through the Font list box to choose your default font. You can select different fonts and see how they look in the Preview area.

4. Scroll through the Font Size list box and select a size. Again, make sure things look OK in the Preview area.

5. When you are satisfied with the font and size, click on the Default button.

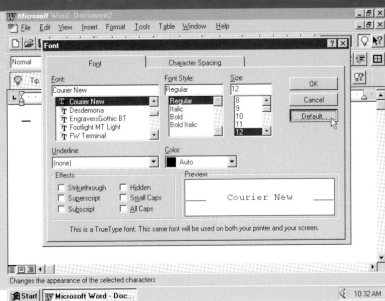

From now on, every new document you start will get the default font and size you just assigned. Of course, you can always override the From now on, every new document you start will get the default font and size you just assigned. Of course, you can always override the default and specify whatever font you want for a whole document or for any selected portion of a document.

MAKE THE TOOLBARS ACTUALLY USEFUL

The idea behind toolbars is to keep the most useful features no more than a single mouse click away, to save you from having to hunt through pull-down menus and so on. It's a great idea, but it doesn't always work that way. First of all, there's so much going on on the screen that all those buttons can be confusing. Second, the toolbar buttons all have little icons on them that are supposed to be perfectly clear, but many of them make no sense at all to a normal person. Third, and most important, the collection of commands assembled on the toolbars are not necessarily the most useful for regular people.

Throughout the rest of this book, my instructions will assume that you've made the recommended changes to your toolbars, however, I'll also tell you the alternatives.

Some of them are there to help sell Word, by illustrating its most advanced or fancy-looking features. Some of those features are things you may never use. Others are features you'll use, but certainly not every day. It defeats the purpose of shortcuts to put arcane features in with saving, printing, and so on.

So let's go through the preset toolbars and decide how useful each button is. (Of course, my opinions might not perfectly suit your working style, so you should be sure to make note of your own preferences as they emerge after you've used Word for a while. Later, you may want to make your own changes to the toolbars.)

Review of Existing Toolbars

When you start Word, two of its toolbars come up automatically across the top of the screen, the Standard toolbar and the Formatting toolbar, as shown in Figure 2.2.

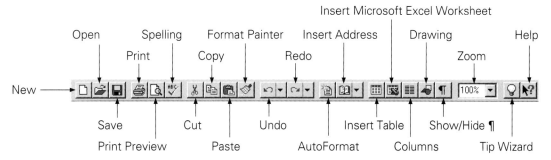

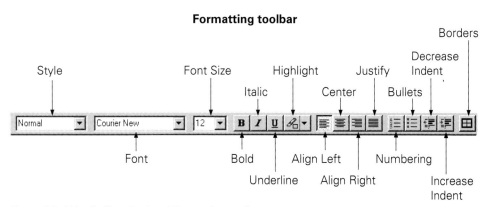

Figure 2.2 Word's Standard and Formatting toolbars

The Standard Toolbar

- **New**, **Open**, **Save**, and **Print** are all very useful and deserve to be there at the top left edge of the screen.
- **Print Preview** is a toss-up. You can see the whole page at any point by going into Page Layout view, but you can look at multiple pages (if that's useful to you) with Print Preview. Then again, do you need a shortcut for that? Print Preview is easily accessible from the File menu, so we'll remove it.
- **Spelling** makes sense being next to the Print button, since it's always a good idea to check your spelling before printing, even though Word now has automatic background spell checking (as explained in Chapter 1).
- **Cut**, **Copy**, and **Paste** all belong where they are.
- **Format Painter** is a useful shortcut for imposing consistent formatting on different parts of your document, especially if you don't intend to learn much about styles (which do the job much better).

- **Undo** and **Redo** are fine where they are.
- **AutoFormat** is another waste of time. It's not too hard to select Format | AutoFormat if you really want the computer to decide how your documents should look. (It's really just there to show off a fancy feature.)
- **Insert Address** can be useful if you've got your e-mail and work groups all set up with Windows 95. If not, it's just a waste of space. We'll keep it just in case.
- **Insert Table**—I could flip a coin on this one. It's a neat effect to allow you to select the number of rows and columns while creating a table, but so what? It's just as easy to do that by selecting Table | Insert.
- **Insert Microsoft Excel Worksheet**—do we really need a special button for this?
- **Columns** is similar to Insert Table. It's not much of a shortcut, but it looks nice.
- **Drawing**—can it. How often are you going to be drawing with the rinky-dink Microsoft Draw program that comes with Word? Not too often.
- **Show/Hide ¶** is useful. Keep it around.

- **Zoom Control** is a good one. I use it all the time.
- **Tip Wizard** is not a bad way to help you learn Word. It's also useful for closing that Tip Wizard window when you get jealous of the space it takes up on the screen.
- **Help**—keep it. Sure, Help is always the rightmost menu choice, and it's easy to get to, but this button gives you context-sensitive help (meaning that you can click on something specific to get help about it).

The Formatting Toolbar

- **Style**, **Font**, and **Font Size** are all decent shortcuts. Keep them around.
- **Bold**, **Italic**, and **Underline** belong within easy reach.
- The **Highlight** button will mainly be useful for work that stays on your screen, since it won't print out too well. It's definitely up there because it's a new feature, but it may come in handy (and I have to admit, it's sort of cool), so keep it around.
- **Align Left**, **Center**, **Align Right**, and **Justify** may be a matter of personal preference. I center things a lot, but I don't mess with alignment very much.
- **Numbering** and **Bullets** are nice automated commands (although they have some tricky effects).
- **Decrease Indent** and **Increase Indent** are moderately useful, depending on what kind of formatting you use, but they're also easy to get to via the menus. They can go.
- **Borders** brings up the Borders toolbar, but you can do this at any point by right-clicking on a toolbar and selecting Borders, so I'd get rid of it.

So what's the score? Here are the toolbar buttons worth eliminating:

Print Preview	Decrease Indent
AutoFormat	Increase Indent
Insert Microsoft Excel Worksheet	Borders
Drawing	

But let's not just be negative. What can we add to the toolbars to make them more useful?

What's Missing from the Toolbars?

Well, starting with the Standard toolbar, we've got the New, Open, and Save buttons. What about **Close**? It's the other most common command. (Of course, every window now has a Close box in its top rightmost corner, but I think it's useful to have New, Open, Save, and Close all in a row together.)

Then there's Word's useful **Shrink to Fit** command. Never heard of it? That's not surprising. It comes up on the Print Preview screen. What it does is slightly fiddle with spacing and other things in your document when the document just barely runs onto a new page at the end. Gotta hate those big, empty final pages. We'll add a Shrink to Fit button to the set of printing-related buttons (Print and Spelling).

Then there are the navigation commands, **Find** and **Go To**. They should be up there. (Yes, you can double-click on the left end of the status bar to use Go To, but I think it deserves a button among similar shortcuts on the toolbar.)

Along with those old editing standbys Cut, Copy, and Paste, how about **Replace** as well, for industrial editing jobs?

We're not going to take much off the Formatting toolbar, but there is one pair of buttons worth adding—double spacing and single spacing. If you ever want to proofread your writing on paper, the old-fashioned way, you'll want to make your documents double-spaced to leave room for written corrections. Might as well have a shortcut for double spacing and for setting your text back to single spacing.

Funny, double spacing was on the toolbar in Word 1.0. I wonder why they took it off?

Change Your Toolbars

OK, enough blather. Let's start messing around with the toolbars.

1. Put the mouse pointer over one of the toolbars.
2. Click the *right* mouse button, and a menu pops up.
3. Select Customize. The Customize dialog box appears with the Toolbars tab already selected (see Figure 2.3).

Removing Buttons

First, eliminate the buttons you don't need.

1. Click on the Print Preview button and drag it off the Standard toolbar.
2. Do the same for the AutoFormat, Insert Microsoft Excel Worksheet, and Drawing buttons.

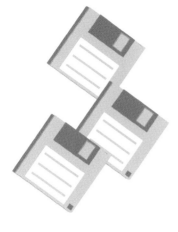

3. Drag Decrease Indent, Increase Indent, and Borders off the Formatting toolbar.

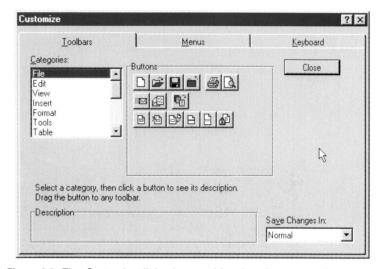

Figure 2.3 The Customize dialog box used for changing your toolbars

Adding Buttons

Now add the new buttons.

1. Make sure that File is selected in the Categories box. In the Buttons area of the Customize dialog box there is a button that shows a closed file folder and an arrow. This is the Close toolbar button, not to be confused with the big button with the word "Close" on it in the right portion of the Customize dialog box. Click on this button and drag it to the Standard toolbar, placing it to the right of the Save button.

2. Oops! That closed up the space that separated the Save button from the Print button. Click on the Print button and drag it slightly to the right to reopen the space.

3. Next click on the Shrink to Fit button in the Customize dialog box. Drag it into place after the Spelling button.

4. Make some room between Shrink to Fit and Cut.

5. Select Edit in the Categories box.

6. Click on the Find button and drag it so that it's on top of (obscuring) the Cut button. (If it falls to the right of the Cut button, drag it to the left.)

7. There is no preset button for Go To in the Customize dialog box, so you have to select All Commands in the Categories list box.

8. Scroll down to EditGoTo in the Commands box that appears, click on it, and drag the little box to the Standard toolbar to the right of the Find button. There's no preassigned icon for Go To, so the Custom Button dialog box appears (see Figure 2.4).

9. Choose an icon that seems appropriate. (I like the pushpin, because Go To helps me pinpoint a location in the document—OK, it's a stretch, I admit it.) Click on the Assign button.

10. Drag the Cut button over to give Find and Go To a little breathing room.

11. Scroll down to and select EditReplace from the Commands box and drag it to the toolbar, just to the right of the Paste button.

12. Click on the Format Painter button on the Standard toolbar and drag it down to the Formatting toolbar (where it belongs), between the Underline button and the Highlighter button.

13. Close up the space between the Replace button and the Undo button. (It's getting crowded, and those are all editing buttons.)

14. Select Format in the Categories list box.

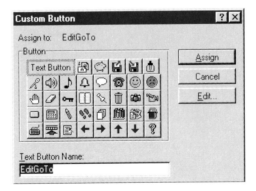

Figure 2.4 The Custom Button dialog box, which allows you to choose plain text or an icon for a new toolbar button

15. Drag the Double Space button and drop it on top of the Align Left button.

16. Drag the Single Space button (not the 1.5 Space button in between Single Space and Double Space) to a position just to the right of the Double Space button.

17. Put a little space between Single Space and Align Left.

18. Click on Close.

There, you're done. That wasn't so bad, was it? Here's what the two toolbars look like now:

Now exit Word to make sure your changes get saved, and then start Word again.

HOW TO RESTORE THE ORIGINAL TOOLBARS

If you later decide that you preferred the original toolbars, or if you'd like to get them back and modify them differently, it's easy enough to return them to their original states.

1. Right-click on any toolbar and choose Toolbars.

2. In the Toolbars dialog box that appears (see Figure 2.5), select the toolbar you want to restore and click on the Reset button.

3. Click on OK.

4. Repeat steps 2 and 3 for as many toolbars as you want to change back.

5. Click on OK.

CLOSE THE TIP WIZARD WINDOW

When you start Word for the first time, the Tip Wizard, a small toolbar with an information window in it, appears just above the Ruler, and the Tip Wizard button in the Standard toolbar appears "pushed in."

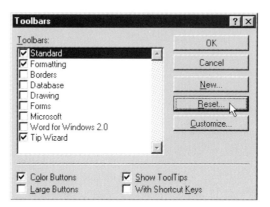

Figure 2.5 Choosing a toolbar and clicking on Reset to return it to its original state

Whenever Word has a suggestion or makes an automatic change for you, the text will appear in the Tip Wizard.

If and when you get tired of seeing the Tip Wizard or of ceding that much space on the screen for the tips, you can close it by clicking on the Tip Wizard button on the Standard toolbar. If the Tip Wizard ever wants your attention (for instance, after Word has made an automatic change and needs your approval), the Tip Wizard button will start flashing. Just click on the button and the window will open again, offering an explanation for the interruption.

CHOOSE YOUR PREFERENCES FROM THE OPTIONS DIALOG BOX

The settings described in this section are somewhat a matter of personal preference, so I won't dictate to you exactly what to do. I'll just lay out the options (and the ramifications) and let you decide for yourself. The title of this chapter promises that you will only have to do these things once ("set it and forget it"), but of course you might change your mind later, in which case you'd need to perform these actions again.

The Options dialog box is Word's nerve center for custom settings. It sports twelve different tabs, each of which governs some aspect of Word's setup. Many other dialog boxes in Word (such as the Print dialog box) have an Options button that leads directly to the appropriate tab of the Options dialog box. Here I'll walk you through some of the essential settings in various tabs of this dialog box. (Have I used the words "dialog box" enough times in a row?)

To begin with, start Word again if you haven't already. Then select Tools | Options. This brings up the Options dialog box (see Figure 2.6).

Losing the Horizontal Scroll Bar

If the View tab is not the one selected, choose it now. In the Window box, consider unchecking Horizontal Scroll Bar. You won't need it much. The idea is to have your text fit on the screen anyway.

Maximizing the Recently Used File List

Click on the General tab. For the Recently Used File List option, choose the maximum (9). This controls how many of your most recently opened documents will appear at the bottom of the File menu. I say show as many as possible. It's awfully convenient.

Turning Off Background Spell Checking

As I mentioned in Chapter 1, the question of whether to allow automatic background spell checking to go on is for you to decide, based on how you prefer to work. Do you like to correct typos as they occur, or does that break your concentration? If you fall into the latter category, you can turn off automatic spell checking in the Options dialog box.

habits & strategies

If you turn off Automatic Spell Checking and later turn it back on, Word will then point out any suspicious words it finds, so from the user's point of view, there's no real difference between the two approaches.

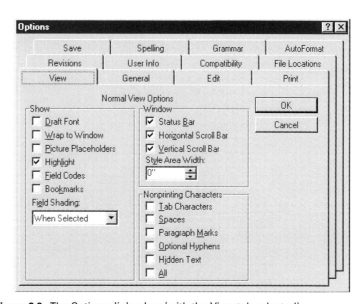

Figure 2.6 The Options dialog box (with the View tab selected)

Click on the Spelling tab. Then uncheck Automatic Spell Checking. You could also check Hide Spelling Errors in Current Document, which instructs Word to continue to check your spelling as you type, but to hide the squiggly lines. When you're ready to fix any spelling errors that may have accumulated, you can return to the Options dialog box and uncheck the Hide Spelling Errors option.

Controlling Text Replacement

Click on the Edit tab. There are several editing options you might want to think about changing. First, there's Typing Replaces Selection. Personally, I keep this on because I find it useful, though it can be frustrating to accidentally replace a selection because you brushed the keyboard. Then again, there's always Undo.

Then there's Automatic Word Selection. I find this frustrating when I want to select just part of a word, so I turn it off, but many people like it because it makes it much easier to select whole words. It's up to you.

I check Use the INS Key for Paste, not so much because I plan to use the INSERT key to do my pasting, but because I find it so annoying if I accidentally go into Overtype mode (by pressing INSERT when I mean to press DELETE or HOME) and then start running roughshod over my precious text. Yes, you can still go into Overtype if you want, even if you reassign the INSERT key. You can do it by clicking on the OVR box in the status bar at the bottom of the screen.

I keep Use Smart Cut and Paste checked, but it can occasionally add to your work. This feature mainly deals with stray spaces when you cut and paste text. It's useful most of the time, except when you don't want a space between the inserted text and the text into which you inserted it.

Choose Save and Backup Preferences

Click on the Save tab. I don't keep Always Create Backup Copy checked because I dislike having two copies of every document floating around, but if you're worried about losing your work, this is a good fail-safe technique. Allow Fast Saves is a trade-off. I use it because it saves time, but it does result in bigger files. If you're worried about your storage space, uncheck it. For the Automatic Save Every option, choose a nice small number of minutes, such as 10 or 15.

Be sure to save regularly no matter what. Every time you pause or take a break, save your work!

Undo is covered in Chapter 1, and Redo and Multiple Undo are explained in Chapter 3.

habits & strategies

Automatic Save is a routine that helps if Word or Windows crashes. If that happens, Word restores the most recent AutoSaved copy of your document the next time you run Word. In normal circumstances, that backup is deleted when you quit Word, so it's no substitute for saving your document.

Decide Where to Save Documents

As you saw in Chapter 1, Word suggests the My Documents folder when you save a document for the first time. This is a fine place to put documents (obviously), but you may prefer to send your documents elsewhere by default.

To choose a different default folder for documents, click on the File Locations tab in the Options dialog box. Then click on the Modify button. This will bring up the Modify Location dialog box, a variation on the familiar Open and Save dialog boxes.

You can change where the dialog box is pointing with the Up One Level button and make a new folder anywhere with the Create New Folder button. When you've chosen the folder you want as your default from now on, click on OK.

When you're done with the Options dialog box, click on OK (or, if you just changed a file location, click on Close).

CHOOSE YOUR AUTOCORRECT PREFERENCES

Some preferences not available from the Options dialog box are those for AutoCorrect. These must be set by selecting Tools | AutoCorrect to access the AutoCorrect dialog box (see Figure 2.7).

definition

AutoCorrect: *Word's AutoCorrect feature corrects the spelling of commonly mistyped words as soon as you press the Spacebar. You add new pairs of words (misspelled and corrected) in the AutoCorrect dialog box.*

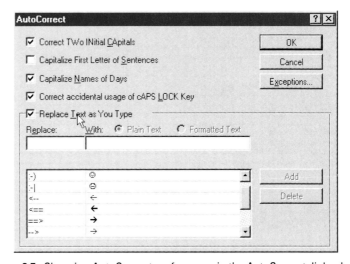

Figure 2.7 Choosing AutoCorrect preferences in the AutoCorrect dialog box

The main function of this dialog box is to enable you to add new AutoCorrect pairs to the list (typically misspelled words, such as *teh*, and their correct spellings, such as *the*). It also gives you fine control over how and when AutoCorrect works.

- To prevent AutoCorrect from "fixing" instances of two capital letters at the beginnings of words, uncheck Correct TWo INitial CApitals.
- To make AutoCorrect capitalize the first letter of what it thinks is any new sentence (usually, any letter after a period and a space), check Capitalize First Letter of Sentences.
- Capitalize Names of Days is self-explanatory.
- Correct accidental usage of cAPS LOCK Key recognizes the typical output of this familiar mishap and corrects it on the fly.
- Finally, if you don't want AutoCorrect following you around and making changes while you're working, you can uncheck Replace Text as You Type (this is effectively equivalent to turning AutoCorrect off).

When you've specified all your preferences, click on OK.

It's still up to you to notice and hit the CAPS LOCK key a second time to turn it off.

PUT A WORD ICON ON YOUR DESKTOP

If you use Word all the time, you may want to have a Word icon live on your desktop to make the program easy to start. First, exit Word, or at least minimize the window. Now you have to find the Word program. Most likely it's in the Winword subfolder of the MSOffice folder. If so, you can get to it by double-clicking on My Computer, then on C:, then on MSOffice, and then Winword.

But the easiest way to get to Word is to use the Find feature on the Start menu.

Winword (or Winword.exe) is the actual name of the Word for Windows program.

1. Click on the Start button.
2. Point to Find.
3. Point to Files or Folders.

habits & strategies

If you ever want to double-click on a desktop icon that's obscured by several open windows, right-click on the Taskbar first and select Minimize All Windows to get a clear shot at the desktop.

4. In the Find: All Folders dialog box that appears, type **winword** and press ENTER. Windows quickly finds the Winword program icon (as well as the folder it's in, and some other related icons).
5. Click on the Winword icon (the blue W) and drag a shortcut onto the desktop.
6. An icon called Shortcut to Winword appears, with the telltale little arrow-in-a-box that indicates a Windows 95 shortcut. Click in the label under the icon, type **Word**, and press ENTER.

Now you've got a handy desktop icon for Word. You also can make desktop shortcuts for important documents using the same method described here. Just search for the filename of the document you want.

PUT WORD ON THE START MENU

Another handy place to put a Word shortcut is directly on the Start menu. Once again, you need to get to the program icon, either by hunting for it through folders or (as I recommend) by using the Find feature from the Start menu. Once you've got your Winword icon visible, click on it and drag it onto the Start menu. It will appear at the top of the menu.

WHAT DO YOU WANT TO DO NOW?

You're ready to roll. Your copy of Word is set up for your convenience, and you know all the basics for creating documents. From here on out, you should be able to skip through the book, picking out only the information you need right now.

Everyday Formatting and Editing

FAST FORWARD

MOVE THE DOCUMENT VIEW WITH
THE VERTICAL SCROLL BAR ➤ *pp 41-42*

- Click on the scroll arrow at the top or bottom of the scroll bar.
- Click in the scroll bar above or below the scroll box.
- Click on and drag the scroll box to a new position.

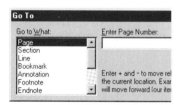

GO TO A SPECIFIC PAGE ➤ *p 42*

1. Double-click on the left end of the status bar, press CTRL-G, or click on the Go To button (if you created one).
2. Type a page number.
3. Press ENTER.

GO TO A SPECIFIC WORD ➤ *pp 42-43*

1. Press CTRL-F.
2. Type the word you're thinking of.
3. Press ENTER.
4. Repeat if necessary.
5. Press Cancel.

SELECT TEXT ➤ *pp 43-44*

- Click and drag to select any amount of text.
- Double-click to select a word.
- Triple-click to select a paragraph.
- Click in the left margin to select a line.
- SHIFT-click or use SHIFT with movement keys to extend a selection.

FORMAT A CHARACTER ➤ *p 45*

1. Make a selection.
2. Right-click and select Font.
3. Choose a font.
4. Choose a size.
5. Select a form of emphasis, if desired.
6. Click on OK.

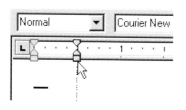

INDENT AN ENTIRE PARAGRAPH ➤ *pp 45-47*

1. Select the paragraph(s) or place the insertion point in a single paragraph.
2. Click on the lowest marker at the left edge of the Ruler.
3. Drag it to the indentation level you want.

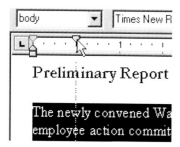

INDENT THE FIRST LINE OF A PARAGRAPH ➤ *pp 45-47*

1. Select the paragraph(s) or place the insertion point in a single paragraph.
2. Click on the highest marker at the left edge of the Ruler.
3. Drag it to the indentation level you want.

COPY FORMATTING ➤ *pp 47-48*

1. Place the insertion point in (or select) the text that has the formatting you want to copy.
2. Click on the Format Painter button on the toolbar.
3. Click on and drag the Format Painter pointer across the text you want to apply the copied formatting to.

REMOVE A SELECTION ➤ *p 49*

- To throw a selection away for good, press DELETE.
- To save a selection for pasting elsewhere, click the Cut button, or press CTRL-X.

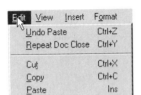

Expenditures for office supplies went dow
drop in office supply expenditures in 1995. Since
the same level and inflation has hovered in the lov
in question, the expenditure drops represent real
slowdown in the rate of lessening expenses in 199
unwelcome pattern. Projections for 1997 show a
savings. Perhaps it is too soon to worry.

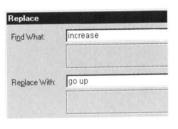

MOVE A SELECTION A
SHORT DISTANCE ➤ *pp 49-50*

1. Click on the selection and hold down the mouse button.
2. Drag the drag-and-drop pointer.
3. Release the pointer at the destination.

MOVE A SELECTION ANYWHERE ➤ *p 50, 51*

1. Press CTRL-X (or CTRL-C to move a copy and leave the
   original in place).
2. Move the insertion point to the destination.
3. Press CTRL-V.

FIND THINGS AND REPLACE THEM ➤ *pp 50-53*

1. Press CTRL-H.
2. Type the text you want to find.
3. Choose the special options for how to treat the text (if any).
4. Select the formatting to find (if any).
5. Click in the Replace With box (or press TAB).
6. Type the text you want to replace the found text with.
7. Select the formatting you want to replace the found
   formatting with (if any).
8. Click on Find Next.
9. Click on Replace, Replace All, or Find Next.
10. Repeat as often as necessary.
11. If Word gets to the end of your document, click Yes to have
    it continue the search from the beginning or No not to.
12. If Word completes the search of your document, click OK in
    the dialog box that appears.
13. Click on Close when you're done (or Cancel, if Word failed to
    find anything that matched).

UNDO A NUMBER OF RECENT STEPS ➤ *p 53*

1. Click on the down arrow next to the Undo button.
2. Scroll through the box that drops down, if necessary.
3. Choose the oldest action to be undone.

This is another "read-it-if-you-need-it" chapter. If you already know how to move around in your documents, make selections, make changes, and do formatting, you're excused from reading this one—go on to Chapter 4. Otherwise, at least skim through this chapter to make sure you're up to speed. I won't make you do any laborious typing or exercises. I'll just spell out all your options and demonstrate a few.

When I said that Chapter 1 covered just about everything you need to know about using Word, I was telling the truth, but once you get past the basics, you'll encounter another set of slightly more refined tasks and goals—things you'll do less frequently but that will become unavoidable. The skills you gained in Chapter 1 are suitable for rough drafts and for harnessing the computer workstation as a writing tool. Now it's time to talk about editing tools, such as those that allow you to make selections, copy formatting, move selections, and replace words—all techniques that are needed to make a document appear complete.

When you're working with computers, there's always a temptation to play with all the available "levers" all the time. My advice is to do the actual writing first. Get it out there "on the page" (saved). Then make another pass to fix, change, tweak, correct, and compromise. Tidy up the language. Make your document presentable.

I'm talking about two sets of things, really: editing and formatting—the brain and the body. I'll spell out the mechanics (the exact how-to, you-are-getting-sleepy-just-do-as-I-say instructions) in this chapter for each specific task. I recommend skimming it, honestly. When you actually want to do one of the things covered here (such as adding formatting or moving a paragraph), dip back into this chapter. You'll find you can use it as a reference.

AUTOMATIC SPELL CHECKING (THOSE WAVY RED LINES)

This came up in Chapter 1, but you may have skipped that. If a bunch of the words in your document are underlined with wavy red lines and you don't know what it's all about, take a look in the Tip Wizard. (If you don't see this feature, click on the Tip Wizard button on the Standard toolbar to open it.) The spell checker has automatically checked your document and has some questions about the underlined words. As explained in Chapter 1, just right-click on each word and choose an option, or retype or correct the error manually. Chapter 2 tells you how to turn off automatic spell checking. (Choose Tools | Options, select the Spelling tab, and then uncheck Automatic Spell Checking.) If you want to know *all* the ins and outs of spell checking, it's covered thoroughly along with other editing aids in Chapter 12.

BEFORE YOU START EDITING AND FORMATTING

To either edit or format your writing in Word, you first need to know how to move around in a document and how to make selections. You probably already know how to do both, because it works the same way in Word as it does in *every other program in Windows 95*. If you already have a firm grasp of this kind of thing, skip ahead to the section "Basic Formatting" and get this chapter over with as fast as you can!

Moving Around in Your Document

For limited movement, use the arrow and other movement keys to the right of the ENTER key. (You can also press NUMLOCK and then use the equivalent keys on the numeric keypad, assuming you have one.) For traversing large stretches of your document, use the vertical scroll bar. To get somewhere specific, you can try using Go To or Find. (Chapter 13 is full of hints for dealing with long documents.)

Using the Keyboard to Make Short Hops

To move your insertion point a short distance, you should rely mainly on the arrow keys. You can lean on them to get them to repeat. Holding down CTRL while pressing an arrow key magnifies the effect of the key. So, while pressing the RIGHT ARROW key moves the insertion point to the next letter, CTRL-RIGHT ARROW jumps the insertion point to the beginning of the next word; CTRL-DOWN ARROW moves not just to the next line but jumps to the beginning of the next paragraph. Other movement keys in the same vicinity of your keyboard include HOME, END, PAGEUP, and PAGEDOWN.

CAUTION

Unfortunately, on many keyboards there are also INSERT and DELETE keys right next to HOME and END. (They're under END and PAGEDOWN on the numeric keypad.) They have nothing to do with moving and can cause you problems. If you accidentally hit one of them, press CTRL-Z right away to undo whatever you done did.

Table 3.1 shows what all the movement keys and various movement key combinations do.

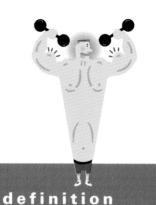

definition

Paragraph: To Word, a paragraph is anything between two paragraph marks, even blank lines and headings. (Click on the Show/Hide ¶ button on the Standard toolbar to see these marks in your document.)

This Key or Combination...	Moves the Insertion Point...
LEFT ARROW	Left one character
RIGHT ARROW	Right one character
UP ARROW	Up one line
DOWN ARROW	Down one line
CTRL-LEFT ARROW	Left one word
CTRL-RIGHT ARROW	Right one word
CTRL-UP ARROW	Up one paragraph
CTRL-DOWN ARROW	Down one paragraph
HOME	To the beginning of the line
END	To the end of the line
CTRL-HOME	To the beginning of the document
CTRL-END	To the end of the document
PAGEUP	Up one screenful
PAGEDOWN	Down one screenful
CTRL-PAGEUP	To the top of the screen
CTRL-PAGEDOWN	To the bottom of the screen
SHIFT-F5	To its previous location

Table 3.1 Movement Keys and What They Do

CAUTION

The insertion point does not move along with the scroll box. If you want to get your insertion point onto the screen you've scrolled to, click in the screen.

Using the Scroll Bar to Go Farther

You probably know how to use the scroll bar already, because it works just like the ones in all the other windows that have them. You click on the arrowheads at the top or bottom of the scroll bar to inch along a little bit at a time. Click in the areas above or below the scroll box to move your view one screenful at a time. Click on the scroll box itself and drag it along the scroll bar to move yourself to a precise spot in the document (or to get in the right ballpark before using the movement keys to find the exact spot). If you drag the scroll box into position, Word will pop up a little box, shown in the following illustration, displaying what page you've gotten to.

ffice Suppl~~ies~~
made prel~~iminary~~
nd in the reuse of

> ### upgrade note
>
> *You may have noticed that scroll boxes now vary in size. (In Windows 3.1 and earlier versions, scroll boxes were always square.) The size of the scroll box shows you what portion of the document you're currently viewing on the screen, taken in relation to the entire length of the scroll bar.*

Using Go To to Get to a Specific Page

Another way to jump to a specific page in a document is to use Go To. If you set up your toolbars the way I recommended in Chapter 2, you can click on the Go To button (remember I assigned the pushpin icon to it) to bring up the Go To dialog box. If not, select Edit | Go To, or double-click on the left end of the status bar, or press CTRL-G.

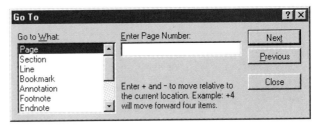

In the Go to What box, you can select parts of your document (other than the top of a page) to go to. By pressing the Next button, you can skip ahead or back one page at a time.

With Page selected in the Go to What box, type a page number and press ENTER to go to the top of that page. Click on Close when you're done using Go To. (The dialog box doesn't close on its own.)

Using Find to Get to a Specific Word or Words

If you're not sure what page you want to go to but you know a specific word or phrase in or near the section you want, use Find. If you set up your toolbars the way I recommended in Chapter 2, you can click on the Find button. Otherwise, select Edit | Find or press CTRL-F. This brings up the Find dialog box (see Figure 3.1).

Figure 3.1 The Find dialog box

Most of the options in this dialog box are overkill for general use. (Some of them are more useful when you're finding text and replacing it with the Replace dialog box, which is explained later in this chapter.) I'll just cover the basics here: type the word or phrase you're thinking of and press ENTER (or click on Find Next) to get to the first example Word finds in your document. To search from the insertion point back to the beginning of the document, select Up in the Search drop-down list box. To search the entire document from beginning to end, select All. Repeat until you get to the section you wanted. Click on Cancel when you get to the spot you were looking for.

Selecting Text

As I mentioned before, you have to have a grip on selecting things before you can edit or format them. Fortunately, there's not much to it. To make simple, short selections, most of the time you'll just click on the I-beam pointer at one end of the text you want to select, hold the mouse button down, and drag the pointer to the other end. The selected text will appear reversed out against a colored or dark background.

Word also gives you all kinds of selection shortcuts, some involving keys along with or instead of the mouse. These are described in Table 3-2.

Once you've clicked at a certain point, you can SHIFT-click elsewhere to select everything in between. Likewise, you can position the insertion point, hold down SHIFT, and then use any of the arrow keys or other movement keys (as explained earlier) to select everything between the original "anchor" position and the new position of the insertion point.

habits & strategies

If you're having trouble dragging over the right amount of text, you might want to check the status of Automatic Word Selection on the Edit tab of the Options dialog box (Tools | Options), as explained in Chapter 2. Experiment with this feature until you find the setting you're comfortable with.

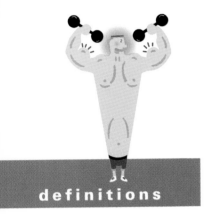

CTRL-clicking: Holding down CTRL while clicking.

SHIFT-clicking: Holding down SHIFT while clicking.

If You Want to Select an Entire...	Use this Shortcut
Word	Double-click anywhere in the word
Line	Click in the left margin. (Hold down the mouse button and drag to select several lines at once.)
Sentence	CTRL-click (hold down CTRL and then click) anywhere in the sentence
Paragraph	Double-click in the left margin or triple-click in a paragraph
Document	CTRL-click or triple-click anywhere in the left margin, or press CTRL-A

Table 3.2 Selection Shortcuts

BASIC FORMATTING

There are all kinds of things you can do to format your documents and make them more presentable, more persuasive. The most common enhancements are easily available from the toolbars and other doohickeys on the screen.

AutoFormat and Its Discontents

Word strains to offer you additional services with every new release of the program, and it has now reached the level of following you around, making suggestions. You've already seen how it automatically checks your spelling. Word will also make automatic formatting changes if you let it, changing straight quotation marks (" and ') to curly marks (" " and ''), creating first-line indents, applying heading styles, making numbered lists, and so on. You can generally override these suggestions in the Tip Wizard if you don't like 'em.

Although AutoFormat existed in version 6 of Word for Windows, you had to invoke it directly (from the Format menu) to get it to work. If you prefer this less obtrusive style, turn off the as-you-type AutoFormat, as explained in the following paragraph.

To prevent AutoFormat from formatting your text as you type it, select Tools | Options, click on the AutoFormat tab, and select AutoFormat instead of AutoFormat As You Type at the top of the dialog box.

Emphasis, Fonts, and Sizes

The general approach to formatting text is to select the text you want to format and then click on the button or select the option that applies the formatting you want. If you don't select something first, the formatting will apply either to nothing or to the word, the paragraph, or the entire document in which the insertion point is currently located, depending on the context. So, for example, to make the title of a report bold, you could select the title and then click on the Bold button on the Formatting toolbar. To make a single word italic, place the insertion point anywhere in it (or select it) and click on the Italic button. The deal is the same for Underline.

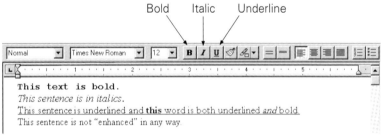

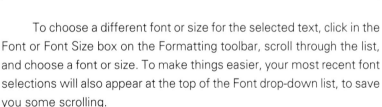

To choose a different font or size for the selected text, click in the Font or Font Size box on the Formatting toolbar, scroll through the list, and choose a font or size. To make things easier, your most recent font selections will also appear at the top of the Font drop-down list, to save you some scrolling.

You can do all of these things and more from the Font dialog box, shown in Figure 3.2. To get to it, select Format | Font or right-click anywhere in your text and choose Font from the menu that pops up.

Choose various options, mix and match, and check the results in the Preview area of the dialog box. When you're satisfied, click on OK.

Indentation

You *can*, of course, indent the first line of a paragraph simply by pressing TAB at the beginning. There's nothing really wrong with this.

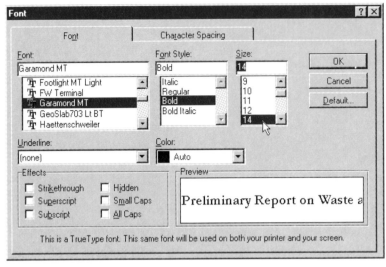

Figure 3.2 The Font dialog box

It's also possible, though, to indent the first line of a paragraph from the Ruler, without adding the tab character to the beginning of the line. As you continue to type, each new paragraph will automatically get the same formatting, with the indented first line. In fact, with AutoFormat on, Word will *sometimes* automatically convert a tab at the beginning of a paragraph into a first-line indent.

The Ruler has indentation markers at either end. The one on the right can be used to indent the right edge of the text from the right margin. The one on the left looks much more complicated:

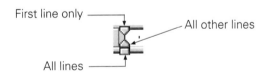

It's really not as tricky as it looks. To indent the first line of the current paragraph, click on the upper handle (which affects the first line only) and drag it right or left. Select several paragraphs to format more than one at a time. To indent the rest of the lines without moving the first line, drag the middle handle (which affects all other lines).

To indent all the lines the same amount, click on the bottom, square handle. What's confusing is that the middle and bottom handles always move together. The difference is that if you click on the middle

In addition to using the Ruler as a tool, you can also read it as an instrument panel for information about the current paragraph. To see the indentation, the tabs, or even the columns in a particular paragraph, move the insertion point into it and look at the Ruler.

handle, the top one won't move with them. If you click on the bottom handle, it will.

Probably the most convenient use for the indentation markers is for indenting both edges of a paragraph some standard amount, such as a half-inch. (This is common formatting for quotations.)

You can also control paragraph indents by entering exact measurements in the Paragraph dialog box. Select Format | Paragraph or right-click and select Paragraph. This dialog box is shown in Figure 3.3. The Paragraph dialog box enables you to do several things at once (change indentation, spacing, and alignment, for example) and to clear up muddled settings by just typing in nice round numbers.

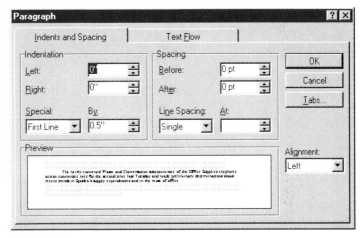

Figure 3.3 The Paragraph dialog box—a good place to straighten out your indentation if you somehow get things messed up on the Ruler

Format Copying

The Format Painter button, which I had you move to the Formatting toolbar from the Standard toolbar in Chapter 2, can copy the formatting of a selection to the next text you select. One of its real advantages is that you can copy several different types of formatting (font, font size, character formatting, color, indentation, spacing, and so on) in one step.

To copy formatting with the Format Painter, put the insertion point in some text that has the formatting you want. If you want to include paragraph formatting, such as indentation, select a paragraph mark (the ¶ character at the end of a paragraph) in a paragraph that contains the formatting you want. Then click on the Format Painter button.

Next, click in a word or click and drag (or use any other selection method) with the Format Painter I-beam to apply the formatting of the original selection to another selection (see Figure 3.4). To "paint" paragraph formatting, just click in the target paragraph with the Format Painter I-beam (or select several paragraphs).

Repeat the process if you double-clicked on the Format Painter button. (It stays active until you click on it again.) Or click on the Format Painter button again to repeat the process a single time.

I call Format Painter the poor person's styles because it enables you to impose a consistent appearance on separated elements in a document. Unlike styles, though, the formatting is "dumb" and can't be updated everywhere by one simple change.

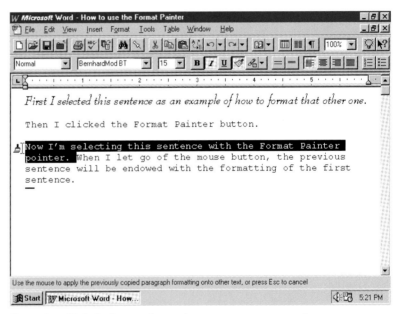

Figure 3.4 "Painting" some formatting onto a new paragraph

SIMPLE EDITING

Inevitably, after the first draft of a document, there are corrections to be made, typos to be fixed, last-minute "constructive criticism" from the boss to be accommodated. Sometimes a document requires a major overhaul. The mechanics of editing consist mainly of cutting stuff, moving stuff around, and replacing stuff.

If you want to be able to track your changes, including cuts, consider turning on revision marks. Revision marks are explained in Chapter 10.

Deleting vs. Cutting

To Word, there is a difference between deleting a selection and cutting it. Deleting means removing it completely (although deletions can be undone). Cutting means removing it from your document but also keeping a copy in reserve.

Something that has been cut can be *pasted* anywhere in the current document (or in other documents or even other programs). Deleted stuff cannot be pasted. (Cutting and deleting can both be undone, though, with CTRL-Z or the Undo button.) Here's a brief description of these actions:

Action	Description
Cut	To remove a selection to a sort of waiting room called the Clipboard.
Paste	To copy a selection from the Clipboard to the location of the insertion point. The Clipboard keeps a copy of the selection until the next Cut or Copy.
Delete	To remove a selection from the document. The removed selection *does not* go to the Clipboard.

To delete a selection, simply press DELETE (or Backspace). To cut a selection, press CTRL-X, click on the Cut button, select Edit | Cut, or right-click on the selection and select Cut. You get the picture.

Moving Things with the Mouse (Drag and Drop)

When you want to move a selection a short distance—to another part of the sentence, below a certain nearby paragraph, and so on—drag and drop is your best bet. When you drag a selection, the pointer gets a gray rectangle attached to it.

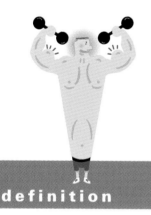

definition

Drag and Drop: *Clicking on a selection, holding down the mouse button, and dragging it (using the special pointer that appears) to the intended destination.*

unwelcome pattern. Projections for 1997 show a return to roughly the 10% level of savings. Perhaps it is too soon to worry.

If you drag a copy, the pointer gets a little plus sign in a box.

If you ever need to drag a *copy* of a selection while keeping the original in place, hold down CTRL while draggin' and droppin'. The little drag-and-drop pointer will sport a tiny plus sign as the only onscreen hint of what you're doing (although the message "Copy to Where?" instead of the usual "Move to Where?" appears in the status bar).

When you drag and drop, notice that Word generally keeps the spacing around the old and new places cleaned up, but it sometimes makes mistakes, so you might occasionally have to add a space (or, more rarely, get rid of one).

Moving Things with Cut, Copy, and Paste

There are so many different ways to cut, copy, and paste that I'll put them into a nice handy table for you (see Table 3.3). Just remember that both cutting and copying put the selection on the Clipboard, but copying leaves the original in place—great for creating small variations on the same theme. Paste takes whatever's on the Clipboard and inserts it wherever the insertion point is at the time. Since the content of the Clipboard stays the same until the next time you cut or copy a selection, you can paste the same selection over and over again.

Just to show you how easy it is to move text with cut and paste, a step-by-step walk-through of how to move a paragraph is on the next page.

Making Systematic Changes with Replace

To replace one thing with another once, many times, or every-where in your document, use Replace. Why would you want to do this?

Method	Cut	Copy	Paste
Keyboard	CTRL-X	CTRL-C	CTRL-V
Menus	Edit | Cut	Edit | Copy	Edit | Paste
Toolbar	✂	📋	📋
Right-clicking on the selection	Cut	Copy	Paste

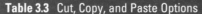
Table 3.3 Cut, Copy, and Paste Options

MOVING A PARAGRAPH step by step

1. Double-click in the left margin to select the paragraph.
2. Click on the Cut button on the toolbar (the one with scissors).
3. Move the insertion point to the destination.
4. Click on the Paste button (the one with a clipboard and document).

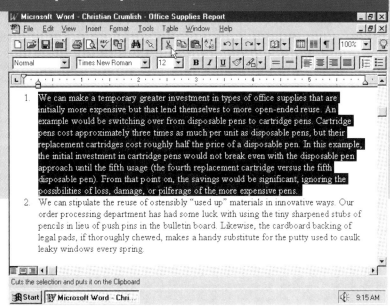

Sometimes you'll decide to change a given piece of terminology with another, you'll want to make a formatting change throughout a document (when you haven't been using styles—tsk, tsk), or you'll want to clean up a document with extra line breaks in it or other irregularities.

If you set up your toolbars as suggested in Chapter 2, click on the Replace button on the Standard toolbar. Otherwise, select Edit | Replace, press CTRL-H, or, if you're already in the midst of a Find operation (as explained earlier), just click on the Replace button in the Find dialog box. Any of these actions will bring up the Replace dialog box (see Figure 3.5).

As you can see, you have a lot of options to choose from in the Replace dialog box. Here's what they all do:

- **Match Case** is handy if you want to replace only those words capitalized exactly like your example word (entered in the Find What box).
- **Find Whole Words Only** will allow you to find just *car* and not *carpet*, for example.

- **Use Pattern Matching** lets you find words that start or end with certain letters, using ? to represent any single character and * to represent any number of characters.
- **Sounds Like**, as you might guess, sets Word to the task of finding words that sound similar to your example.
- **Find All Word Forms** lets you find other parts of speech related to the example word. For example, if your example word is *increase*, Word will find the words *increase, increasing, increased, increases,* and so forth.
- The **Format** button allows you to choose a format to find and one to replace it with—any character or paragraph formatting can be found and replaced.
- The **Special** button has Word look for and/or replace special characters, such as tabs, paragraph breaks, and so on.

Once you've made your choices, click on Find Next to find your first example. If it looks like something you want to replace, click on Replace. The selection will be replaced, and the next example will be found. To skip a selection (leaving it unchanged), click on Find Next again instead of Replace. To go ahead and change every instance of your example word in the document without seeing each one (which is risky, unless you're sure of yourself), click on Replace All.

If Word reaches the end of your document after starting somewhere in the middle, a dialog box will appear. Click Yes to continue the search from the beginning, or No to end it there. If Word gets to the

Figure 3.5 The Replace dialog box, used for finding things and replacing them

end of your document without finding what you want, it will display this message, "Word has finished searching the document." Click on OK.

When it's done, Word will tell you how many changes it made, if any. Click Close (or Cancel, if Word never found anything) to close the Replace dialog box. If you goofed somehow during your replace operation, you can always undo the changes immediately (by pressing CTRL-Z once for each change, or just a single time if you used Replace All).

You may notice that the Find What and Replace With boxes have drop-down lists attached to them. Word keeps track of all the words or phrases you've entered in these boxes during your current editing session. To repeat a find or replace, simply click the button at the right end of the box in question and choose one of the earlier entries.

Undoing Complicated Procedures

You already know how to undo your most recent mistake—just press CTRL-Z, select Edit | Undo, or click on the Undo button. If you undo something by mistake (or hit the Undo key too many times), click on the Redo button (to the right of Undo) to redo the last undone thing. If you want to undo something that was done a few actions ago, click on the little drop-down arrow to the right of the Undo button. A list of your recent actions will drop down.

You can scroll through the list if necessary. Select the action you want to undo and Word will turn back the clock to the point of that earlier action. You'll lose the things you did afterward, even if they were OK, so there's a tradeoff involved here.

CHOOSE A PROJECT

You're now safely out of the primer zone. At this point you can think about any of the more complicated tasks you need to accomplish and jump directly to whichever chapter answers your questions. If you're not sure where to look, check the index—it's pretty thorough and you don't have to know Word or computer jargon to use it. If you have no challenging tasks to deal with immediately, put the book aside until you do!

CHAPTER 4

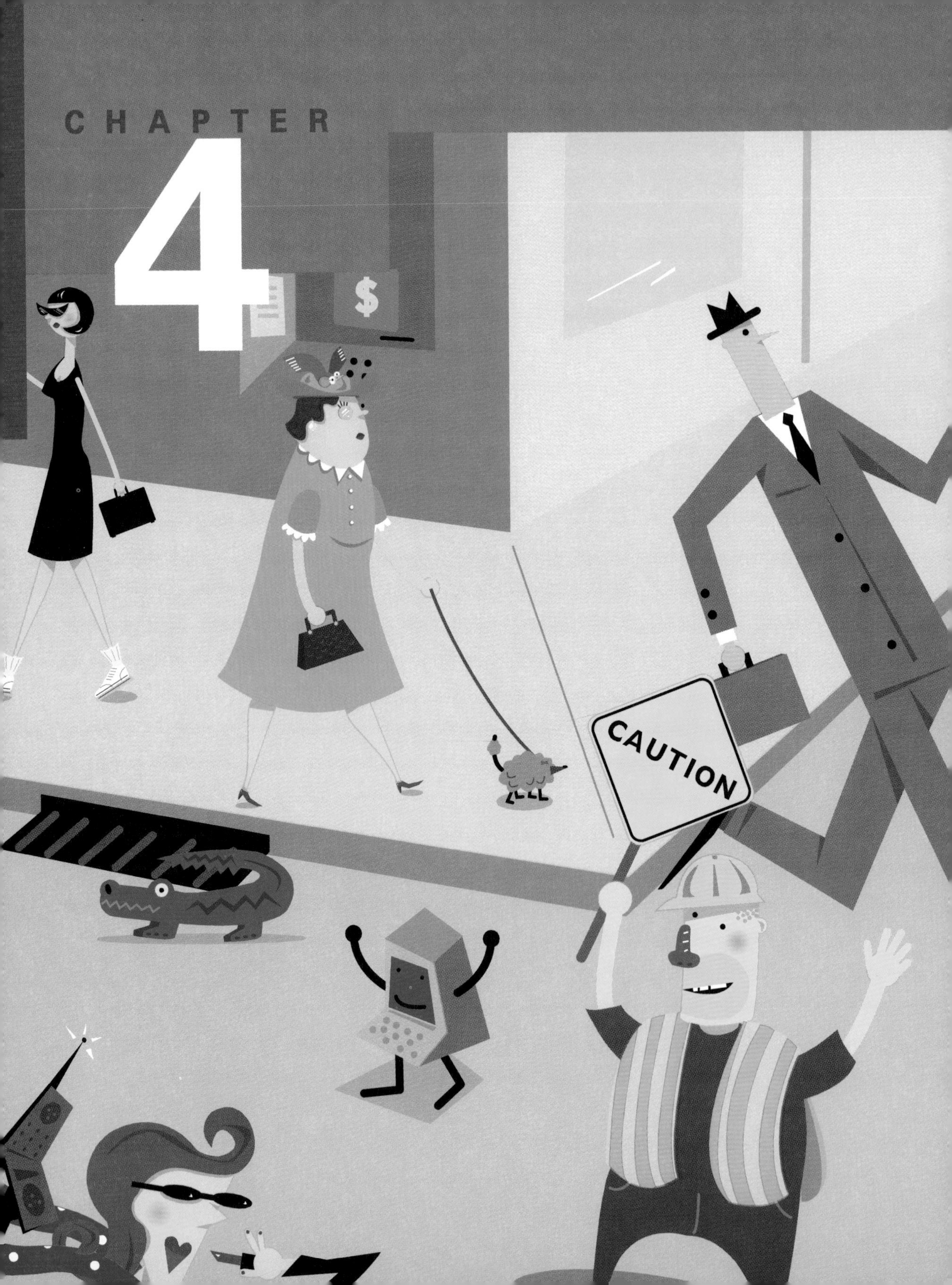

Reusing Documents and Simple Procedures

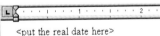

letrhed

June 19, 1996

Wendell Maas
3323 Marina del Mar
San Harmonica, CA 92101

File name: rejection (boilerplate)

Save as type: Word Document

<put the real date here>

<put the recipient's address here>

Dear Mr/s. <recipient's last name>

CREATE AND INSERT
BOILERPLATE WITH AUTOCORRECT ➤ *pp 58-59*

To create the boilerplate:
1. Select the text you want to reuse.
2. Click on Tools | AutoCorrect.
3. Type an abbreviation.
4. Click on Add.
5. Click on OK.

To insert the boilerplate:
1. Type the AutoCorrect abbreviation.
2. Press ENTER or the Spacebar.

MAKE A DUMMY DOCUMENT
TO USE AS BOILERPLATE ➤ *pp 59-60*

1. Click on File | Save As.
2. Type a name for the dummy document.
3. Click on Save.
4. Strip out (cut) specific information you don't need
   in the dummy.
5. Include instructions.
6. Save the document again. (Click on the Save button
   on the toolbar.)

USE A DUMMY DOCUMENT
AS A BASIS FOR A NEW ONE ➤ *pp 59-60*

1. Open the dummy document.
2. Select File | Save As.
3. Type the name of the new document.
4. Replace the dummy information with specifics.
5. Save the copy.

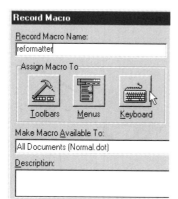

File name:	rejection (boilerplate)
Save as type:	Word Document
	Word Document
	Document Template
	Text Only

Record Macro

Record Macro Name:
reformatter

Assign Macro To

Toolbars   Menus   Keyboard

Make Macro Available To:

All Documents (Normal.dot)

Description:

MAKE A TEMPLATE FROM A DOCUMENT ➤ *p 61*

1. Click on File | Save As
2. Type a new name for the template.
3. Click in the Save as type drop-down list box.
4. Select Document Template.
5. Click on Save.

RECORD A MACRO ➤ *pp 62-65*

1. Double-click on the word REC in the status bar.
2. Type a name and a description for your macro.
3. Click on the Keyboard button.
4. To create a shortcut for the macro, experiment with keyboard combinations until you find one that's not already taken. (Try CTRL-SHIFT-something.)
5. Click on Assign.
6. Click on Close.
7. Carefully execute the procedure.
8. When you're done, leave the insertion point in a sensible place for repeating the macro.
9. Double-click REC again. (If you made any mistakes, use Undo and then repeat from step 1.)

Boilerplates are "good for you," but you might not want to bother with them. Fine with me. This isn't the dentist's office, where I make you feel guilty. Use them only when you're fed up with a repetitive task and feel that "there's gotta be a better way."

For more on the AutoCorrect dialog box, see "Choose Your AutoCorrect Preferences" in Chapter 2.

I've said it before and I'll say it again: Computers are no good unless they can save you some work (at least in the long run). A lot of writing projects are routine, especially in the office or in any organizational setting (volunteer groups, clubs, subversive underground cells). This means you can often reuse text for ordinary situations. Reusable text is known as *boilerplate.*

One common example of boilerplate text is letterhead. For that matter, even a simple name and address can qualify as boilerplate. Another typical kind of boilerplate is a form letter, such as a publishing house's rejection letter, sadly enough.

But boilerplate is just the name of the solution, not a specific command or method in Word. There are several common ways to create boilerplate text and use it. Each method is more or less appropriate for different situations.

A simple boilerplate can be made with AutoCorrect. Longer boilerplate text can be made by saving a dummy copy of a document and keeping it around as a basis for later documents. Word also has *templates,* which are more sophisticated versions of this type of blank, dummy document, but you don't need to mess with them unless you have some pretty sophisticated goals in mind.

CREATING BOILERPLATE WITH AUTOCORRECT

To make some text into boilerplate text with AutoCorrect, first select it. (I have to assume that you've written it at least once before. If not, do that first, of course.) Then select Tools | AutoCorrect. This brings up the AutoCorrect dialog box.

Type an abbreviation for the boilerplate. Try to make the abbreviation something unusual, such as an incorrect spelling (for example, "letrhed" for your letterhead), so that you don't accidentally insert boilerplate when you really mean exactly what you're typing.

Finally, click on the Add button. When you next want to insert your boilerplate in a document, type the abbreviation, then press ENTER (or the Spacebar). Your abbreviation will automatically be replaced by the boilerplate you stored before.

letrhed

June 19, 1996

Wendell Maas
3323 Marina del Mar
San Harmonica, CA 92101

"Real" Word document templates are explained in the upcoming section, "Making a Real Template."

USING A DUMMY DOCUMENT AS BOILERPLATE

I won't call something a *template* unless it's a bona fide Word template, because I don't want to confuse you by sometimes using a word as jargon and sometimes using it for its real meaning. (But to me, any document saved and used as a basis for spin-offs is a template.)

The most important thing I can tell you about this type of operation is that you should *make a copy of the document first—before* you strip out the specific information and turn your sample document into a dummy. Why? Because you'll start gutting some key document, saving only the parts that are needed for the dummy, and then if you're anything like me, without thinking you'll just go right ahead and accidentally *save* the dummy, without specifying Save As, and you'll have accidentally replaced that key document with an empty husk. This is much worse than accidentally deleting a document, because the document actually still exists but the old contents are scattered randomly all over your hard disk. If anything like this does happen to you, get ahold of a useful file-recovery program, such as Norton Utilities, with which you can piece together fragments by searching the entire disk for key words (not much fun, but often better than rewriting).

Make a Copy First

Begin by opening the document you want to base your new dummy on. And how do you make a copy? With Save As, of course (as explained in Chapter 1). Quickly, then, select File | Save As.

This brings up the Save As dialog box (see Figure 4.1). In the File name box, type a new name for the document, one that you'll recognize later when you need to use it as a basis for a new copy. Click on the Save button.

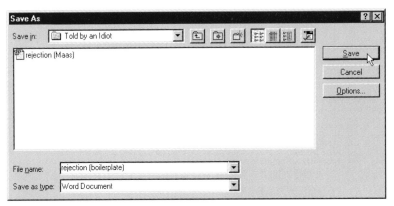

Figure 4.1 Typing a name for a dummy document copy in the Save As dialog box

Then go ahead and strip out any specific information in the document, saving only the material you plan to reuse. It's a good idea to leave some kind of instructions in the parts of the dummy that will have to be filled in for a particular copy, to make sure you don't later leave any embarrassing lacunae (see Figure 4.2). When the dummy document is ready, save it again. (Click on the Save button on the toolbar.)

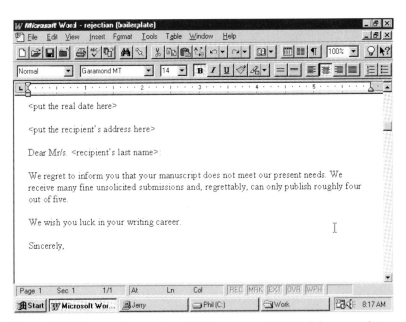

Figure 4.2 A dummy document containing comments that tell the user what details to add

Make a Copy Again When the Time Comes

The same sort of advice holds when the time comes to use the dummy document to create copies: Use Save As to save the dummy as a new document before filling in the details. It's too easy to accidentally work only on the dummy, and then either have to clean it up again next time or—worse yet—end up superseding some work by repeatedly saving over the same copy.

Once again (with feeling): Open the dummy document. Select File | Save As. Type a distinct name for your new document. Click on the Save button. There—your dummy document is safe for next time.

MAKING A REAL TEMPLATE

Even bothering to think about—let alone learn anything about—Word's actual *template* feature could inherently complicate your life and turn a simple writing task into a philosophical discourse about types and tokens. However, templates *do* have their advantages. The main advantage is that they're very hard to accidentally overwrite. Once you've preserved your boilerplate document as a template, it's designed to spin off new documents without altering the original. So, if you really want to save a copy of a sample document as an actual Word document template, select File | Save As, type a new name for the document, and then click in the Save as type box and select Document Template. Then click on Save.

Once you choose the Document Template type, Word should automatically point at your Templates folder in the Save As dialog box. If it doesn't, switch to that folder yourself. (It's most likely inside the MSOffice folder.)

If you want to include self-updating information (such as a date field) in a template, you'll want to use the Insert | Field command, as touched on in Chapter 8. Some of the built-in templates and *wizards* (special kinds of templates that interview you and automatically create documents for you) use these kinds of fields, as do mail merge documents. (Mail merge is torn down to size in Chapter 9.)

Why bother, though, making a real template, unless you need to use Word in some sophisticated way that requires your document to have its own special toolbars, forms, sets of macros, and even dialog boxes?

CREATING A NEW DOCUMENT BASED ON A TEMPLATE

When the time comes to start a new document based on your template, don't start by clicking on the New button on the Standard toolbar. That button's great, but it skips the stage where you get to choose a template. (Actually, that's why it's great.) Instead, select File | New. This brings up the New dialog box (see Figure 4.3). Select your template, and click on OK. Word will start a new document based on your template. (The other tabs in this dialog box include built-in templates that come with Word.)

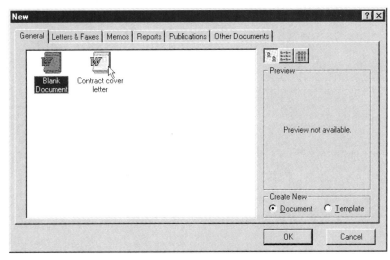

Figure 4.3 Choosing a template in the New dialog box

RECORDING A FEW SIMPLE STEPS

Did you notice that I didn't mention *macros* in the heading? Didn't want to scare you off. This section is really about simple macro recording and playback, but I won't *make* you do it. If the idea gives you the creeps, you're exempt. Off to Chapter 5 with you.

All along I have been emphasizing that anything you find yourself doing over and over could probably be delegated to the computer. Take this idea a step further now, and think about playing around with the macro recorder a little. A macro can record the typing of a piece of

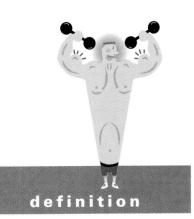

definition

Macro: *A recorded sequence of steps or commands that can be played back to reproduce the original steps, much like a player piano roll.*

**habits &
strategies**

*It is possible to "pause" while
recording a macro, perform
steps that will go unrecorded,
and then resume, but that period
of discontinuity is likely to
destroy the usefulness of the
macro unless you dot all your i's
and cross all your t's.*

boilerplate and then play it back at any point. Since there are easier ways to make and use boilerplate text, you won't need to call on macros for that purpose. But there are other repetitive computer and Word tasks than just typing. For example, certain editing tasks become repetitive, especially when you are "cleaning up" a document or converting some of the contents of an old document into a new format.

Do Your Housecleaning First

To record a macro, you have to run through the task sequence manually with the macro recorder turned on. Then the computer can imitate what you did whenever you invoke the macro. To make the recording process go smoothly, make sure that the portion of the document you'll be working on when you record is free of errors and is typical of the kind of passage you'll be using the macro on. If you think your *computer* takes everything literally, wait till you record a macro. If it could record you scratching your nose, it would include that in the steps it saves.

If you have to add little correcting steps while recording a procedure, the macro recorder will pick all of that up and replicate those extra steps each and every time. Recording a macro is sort of like performing an ancient religious ceremony that must be started over if a single step goes astray. Practice the sequence a few times to get it together without having the "cameras" rolling.

Lights...Camera...

Put the insertion point in the sort of place it will be when you want to run the macro (so you don't end up recording the steps to get it into position), and then double-click on the word REC on the status bar. (This is a welcome shortcut for selecting Tools | Macro and then clicking on Record.)

This will bring up the Record Macro dialog box (see Figure 4.4). Type a name for your macro, something short and pithy. You might have to remember what it is, based on its name, months from now. To help in that eventuality, type a description of the macro in the Description area near the bottom of the dialog box. Then click on the Keyboard button in the Assign Macro To area. This brings up the Customize dialog box (see Figure 4.5).

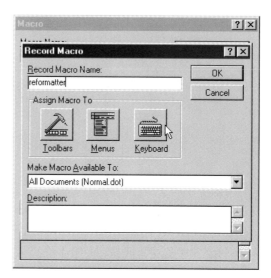

Figure 4.4 Typing a name for a macro and clicking on one of the Assign Macro To buttons to create a handy shortcut

habits & strategies

Definitely create some shortcut for the macro. Usually the keyboard shortcuts are the least obtrusive. (Your best bets for unused key combinations are CTRL-SHIFT with letters.) I'd advise you to add a macro to a menu or a toolbar only if it's something you're really going to use all the time.

Press some combination of keys. If the key combination you tried is already in use, its action will appear under the words Currently Assigned To (under the Press New Shortcut Key box). When you've got a good one, click on Assign. Then click on Close.

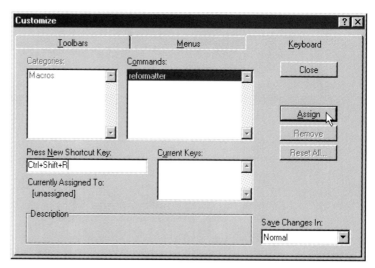

Figure 4.5 Pressing a shortcut key combination to assign it to the macro that will be recorded

Action!

You're now recording a macro. Quiet on the set! You'll notice a few reminders on your screen. First of all, there's a miniature Macro Recorder toolbar floating on the screen. (Actually, only the word Macro is really visible in its title bar.)

Stop ————————  ———————— Pause

 This toolbar sports a Stop button and a Pause button. The word REC in your status bar should now be bold. Also, your mouse pointer now appears as a pointer-and-cassette combination, as shown here, both to remind you that you're recording and that the Macro Recorder can't record text selection done with the mouse. (It can record menu selections and choices in dialog boxes made with the mouse, though.)

Perform your procedure carefully. Leave the insertion point in the best place to repeat the process when you're done (in case you'll want to use the macro over and over without repositioning the pointer between each use). Finally, click on Stop on the Macro Recorder toolbar or double-click on REC again.

Playback Time

When you want to use the macro, position the insertion point and then press the key combination. (If you forget your key combination, and then clicking on Play.) Repeat as needed.

WHAT TO DO NOW

 Chapter 5 deals with the special formatting requirements for reports and formal documents. If that's not your cup of tea, decide what's the next pressing goal you want to achieve with Word, and head for the chapter that gets you to it. If nothing's that pressing, get your nose out of the book and go talk to someone.

MAIL

Producing a Simple Report

INCLUDES

- Adding headers, footers, and page numbering

- Assigning headings

- Using simple styles

- Creating a title page

- Using automatic indentation

- Changing alignment, line spacing, and margins

- Creating numbered and bulleted lists

- Using the Shrink to Fit feature

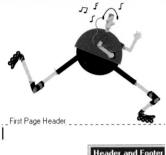

FAST FORWARD

First Page Header

Header and Footer

Preliminary Rep

ADD A HEADER OR A FOOTER ➤ *pp 71-72*

1. Select View | Header and Footer. (To make a footer, click on the Switch Between Header and Footer button.)
2. Type the text you want in your header. Press TAB to move to the center and right side.
3. Click on the Page Number button if you want to add a page number.
4. Click on the Date button if you want to add the date (which will be automatically updated every time the document is opened).
5. Click on Close.

START A HEADER OR A FOOTER
ON THE SECOND PAGE ➤ *pp 72-73*

Follow the steps in the previous Fast Forward item for adding a header or footer.

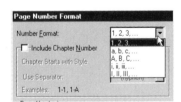

1. Select File | Page Setup (or click the Page Setup button on the Header and Footer toolbar).
2. Click on the Layout tab of the Page Setup dialog box.
3. Check the Different First Page check box.
4. Click on OK.

NUMBER YOUR PAGES ➤ *pp 73-75*

1. Select Insert | Page Numbers.
2. Choose a position and an alignment for your numbers.
3. If you want a special numbering format, click on the Format button. (If not, skip to step 5.)
4. Choose a format from the Number Format drop-down list box and then click on OK.
5. Click on OK.

CREATE A STYLE ➤ *p 76*

1. Format a paragraph.
2. Select it.
3. Click in the Style box on the Formatting toolbar.
4. Type a name for your new style.
5. Click on OK.

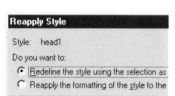

CHANGE A STYLE "ON THE FLY" ➤ *pp 76-77*

1. Make your changes to the paragraph that's currently formatted with the style.
2. Click in the Style box.
3. Press ENTER.
4. Make sure Redefine the style using the selection as an example? is selected in the Reapply Style dialog box that appears.
5. Click on OK.

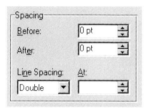

CHANGE THE LINE SPACING ➤ *pp 78-79*

1. Select Format | Paragraph.
2. Select the Indents and Spacing tab.
3. Click in the Line Spacing drop-down list box in the Spacing area of the Paragraph dialog box.
4. Select one of the options.
5. Click on OK.

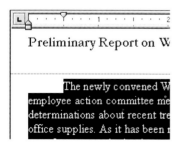

CREATE AN AUTOMATIC PARAGRAPH INDENT ➤ *pp 79-81*

1. Place the insertion point in a typical paragraph.
2. Click on the indentation marker (the upper one) at the left end of the Ruler, and drag it to the indentation level you want.
3. Click in the Style box on the Formatting toolbar.
4. Type a new name for your paragraph style.
5. Assign this style to all normal paragraphs.

CHANGE A
PARAGRAPH'S ALIGNMENT ➤ *p 81*

After placing the insertion point in a paragraph (or selecting several paragraphs):

- Click on the Left button to return to left-justified, ragged-right alignment (the default).
- Click on the Center button to center the selection.
- Click on the Right button to impose right-justified, ragged-left alignment.
- Click on the Justify button to align the selection at both margins (with full justification).

SPECIFY MARGINS ➤ *p 82*

1. Select File | Page Setup.
2. Click on the Margins tab of the Page Setup dialog box.
3. Enter the top, bottom, left, and right margins you want, in inches.
4. Click on OK.

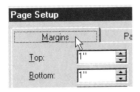

CREATE A NUMBERED LIST ➤ *pp 82-83*

1. Start a new paragraph with the number 1, a period (or hyphen or closing parenthesis), and a space (or tab).
2. Type the first item in the list.
3. Press ENTER. Word starts the next paragraph with the number 2.
4. Type each item in the list, pressing ENTER after each one.
5. Press ENTER twice when you get to the end.

CREATE A BULLETED LIST ➤ *pp 82-83*

1. Click on the Bullets button on the Formatting toolbar.
2. Type the first item in the list.
3. Press ENTER. Word starts the next paragraph with another bullet.
4. Type each item in the list, pressing ENTER after each one.
5. Press ENTER twice when you get to the end.

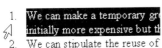

Once your document is past that rough-draft stage and has been treated to the basic niceties of formatting and editing, there's a slightly higher level of polish you might want to achieve for reports, handouts for presentations, and the like—you know, those situations in which you might need the edge that a cleanly designed document can give you.

ADDING A HEADER OR FOOTER

Actually, you can have page numbers without fiddling with headers and footers. If you don't want anything besides numbers at the top or bottom of each page, skip to "Numbering the Pages."

For any document with more than a couple of pages, a header or a footer is a must. Imagine what would happen if the document were dropped on the floor, its pages scattered and mixed with other paperwork. How easy it would be to reassemble if every page had a small header identifying the document and the page number!

Why the View Menu and Not the Insert Menu?

To add a header or a footer (or both), you have to pull down the View menu and select Header and Footer. Why is this command not on the Insert menu? Beats me. Don't try to understand it.

This drops you temporarily into *page layout view* (as indicated by the vertical ruler on the left side of the window and the appearance of the edge of the page at the top), with the header "active" and a little Header and Footer toolbar, shown here, floating partly over the header and partly over the grayed-out contents of the document. If you intend to create or edit a footer, click on the Switch Between Header and Footer button. You'll be taken to an analogous area at the bottom of the page.

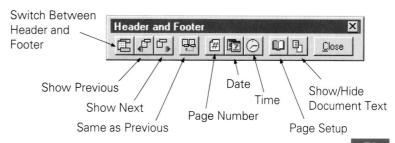

Switch Between Header and Footer

Show Previous
Show Next
Same as Previous
Page Number
Date
Time
Show/Hide Document Text
Page Setup

Naturally, the details of the text, the insertions, and the formatting of your header (or footer) will depend on your needs. What follows is a step-by-step explanation of how to make one specific type of header.

CREATING A TYPICAL HEADER step by step

1. In the header area, type the name of the document or an identifying abbreviation.

2. Press TAB twice.

3. Click on the Page Number button on the Header and Footer toolbar.

4. Select the whole header.

5. Click on the Underline button on the Formatting toolbar.

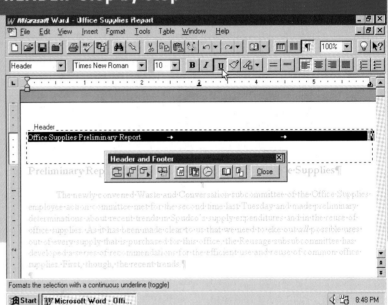

When you're done with your header or footer, click on the Close button on the Header and Footer toolbar. This will return you to normal view (unless you were in page layout view to begin with).

Starting Headers and Footers on the Second Page

Making a title page is explained later in this chapter.

Normally you don't want a header or footer on the first page of a document. The first page of a document usually has a clear title or other identifier.

If you want no header or footer on the first page of your document, select File | Page Setup, or click the Page Setup button on the Header and Footer toolbar. This brings up the Page Setup dialog box. Click on the Layout tab if it's not already in front. Then check the Different First Page check box (see Figure 5.1).

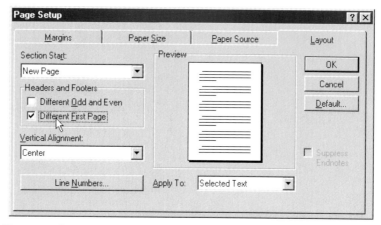

Figure 5.1 Checking the Different First Page check box to have a header start on page 2

Now click on OK. To see the results, select View | Headers and Footers. You'll see the now blank header area for page 1. Notice that the label at the top of the header area on page 1 is First Page Header. Click on the Show Next button on the Header and Footer toolbar. You'll be taken to the top of page 2, where you'll see the header you created earlier. (This one is still labeled Header, as will be true for all pages except page 1.) Click on Close.

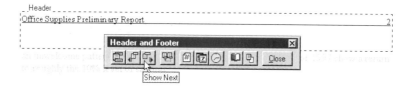

NUMBERING THE PAGES

If you want to add page numbers without any of the other accoutrements of headers and footers, or if you want some elaborate type of page numbering, there's a separate command for that. (Yes, you could also create a header or a footer and then only insert a page number.)

Positioning the Page Number

To number your pages, select Insert | Page Numbers. This brings up the Page Numbers dialog box.

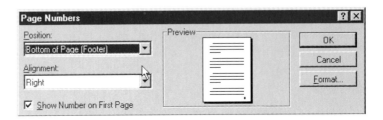

Choose a position for the page numbers (Top of Page or Bottom of Page) and an alignment (Left, Center, or Right). You can also decide whether or not to have page numbers appear on the first page. If you want some special kind of numbering (such as roman numerals, letters, or a combination of chapter and page numbers), click on the Format button. This brings up the Page Number Format dialog box (see Figure 5.2). Choose the number format you want from the drop-down list box, and then click on OK. When you're satisfied with your page-numbering selections, click on OK.

If you want something tricky, such as a hyphenated number indicating chapter and page numbers (when there are several chapters in a document), you have to divide your document into sections. Sections are explained in Chapter 13.

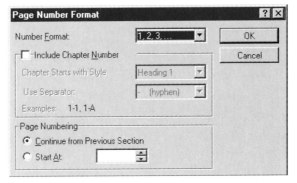

Figure 5.2 The Page Number Format dialog box, which is useful for more exotic page-numbering options

Numbering Pages in Relation to a Total ("Page 2 of 19")

To include running page numbers expressed in relation to a total number of pages, insert your page numbering in a header or footer (using View | Header and Footer, as explained earlier in this chapter). After inserting the page number code with the Page Number button, press the Spacebar, type **of**, and then type another space.

Select Insert | Field. In the Field dialog box (see Figure 5.3), choose Document Information in the Categories box to the left, and then select NumPages from the Field Names box on the right. Then click on OK. This will insert the total number of document pages in your header or footer. It will also automatically update the total if the number of pages in your document changes.

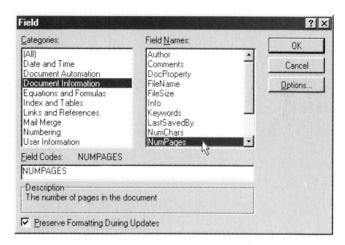

Figure 5.3 Use the Field dialog box to insert a code representing the total number of pages in a document

habits & strategies

Word comes with a set of heading styles, called Heading 1, Heading 2, and so on. They're not very elegant, but they'll do in a pinch. If you make up your own heading styles, be sure to give them names that differ from the preexisting styles.

USING STYLES TO IMPOSE A SIMPLE DESIGN

If you want to make your document really presentable, you should experiment with different fonts and sizes for the text. There is an easy way to do this. The basic principle is to make similar elements *look* similar. You start by defining different styles for the different types of elements in your document, such as headings. Then you assign the appropriate style to every text element in your document. This enables you to change the appearance of every instance of a particular element at once, simply by changing the style.

The most common design element in a document is the heading. Sometimes you will have a document with only a single level of heading, and at other times your documents will have several levels.

Defining a Style

Defining a style is easy. Simply format some text manually with the font, size, and emphasis you want. (You can also choose other paragraph formatting, such as spacing, alignment, and indentation, all of which are explained later in this chapter.) Then, with the insertion point still in the text you want formatted, click in the Style box at the left end of the Formatting toolbar, type a name for your new style, and press ENTER. The following illustration shows a heading style being defined:

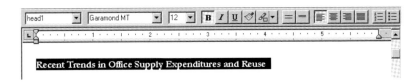

Keep in mind that when you create a style this way, it is associated *only* with your *current* document and not with the Normal template. This means that any subsequent documents produced with the Normal template will not have that style.

Assigning a Style

To assign your newly defined style to other parts of your document, first select an element to which you want to apply the style. Then select the style name in the Style drop-down list box (on the Formatting toolbar). And repeat. What could be easier?

Changing a Style

If you decide that you want to try a variation on the style, simply select any example of the style and make manual changes to the format. (You'll usually use the Formatting toolbar to do this.) Then select the style name in the Style box and press ENTER. Word will display the Reapply Style dialog box, shown here, which offers you two options.

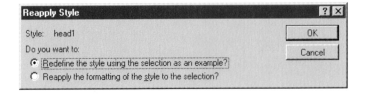

CAUTION

Changing the format of an existing style to create a new style means replacing the original formatting choices, so don't do this unless you're prepared to lose the old style in favor of the new.

Make sure that the first option (Redefine the Style using the selection as an example?) is selected, and then click on OK. All the other elements using this style will change to reflect the new formatting you just applied (see Figure 5.4).

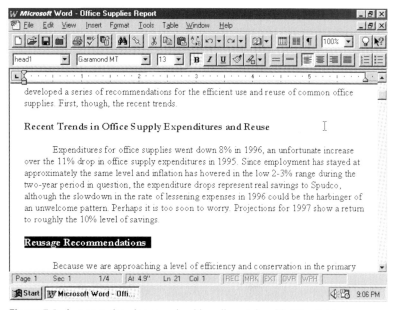

Figure 5.4 A report showing a revised heading style with 13-point type, instead of the 12-point type the head1 style originally had

MAKING A TITLE PAGE

Some documents are so *serious* and formal that they require a separate cover page that announces the document's title and the names of the people responsible. Because of all the blank space that usually appears on such a page, the usual way to lay out a title page is to center the text on it vertically. This is a little tricky in Word because, by default, the vertical alignment of text on a page applies to the document as a whole.

There is a way to get around this problem: divide the document into two sections. Word will allow you to assign different vertical alignments to separate sections within the same document. For our purposes, the first section will consist of only the title page, and the second section will contain the rest of the document.

First, make sure you're in Normal view (select View | Normal). Then position the insertion point at the beginning of the first line of text that will appear after the title page. (This is usually just under the title, or at the top of the page if there is no title yet.) Then select Insert | Break. This brings up the Break dialog box.

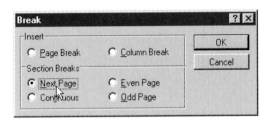

Click on the Next Page option in the Section Breaks area. Then click on OK. An end-of-section marker will appear just before the regular text of the document (after the title, if there is one already). Move the insertion point up before the break.

Preliminary Report on Waste and Conservation of Office Supplies
================End of Section================

habits & strategies

If you create the section break after there's already a "different first page," that feature will repeat in the second section (though you can go to the second section and turn it off again).

Select File | Page Setup. This brings up the Page Setup dialog box. Click on the Layout tab if necessary. Check the Different First Page check box. (You don't want headers or footers on the title page, do you?) Then click in the Vertical Alignment box (just below the Headers and Footers area) and select Center from the drop-down list. Then click on OK. Your layout is done, although you may still need to add more material to the title page to give it the extra oomph you're looking for. Figure 5.5 shows the first two pages of a report in page layout view at 40% so that you can see the centered title page and the first page of the report with a header.

CHANGING THE LINE SPACING

Some documents, especially early drafts, work best if they are double-spaced. If you pass around a document (on paper) to others for comments, double spacing will allow your colleagues to jot down their oh-so-helpful advice between the lines. To change the spacing of a

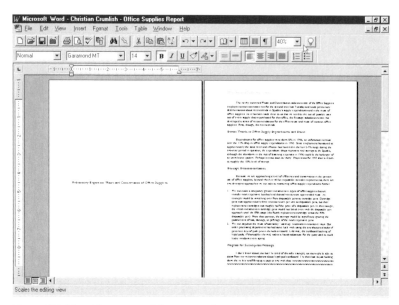

Figure 5.5 The title page and first page of a report

portion of your document, first select the portion you want to change. (Merely placing the insertion point in a paragraph will enable you to double-space that sole paragraph. Select the entire document if you wish to double-space it all.)

If you set up your toolbars the way I recommended in Chapter 2, you can then simply click on the Double Space button on the Formatting toolbar. When it's time to return a document to single spacing, click on the Single Space button on the toolbar.

The Paragraph dialog box is also the place for setting up extra spacing before and/or after a paragraph.

If you want some kind of spacing other than double spacing, or if you are using the default toolbars, select Format | Paragraph. This brings up the Paragraph dialog box (see Figure 5.6). Click on the Indents and Spacing tab if necessary. Then click in the Line Spacing drop-down list box in the Spacing area and select Double or one of the other options. Then click on OK.

AUTOMATIC FIRST-LINE INDENTS

You can always indent the first line of a paragraph manually by pressing TAB at the beginning of the paragraph. You can establish a

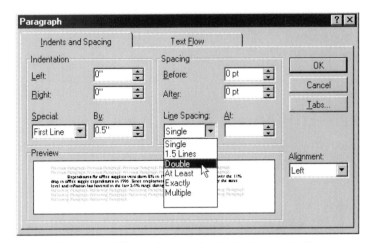

Figure 5.6 Choosing a different line spacing in the Paragraph dialog box

first-line indent for all future paragraphs by dragging the paragraph indent marker on the Ruler into position. But the only way to have the first line of regular paragraphs indent automatically without causing all the other elements (including headings) to also be indented is to establish a special style for body text, distinct from the Normal style that every paragraph gets by default if it isn't given a specified style.

upgrade note

In fact, in some situations, Word will interpret a tab at the beginning of a document as a request for a first-line indent and will change the indentation marker on the Ruler automatically. This AutoFormat feature is new in version 7.0 of Word.

Chapter 12 has more on the trickier aspects of styles.

To establish a special style, select a paragraph, give it a first-line indent on the Ruler, and then click in the Style box on the Formatting toolbar. Type a style name, such as **body**, and press ENTER (see Figure 5.7). From then on, to indent any paragraph, just select the body style (or whatever you called it). You can also define other styles, such as your heading styles, so that the paragraph that immediately follows automatically gets the body text style.

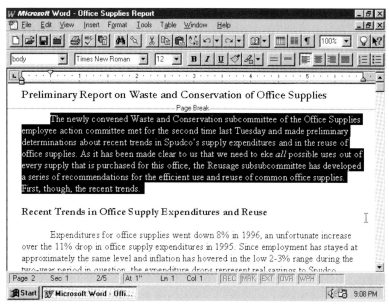

Figure 5.7 Creating an automatically indented paragraph style

CHANGING A PARAGRAPH'S ALIGNMENT

By default, normal paragraphs in Word are left-aligned, meaning that they are aligned along the left side and "ragged" (not aligned) along the right. Changing the alignment of a paragraph or of any selection is a snap. Say you want to center a heading (or a caption, or a quotation, or whatever). Click in the text, and then click on the Center button on the Formatting toolbar. (The Justify button aligns text along both the left and right margins at the same time by varying the amount of spacing between the words—and to a lesser extent between the letters themselves.)

Align Left   Center   Align Right   Justify

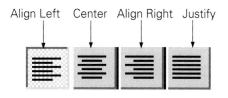

SETTING UP MARGINS

By default, Word gives you 1-inch margins at the top and bottom of each page and 1 1/4–inch margins at left and right. To specify different margins, select File | Page Setup. (It doesn't matter what you've selected in your document, but if your document has sections, make sure that the insertion point is in the section you want to affect.) This brings up the Page Setup dialog box. Click on the Margins tab if necessary (see Figure 5.8). Then click in the Top, Bottom, Left, and Right boxes and enter the margin sizes you want (in inches). When you are done, click on OK.

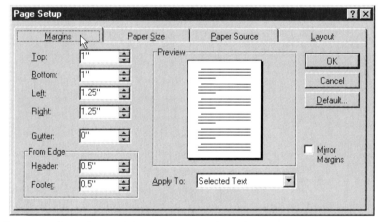

Figure 5.8 Choosing the Margins tab in the Page Setup dialog box to establish new margins for a document

CREATING NUMBERED AND BULLETED LISTS

With numbered and bulleted lists you can often take an argument or explanation and boil it down to a set of easy-to-grasp key points. Word can handle either kind of list automatically, adding a number or bullet to each new item in the list. It will *increment* the numbers (increase them by 1 each time) automatically as well. If you cut and paste items in a numbered list, Word will renumber them for you. Note that this will not happen if you have AutoFormat turned off.

In fact, if you type a new paragraph starting with a number, as soon as you press ENTER Word will assume that you are starting a

definition

Bulleted list: A list of items, each of which is (most commonly) preceded by a centered dot, although other symbols (squares, arrowheads, pointing fingers, faces, shapes, etc.) can be used.

numbered list and will turn the number you typed into one of its magical elements that's not really a character (meaning you can't select or delete it directly since it actually resides in the paragraph mark). If you've got the little Tip Wizard window closed, the light bulb button at the right end of the Standard toolbar will start flashing. If the window is open, Word will let you in on its assumption and offer you the chance to undo it.

There will be times when you won't want what you typed to be treated as a numbered list. (For example, Word will interpret the area code of a phone number, if typed in parentheses at the beginning of a line, as the first number in a numbered list!) Click on the Change button in the Tip Wizard window to undo the action.

Change button

> Word automatically converted your typing to a Numbered List item. You can undo this with the Change Button, or press the Show Me button for more info.

habits & strategies

Numbered and bulleted lists will end if you press ENTER twice. If you want extra spacing between list items, select the list, choose Format | Paragraph, and enter the amount for spacing before or after each paragraph.

upgrade note

Word 6.0 and earlier versions didn't automatically turn your typing into numbered lists, but otherwise, numbered and bulleted lists work pretty much the same way they used to.

To start a numbered list from the Formatting toolbar, click on the Numbering button. To start a bulleted list, click on the Bullets button. The button you pressed will appear "pushed in" the way the Bold, Italic, and Underline buttons do when they are clicked. Type the first item in your list, and then press ENTER.

Numbering  Bullets

Each new paragraph will get a number or bullet, depending on which button you clicked. When you get to the end of your list, press ENTER again and then click on whichever button you clicked on to start the list. The button will become "unpressed," and the previous paragraph style will again prevail.

Rearranging a Numbered List

To rearrange the items in a numbered list, select the item(s) you want to move and then use drag and drop or the cut-and-paste techniques described in Chapter 3. When you complete a move, the numbers will correct themselves "automagically".

Fine-Tuning Automatic Lists

To choose different numbering or different indentation styles for your lists, you have to get your hands a little dirty (though you still don't really have to understand how Word handles the items). Right-click on any paragraph in the list you want to micromanage, and choose Bullets and Numbering from the menu that pops up. (This method can also be used to start a new bulleted or numbered list.) This brings up the Bullets and Numbering dialog box (see Figure 5.9).

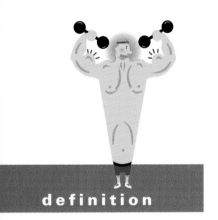

definition

Hanging indent: When the first line of a paragraph is indented less than the rest of the lines. (The first line "hangs" further to the left than the rest of the paragraph.) This is also called a negative indentation.

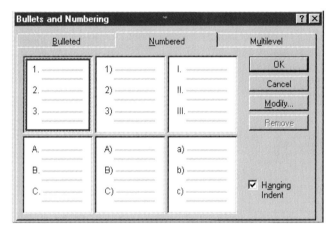

Figure 5.9 The Bullets and Numbering dialog box, used for choosing bullet styles, numbering formats, or elaborate level arrangements

For a list you've just typed, the appropriate tab should come up automatically. For lists within lists, check out the Multilevel tab. The Bulleted tab gives you a choice of dingbats, the Numbered tab offers a choice of numbering styles, and both provide a check box that allows you to opt against the default *hanging indent*.

On each of the tabs, you can also click on the Modify button to gain even more control over the fine points of the list style. For example, clicking on Modify on the Numbered tab brings up the Modify Numbered List dialog box, whose most important option is Start At. This feature allows you to change the starting number of the list (which is great for continuing a list after an intervening paragraph). The determined user can also affect the type of numbering, the characters (such as periods or parentheses) used before and/or after the numbers, the alignment of the numbers, the indentation, the space after the numbers, and the ubiquitous hanging indent.

USING SHRINK TO FIT TO AVOID NEARLY EMPTY PAGES

It never fails that a document you're about to print will turn out to go just barely onto that ninth page, wasting paper now and when you make 27 photocopies of your report for the meeting. That last page, with only a sentence and a half on it, looks a little lame, too. One of Word's cooler features—Shrink to Fit—solves this problem.

If you set up your toolbars the way I suggested in Chapter 2, the Shrink to Fit button is on the Standard toolbar, just to the right of the Spelling button. (If you didn't create this button, you can get to this feature by clicking on the Print Preview button.)

Click on the Shrink to Fit button and Word will change the formatting of your document as subtly as possible. It fiddles with line spacing, font sizes, and so on, to squeeze out that little overrun and force your document to end near the bottom of the previous page. If you don't like the results, press CTRL-Z to undo them immediately.

WHAT NEXT?

If this chapter has not satisfied your report-designing ambitions, try skipping ahead to Chapter 12, where you'll find the keys to designing elegant, sophisticated documents, or Chapter 14, for advice on producing and maintaining professional-quality publications. For heavy-duty, lengthy, complicated documents, see Chapter 13.

habits & strategies

It's a good idea to save your document (by clicking on the Save button) before making any major formatting changes.

You Need a Universal Translator

INCLUDES

- Getting someone else's document onto your computer

- Opening documents created with other word processing programs

- Opening a document that Word can't translate

- Saving a document imported from another word processing program

- Saving your Word documents in other formats

- Saving your Word documents in common formats

FAST FORWARD

GET A DOCUMENT ONTO
YOUR COMPUTER ➤ *p 91*

1. Put the disk containing the document into your disk drive.
2. Run your virus scan software.
3. Open the floppy disk drive window.
4. Drag the document onto your desktop.

OPEN A NON-WORD
DOCUMENT IN WORD ➤ *pp 92-93*

1. Start Word.
2. Click on the Open button on the Standard toolbar.
3. Click on the Up One Level button a few times to work your way up to the desktop.
4. Click in the Files of type list box and choose All Files (unless you can already see the document you want to open).
5. Double-click on the document you want to open.

OPEN A DOCUMENT OF ANY TYPE ➤ *pp 94-95*

- If the document icon looks like a Word document icon, double-click on it and Word will start up (if it isn't already started) and open the document.
- If the document is not a Word document, Word may still be able to open it.

OPEN A DOCUMENT IN A
FORMAT WORD DOESN'T RECOGNIZE ➤ *pp 94-95*

1. Double-click on the document icon.
2. Choose winword in the Open With dialog box that appears.
3. Click on OK.

OPEN A DOCUMENT THAT
WORD CAN'T TRANSLATE ➤ *p 96*

- Try opening the document in another word processing program, such as WordPad.
- Ask the person who gave you the document to save it in a format that Word can understand (such as Text Only).

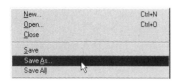

SAVE AN IMPORTED DOCUMENT
IN WORD FORMAT ➤ *p 96*

1. Select File | Save As.
2. Choose Word Document in the Save as type drop-down list box.
3. Click on Save.

SAVE A WORD DOCUMENT IN
ANOTHER FORMAT ➤ *p 97*

1. Select File | Save As.
2. Click in the Save as type drop-down list box and choose the format you want.
3. Type a different filename for the document.
4. Click on Save.

SAVE A DOCUMENT IN A
UNIVERSAL FORMAT ➤ *p 97*

1. Select File | Save As.
2. Choose Text Only or Rich Text Format in the Save as type box.
3. Type a different filename for the document.
4. Click on Save.

CAUTION

Look around your office or wherever you use your computer. Although you might have many computers around you, they might not be the same type as yours. (For instance, some may be Macs.) The other IBM-type PCs may not have Windows installed, and even the ones that do may have other word processing programs on them, such as WordPerfect. Now think about all the computers outside your workplace that produce documents of every type and stripe. Inevitably, the time will come when someone will hand you a disk that contains a document created on some different computer or in some other word processing program and ask you not only to put the document on your computer or print it out, but also to edit the dang thing in Word for Windows.

It's almost as if someone has handed you a wax cylinder from Thomas Edison's day and asked you to make a cassette tape copy of the music encoded thereon. Computer generations evolve about every 18 months, so this analogy is not too far-fetched. Oh, and by the way, can you take this huge stone with hieroglyphics carved on it, scan it in, run a character-recognition program, update the information, and have a report on my desk by 5? Thanks.

Fortunately, the little elves at Microsoft have worked long and hard to make Word compatible with a wide range of earlier and competing word processing formats, as well as with documents created on other computers. Your approach to the translation issue depends on whether you're trying to work with someone else's document or trying to give someone with a different system a copy of one of your documents. I cover both sides of the transaction in this chapter.

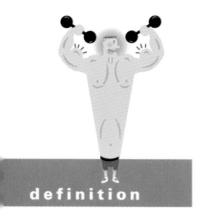

definition

Import: *To open in one program a document that was created in another.*

habits & strategies

A good place to keep a document that you are importing or getting ready to send to someone else is on your desktop. You can get to it easily, and you can click on and drag the icon without having to hunt around for its original folder.

GETTING THE DOCUMENT ONTO YOUR COMPUTER

Generally, someone will hand you a document on a disk (although more and more often nowadays documents are arriving via e-mail or in some other electronic form) and you'll need to import it somehow into Word. If the disk is from a PC, go ahead and put it in your disk drive. Then open the floppy drive window. (Double-click on My Computer and then double-click on the floppy drive icon.) Drag onto your desktop the document (or documents) you need to import into Word (see Figure 6.1). The original files will stay on the disk unless you hold down SHIFT while dragging.

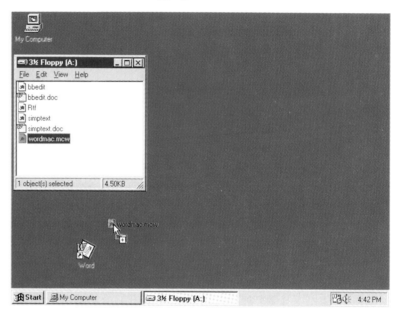

Figure 6.1   Dragging documents from the floppy disk window onto the desktop

If you put a shortcut to your disk drive on the Start menu, you can open a disk easily from anywhere, instead of having to use My Computer to access your floppy drive icon. To add the shortcut, just drag the appropriate icon onto the Start button.

TRYING TO OPEN THE DOCUMENT

You can often open a document that was created in one of the common word processing formats by just using the normal file opening routine to import it into Word. Word will recognize the format and automatically convert the document on the fly. Here's how it works.

First, click on the Open button on the Standard toolbar. This brings up the Open dialog box. Click on the Up One Level button a few times to work your way up to the desktop.

The main window in the Open dialog box typically shows only those files whose extensions are .doc, which is the extension that Word automatically gives to its document files. (File extensions might not be visible in this window, but they are there nonetheless and Windows still uses them to help determine file type.) Many documents, even those not created in Word, have that extension. But an equal number of documents have different extensions or no extension at all. To see all the documents on your desktop, regardless of their extensions, click in the Files of type drop-down list box and choose All Files (see Figure 6.2). Documents of every type will then appear in the window.

See the Upgrade Note later in this chapter to find out how to make file extensions visible.

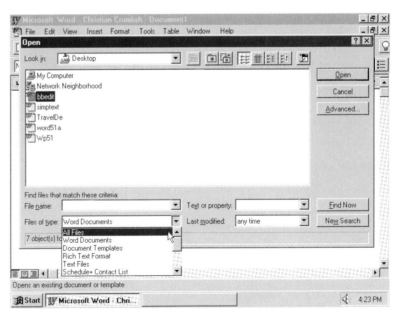

Figure 6.2 Changing the display in the Open dialog box from only .doc files to files of all formats

Then simply go ahead and select the document you want to open and click on the Open button. Most of the time, Word will know what to do and will go ahead and open the document without giving you any trouble. It may take awhile, though. As Word performs the conversion, you'll see a message in the status bar telling you that Word is converting your document.

If your document has an unusual file format or a misleading extension, Word may pop up the Convert File dialog box, shown here, asking you to specify the format of the original file. Choose the one you think is correct and click on OK.

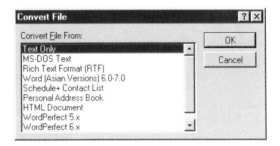

If Word "chokes" on the file, it will present you with a message box saying "The file is not the right file type." Click on OK in this box. (What other choice do you have?) When Word pops up the "choke" message box, it might mean that it just cannot open the document. If so, your best bet is to ask the original creator of the document to try saving it in a different format, one that both her word processing program and yours understand. For more on that option, see "Saving a Document in a Lingua Franca," at the end of this chapter.

CLICKIN' OR DRAGGIN' THE DOCUMENT ICON

In Windows, the easiest way to open a document is to double-click on its icon. You don't have to have Word already running to do this. Windows will start up whatever program is needed to open the item you double-click on. For this to work smoothly with Word, however, the icon must be a Word document icon (a dog-eared page with a blue W floating on its left edge).

CAUTION

Technically, a document can look like a Word document without being one. Word will still attempt to open the document, but it may fail if the document's format is not one that Word can translate.

Double-Clicking on a Word Document Icon

If you double-click on a Word document icon, Word will start (if it's not already running) and automatically open that document.

Word can handle any document created in an earlier version of the program (any version number earlier than 7.0) with no trouble. It won't even mention to you that it's translating the document. If you need to return the document to someone who is using a version of Word earlier than 6.0, make sure to save it again in that person's original format before giving it back (as explained in "Preparing Your Own Documents for Other People," later in this chapter).

upgrade note

The appearance of a document icon is based on its (usually) hidden extension. (This means that a WordPerfect document whose filename ends in .doc will appear to be a Word document.) If you miss those old DOS extensions, you can turn them on again in the Options dialog box that can be accessed from the View menu of any folder window.

Double-Clicking on a Non-Word Document Icon

If a document appears to have been made in another word processing program, such as WordPerfect, double-clicking on it will start that program instead.

Wordperf

If the document is unrecognized, it will sport the generic Windows icon.

bbedit

CAUTION

Windows usually recognizes a document type only if the program that created the document is on your computer. Occasionally, Windows recognizes a document type after the source program has been removed. If you try to open such a document, Windows tells you it's missing something and will refuse to comply.

If you double-click on the icon, a Windows dialog box called Open With will appear. This dialog box asks you to choose the program you want to use to open the unrecognized document (see Figure 6.3).

Scroll through the list of programs in the Choose the program you want to use list box, and click on winword. Don't check off Always use this program to open this type of file unless you know all the ramifications of doing so. Then click on OK. If Word is unable to interpret the document correctly, it will pop up a dialog box to let you know.

Right-Clicking on an Unrecognized Document Icon

The easiest way to open an unrecognized document in Word is to right-click on the document icon and then choose Open With from the menu that pops up. This also brings up the Open With dialog box that is shown in Figure 6.3. Again, if Word is unable to interpret the document correctly, it will let you know.

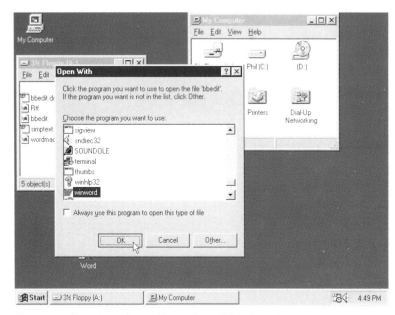

Figure 6.3 Choosing winword in the Open With dialog box to open an unrecognized document.

Dragging a Document Icon onto the Word Icon

An easy way to open a document created in another recognized word processing program is to drag the document icon onto the Word program icon (or, ideally, onto a Word shortcut on your desktop). Word will start up (if it's not already running) and open the document, if it's able to. Chapter 2 explains how to put a shortcut to Word on your desktop.

IF WORD IS UNABLE TO OPEN A DOCUMENT

There will be times when you will receive a document that you simply can't open. There are two things you can try in such a situation: First, try to open the document in some other program, such as WordPad or another word processing program. This intermediate step might provide the missing link. Save the open document in WordPad (or your other word processing program) as a Word document (give it a different name). Expect more minor flaws and inaccuracies in the format than would occur in a normal import.

If that doesn't work, ask the owner of the original document to save it in a format that you both have in common. You can scroll through the Files of type drop-down list box in the Open dialog box to see what formats Word speaks. Ask the other person to check his or her Save As dialog box (or the equivalent) for formats that the source program can produce. Look for formats in common. At the very least, you should both be able to handle text files (though you'll lose all your formatting). Better yet, you might both be able to save in Rich Text Format, which will preserve most of the formatting.

SAVING IMPORTED DOCUMENTS

Word remembers the format of an imported document. If you just click on the Save button or select File | Save when you are done working with the document, Word will keep the document in its original format. To turn the thing into a Word document (which is worth doing, in my opinion, if you need to keep it around), select File | Save As.

When the Save As dialog box comes up, choose Word Document in the Save as type drop-down list box. Then click on Save. From then on, your file will be a bona fide Word document.

If you open a document in another program, you might have to clean up a lot of extraneous coding from the document's native format.

See "Saving a Document in a Lingua Franca," at the end of this chapter, for more on Rich Text Format.

SAVING IN ANOTHER FORMAT

The kindest thing you can do is save your Word document in the exact format that the other person uses. Word can imitate a large set of other word processing programs for this purpose. (The results are not always 100 percent accurate, but what is?)

To save a Word document as another type of document, select File | Save As. Then click in the Save as type drop-down list box and choose from the many other formats available. Type a new name for your document (to preserve the original copy in Word format) and then click on Save.

SAVING A DOCUMENT IN A LINGUA FRANCA

In the worst-case scenario, you and your co-worker will have word processing programs that have no formats in common. In that case, you can still save your document in Text Only format (which is usually a better choice than Text Only with Line Breaks, since it preserves the original paragraphs). Every word processing program on the planet can read text documents, but all your formatting will be lost. A better choice is Rich Text Format, which Word can produce. It's a kind of plain text format with a lot of special codes to indicate different types of formatting. If your colleague's word processing program understands RTF (as it's called), you're in business.

Either way, select File | Save As, drop down the Save as type list box, and choose the common format (Text Only or Rich Text Format). Give the document a different name, to avoid eradicating the original, and click on Save.

TAKE A REST OR MOVE ON

By now you're probably tired of Word. This might be a good place to knock off for a while. The next chapter tells you what to do if you've lost track of a document on your computer. After that, the rest of the book covers how to handle heavy-duty tasks and highly organized documents.

habits & strategies

If Word can't produce a document in exactly the format that your colleague's word processing program expects, offer him the list of formats that Word can produce and see whether his word processing program can import any of them.

CHAPTER

7

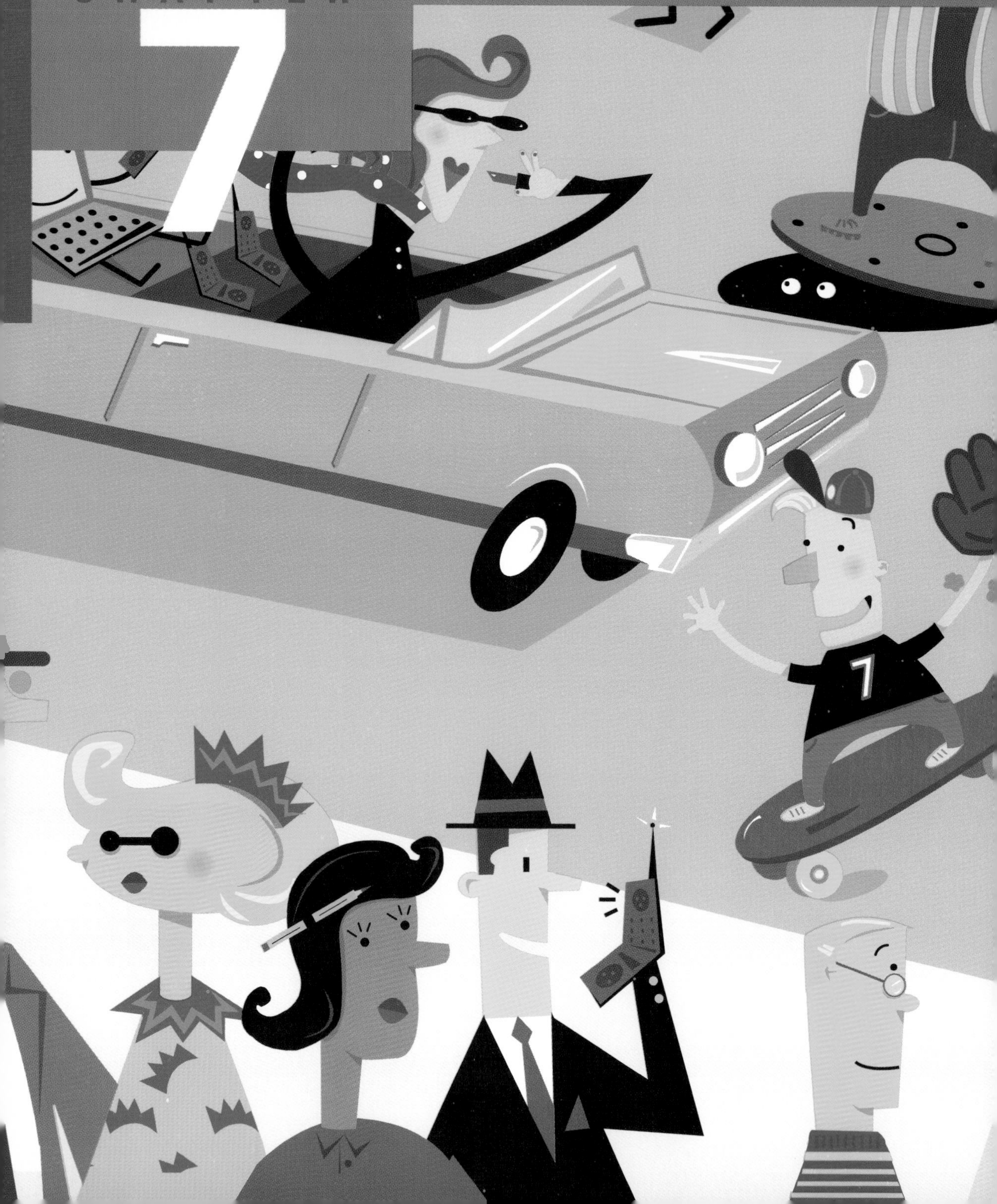

Finding Stuff That's Lost Inside Your Computer

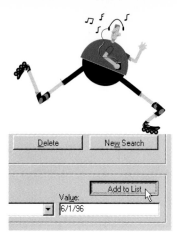

FAST FORWARD

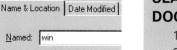

SEARCH FOR DOCUMENTS
FROM WITHIN WORD ➤ *pp 20-22*

1. Click on the Open button on the Standard toolbar. Click on the Advanced button in the Open dialog box.
2. Click on the Delete button if you don't want to use the supplied criterion.
3. Choose a property, a condition, and a value in the Define more criteria area.
4. Click on the Add to List button.
5. Repeat steps 4 and 5 as often as you need to.
6. Choose a folder in the Look in drop-down list box. Click on the Find Now button.

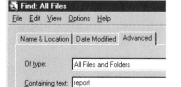

SEARCH FOR A
DOCUMENT IN WINDOWS ➤ *pp 20-22*

1. Click on Start | Find | Files or Folders.
2. Click on the Name & Location tab.
3. Type a filename or part of a name.
4. Choose a folder to start the search in the Look in list box.
5. Click on the Find Now button.

SEARCH BY CONTENTS ➤ *pp 20-22*

1. Click on Start | Find | Files or Folders.
2. Click on the Advanced tab.
3. Type the text you're looking for in the Containing text box.
4. Click on the Find Now button.

SAVE THE RESULTS OF A SEARCH ➤ *pp 20-22*

1. In the Windows Find dialog box, select Options | Save Results.
2. Select File | Save Search.

CHECK THE RECYCLE BIN
FOR MISSING FILES ➤ *pp 20-22*

1. Double-click on the Recycle Bin on the desktop.
2. Scan the list of files (they should be in alphabetical order).

Documents get lost inside computers. It's a fact—sad, but true. Yes, it helps if you maintain an organized folder structure and if you're always careful to save your documents in the correct folders. But no matter what, sometimes files just aren't where you think they are. Fortunately, program developers have started to recognize this fact instead of catering to an idealized user (geeky, just like them), and you now have several decent ways to hunt for missing documents.

It always happens at the worst time, too. Just when someone from accounting is hollering for some backup paperwork, or when your boss needs to see that report you thought you were done with last October. That's when you can't find what you need. Don't let the pressure get to you. Keep cool and follow the steps in this chapter, and you'll find your missing work.

SEARCHING FOR DOCUMENTS FROM WITHIN WORD

Word's document-finding feature, Advanced Find, is available from the Open dialog box. Click on the Open button on the Standard toolbar to get to the Open dialog box. Then click on the Advanced button on the right side of the Open dialog box, below the Open and Cancel buttons. This brings up the Advanced Find dialog box (see Figure 7.1).

In the Find files that match these criteria area (the top half of the dialog box), there should be one criterion listed (based on what was selected in the Files of type list box in the Open dialog box). The criterion is usually "Files of type is Word Documents" (which I know doesn't sound grammatical). Word is building a list of criteria by which to filter the possible documents and come up with a short list of documents that meet all your requirements. The list always starts with Word Documents, but you can add as many additional criteria as you like and even remove this one basic criterion as well as others you've added. To remove a criterion, just select it and click on the Delete button.

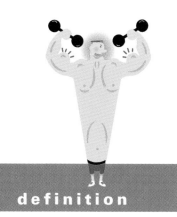

definition

Criterion: *A rule or test applied to a set of objects under consideration. Only those objects that match the criterion or criteria—for example, Word documents created before a certain date and containing some specific text—will be selected.*

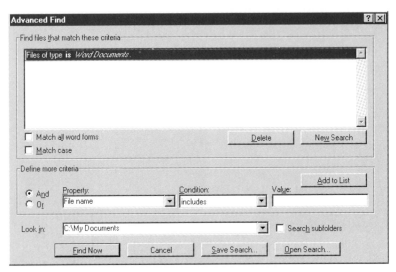

Figure 7.1 The Advanced Find dialog box

To search for a document based on text contained in it, add this criteria: Text or property (in the Property box), includes (in the Condition box), [the text to look for] (in the Value box). A search that includes this kind of criteria can take awhile.

Describing the Document to Search For

You can add more criteria to the list if it will further limit the number of documents that will match, helping you zero in on your missing document sooner. To do so, first choose either And or Or in the Define more criteria area. Choose And if you want to see only documents that match both criteria. This is the stricter way to combine two criteria. Choose Or to see documents that match either of the criteria.

Then choose a property, a condition, and a value. The type of condition you choose and value you enter depends on the property you've chosen. Choose a condition (such as "includes" or "on or after") from the Condition drop-down list box. The value might be a date, some text to be found inside the document, a file size, or something else. Then click on the Add to List button to add your new criterion to the box at the top. Repeat this process as often as necessary to refine your search. Figure 7.2 shows an Advanced Find dialog box that has had "File name includes win" added and in which a third criterion—creation date on or after 6/1/96—is in the process of being added.

Specifying Where to Search

At the bottom of the Advanced Find dialog box, you can specify a folder in which to start the search, though if you leave it at C:\ you can be sure that your whole hard disk will be searched. By default, the

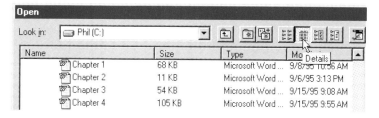

Figure 7.2 Adding criteria to the search constraints

Search subfolders option is checked. If you uncheck it, the search will end in the Look in folder. With it checked, all folders inside the Look in folder, and inside them, and so on, will also be searched.

Starting the Search

To begin the search, click on the Find Now button. The Advanced Find dialog box will disappear and the documents Word finds will appear in the Open dialog box.

Word will throw all the documents it finds, regardless of what folders they "live" in, into the same window in the Open dialog box. To distinguish documents with the same name, click on the Details button (fourth from the right at the top of the dialog box) to show all information about each document, including the *path* (the complete list of folders leading to it).

Remember to click on the List button (just to the left of the Details button) when you want to return the dialog box to its normal mode.

Advanced Find can be complicated and confusing, so the step by step below gives you a complete run-through. In this example, assume that you're looking for a document that you know you created before September 1996, whose title has the word *report* in it somewhere, and which contains the word *widgets* somewhere in the text of the document itself. Start by selecting File | Open and clicking on the Advanced button in the Open dialog box to get to the Advanced Find dialog box.

ADVANCED FIND step by step

1. Click in the Value box and type **report**.

2. Click on Add to List.

3. Choose **Creationdate** in the Property box, choose **on or before** in the Condition box, and type **September 1996** in the Value box.

4. Click on Add to List.

5. Click in Property and choose **Contents**, and click in Value and type **widget**.

6. Click on Add to List.

7. Click on Find Now.

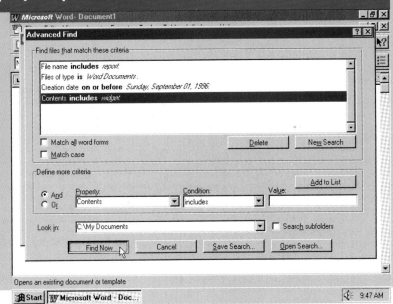

SEARCHING FOR DOCUMENTS WITH WINDOWS 95'S FIND FEATURE

An alternative to Word's Advanced Find feature is the powerful Find feature that comes with Windows itself. You might use this Find feature when you haven't started Word yet, or you might end up preferring it to Word's approach.

To try the Windows Find feature, click on the Start button, choose Find, and then choose Files or Folders.

Searching by Filename

In the Find dialog box that appears, type a filename or part of a name and then click on the Find Now button. Find will start searching. While it's working, the image of a magnifying glass will move in a circle with an image of a document appearing and disappearing underneath it.

A window will open at the bottom of the dialog box, and files will start appearing in it as they are found (see Figure 7.3). You can stop the search at any time (if, for example, you see the document you're looking for) by clicking on the Stop button. The window that shows the found documents behaves as any Windows folder window does: the icons in it can be double-clicked, copied, and so on.

To change the search criteria or start a new search, click on the New Search button. Windows will warn you that this will clear the results of the first search. Click on OK. (If you do want to save the results of your first search, see "Saving the Results of a Search," later in this chapter.)

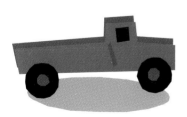

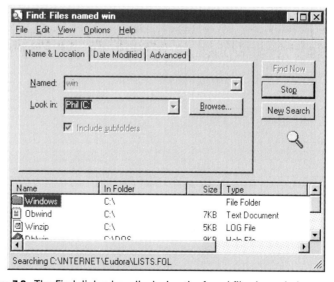

Figure 7.3 The Find dialog box displaying the found files in a window

Searching by Date or Contents

To constrain the search based on the document's creation date or the date on which it was last modified, click on the Date Modified tab in the Find dialog box.

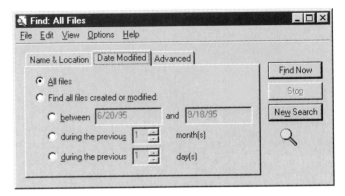

Provide the information requested and click on the Find Now button.

To search for a document based on some text that is contained within it, click on the Advanced tab and then enter the text you're looking for in the Containing text box. You can also specify types of files (for instance, Microsoft Word documents only) in the Of type box, and you can specify size limitations in the Size is box.

Saving the Results of a Search

If you have the funny feeling that you're going to end up wanting to reuse the results of this search sometime in the near future, you can save it. Because the window that shows the results of a Find search works just like any other folder window, you can save it and use it as if it was a folder. To do this, from the Find dialog box select Options | Save Results and then File | Save Search. Windows will save an icon on your desktop called Files named such-and-such, which you can double-click on whenever you want to access those found files again.

CHECKING THE RECYCLE BIN

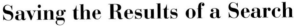

If your document is missing because it has been deleted (or thrown in the Recycle Bin) accidentally, it won't show up when you try to find it either within Word or in Windows 95. So, as a last resort, you should open the Recycle Bin and look inside. To do so, double-click on the Recycle Bin icon on the desktop.

A window much like a folder window will open, showing the deleted files (see Figure 7.4). The files are probably in alphabetical order. (If they're not, click on the Name button at the top of the window to sort the files by name.) Scan through, scrolling if necessary, until you see the file you're looking for. If you find it in there, simply drag it out of the window onto the desktop and then put it in a safe place so that you won't lose it again.

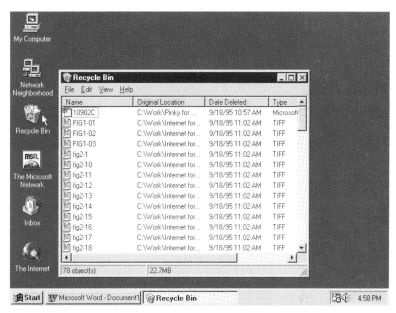

Figure 7.4 The Recycle Bin window, showing all the files that are gone but not yet forgotten

If you haven't found that missing document by now, it's gone. Check any backup disks you or anyone else might have made from your computer, as well as your pile of stray disks. There are file recovery programs (such as those included with the Norton Utilities package) that can scour your hard disk even for scraps of obliterated programs containing key words, so if you have the patience for such an approach, you still might recover some of your missing work.

THE REST OF THE BOOK

The remaining chapters all deal with various specific projects you might want to undertake with Word. Don't slog through them until or unless you actually need to know how to make a form, or send out a mass mailing, and so on.

CHAPTER 8

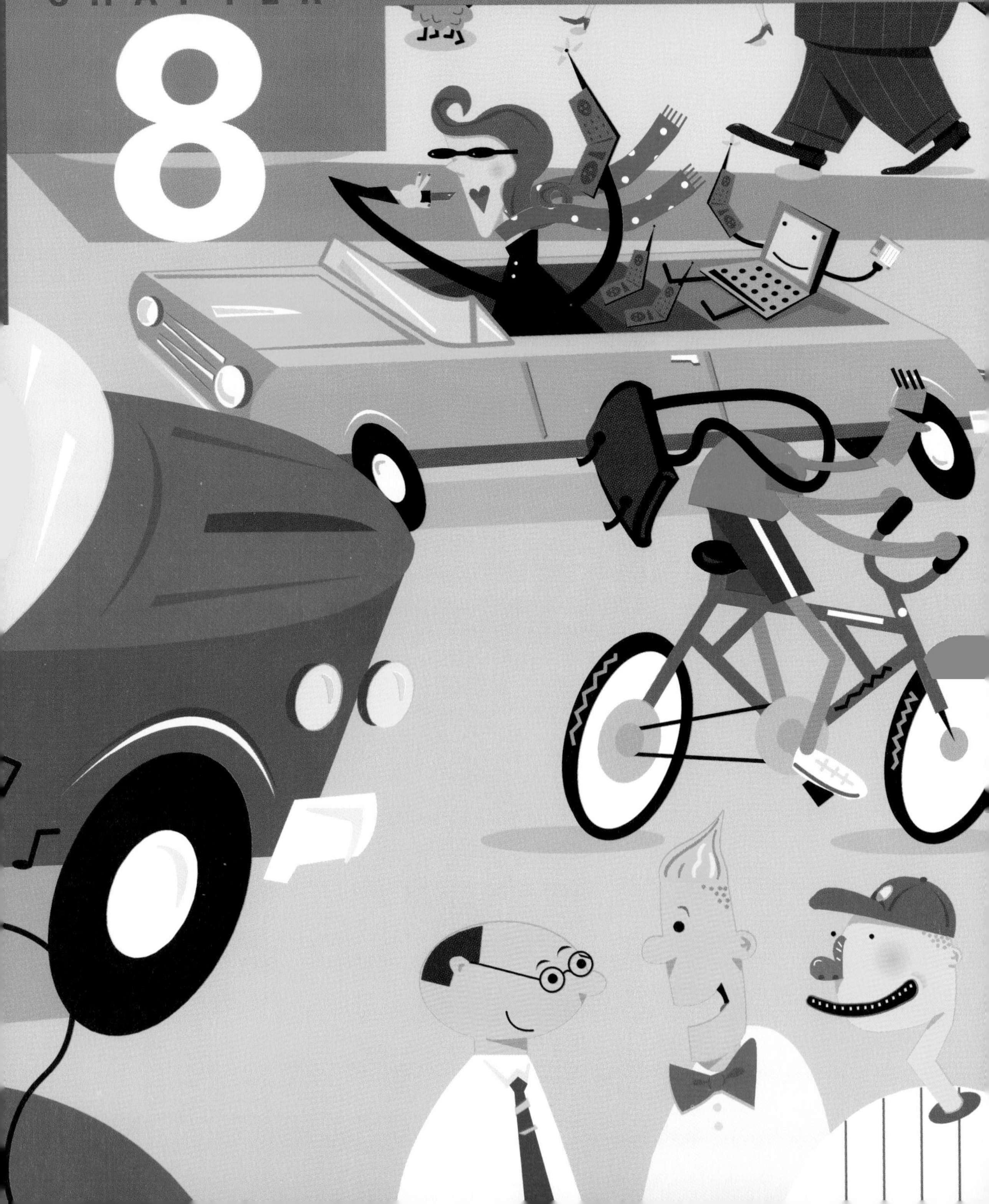

Designing and Reusing Forms

FAST FORWARD

PARKING

INSTRUCTIONS: Complete all bla
incomplete applications cannot be

Insert Table

Number of Columns: 12
Number of Rows: 20
Column Width: Auto
Table Format: (none)

INSTRUCTIONS: Complete all
incomplete applications canno

Name:
last
Home
Addres
s:
number street
Depart
ment:

vork location pho
Employee I.D. Number:
license no. stat
MPORTANT
s are subject to revocation if incorrect information
I that the parking permit issued to me **does not** g

Signature of Applicant

ADD INFORMATION TO
THE TOP OF A FORM ➤ *p 113*

Before you insert the table that will make up the main part of your form, type the information you need at the top of the form, such as the name of the form, the name of the organization the form is for, and any necessary instructions.

INSERT A BIG TABLE ➤ *p 113*

1. Choose Table | Insert Table.
2. Type the number of columns and rows.
3. Click on OK.

FIT THE TEXT INTO YOUR FORM ➤ *pp 113-116*

- Experiment with different font sizes.
- Drag column dividers to widen or narrow columns.
- Select and change individual rows for more fine-tuned adjustments.
- Merge cells when necessary to create wider areas.
- Add and delete columns where needed.

ADD LINES TO A FORM ➤ *pp 116-117*

1. Right-click on any toolbar and choose Borders.
2. Select a cell or cells.
3. Choose a line width.
4. Click on a border button to apply a border to one or more sides of the selection.
5. Repeat as necessary.

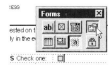

ADD SHADING TO A FORM ➤ *pp 117-118*

1. Select a cell or cells.
2. Choose a shading value from the Borders toolbar.
3. Repeat as necessary.

MAKE AN ONSCREEN FORM ➤ *pp 118-121*

1. Right-click on any toolbar and choose Forms from the menu that pops up.
2. Insert text fields, check-box fields, and drop-down fields as needed.
3. Protect the document.
4. Save it as a template.

USE AN ONSCREEN FORM ➤ *p 121*

1. Choose File | New.
2. Choose the template for the onscreen form you want to use.
3. Click on OK.
4. Have the user fill out the form.
5. Save the form.
6. Print the form, if necessary.

All organizations, from the glacial bureaucracy to the entrepreneurial home-office sole proprietorship, rely on forms. Nobody really likes forms much. They never give you enough room. They represent paperwork in its purest form. But face it: without 'em, the whole world would run on Post-it™ notes and cocktail napkins.

The simplest forms, such as straightforward invoices, require no special tricks for assembly. You just type some categories, leave room or make long underlines for the user to fill in the blanks, and presto! You have created a form. Beyond this rudimentary level, though, the creation of a form requires you to know a bit about tables and how to apply borders (lines) on the page. If you're truly ambitious and forward-looking, with a little extra effort you can create onscreen forms, complete with automated check boxes and drop-down lists of choices.

See Chapter 14 for more information about the fanciest document design techniques.

PLANNING YOUR FORM

The first step in creating a form with Word is to sketch out a dummy on paper. That's right—step away from your computer, grab a piece of scrap paper, and pick up a pencil. Get a sense of how many lines of information your form will need. How many items should go side by side? Where will you want boxes and bordered areas? What wording will you use and what text should be the most prominent? You don't have to, however, polish the thing at this stage.

CONSTRUCTING YOUR FORM

Tables are essential for keeping columns aligned and creating boxed areas. For a simple form, a relatively small table with just a few columns and rows will do the job without requiring a lot of tweaking. For a complicated form, you can either create several tables and massage them separately or start with one mega-table and work on various parts of it to create the different areas. If you're going to make one big table, start by figuring out the largest number of boxes or areas that will need to go side by side on a single line. This is how wide the table will need to be.

Tables are discussed in other contexts in Chapter 12. .

Adding a Title and Other Information at the Top

Before you go ahead and insert a table, type the information you need at the top of the form, such as the name of the form, the name of the organization the form is for, and any necessary instructions.

PARKING PERMIT APPLICATION

Spudco Industries, Worldwide

INSTRUCTIONS: Complete all blanks and check (✓) applicable boxes. We regret that incomplete applications cannot be processed.

Now you're ready to insert a table.

Inserting a Table

There's a Table shortcut button on the Standard toolbar, but for tables with more than just a few columns you're better off using the Table menu. For example, if your form at some point needs to show more than eight items side by side, you might not be able to create a table that wide with the Insert Table button (the exact number depends on your screen resolution). Instead, choose Table | Insert Table.

In the Insert Table dialog box that appears, type the number of columns you want, and specify a generous number of rows (it's easy enough to add or remove rows later). Then click on OK.

Don't be daunted by the huge gridwork that appears (see Figure 8.1). Those gridlines are just there to guide you. They don't print out.

Fitting Text into the Table

Now it's time to start entering the text for the form and playing with the font sizes and column widths to get things to fit. Work your way down from the top and be generous with rows. The table columns are all quite narrow at this point, but in most of the rows of your form you won't need to use all the columns, so you can widen columns when necessary to make important text fit. To widen a column, put the mouse pointer over a column divider and then drag it (see Figure 8.2).

Table columns follow some puzzling rules when you start resizing them. Generally, the column dividers to the left of the divider being

CAUTION

Tables differ from spreadsheets in at least one important way: pressing ENTER in a table cell will insert a new blank line into the cell, increasing its height instead of simply confirming the contents of the cell.

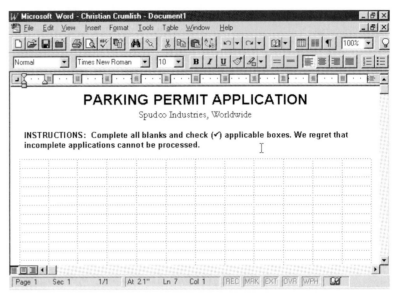

Figure 8.1 The huge raw table that will be carved and molded into a form

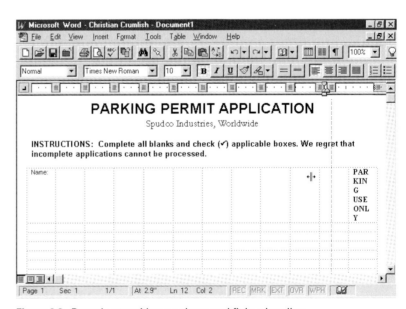

Figure 8.2 Dragging to widen a column and fit in a heading

dragged don't move, so the column immediately to the left of the divider shrinks or widens as needed. All columns to the right of the divider being dragged shrink or widen in proportion to their initial widths. If you hold down SHIFT before dragging, the dividers to the right of the divider being dragged won't move, so the column to the right of the divider will widen or shrink as needed.

When it comes time to format the text in a table, you can select an entire column by holding down ALT and clicking in the column. Another method is to place the insertion point at the top of the column and, when the pointer turns to a black downward-pointing arrow, click to select the column.

You may also need to adjust the size of the various text entries to get things to fit nicely. Normally, any text too wide for a cell will wrap as it would in a paragraph, adding as many new lines as necessary until the text fits. The row height will automatically expand to accommodate the extra lines of text. To change the text size, select the text in question and type a new size in the Font Size box on the Formatting toolbar.

As you work your way down the form, you will come to rows in which you want to widen an individual cell without widening the entire column throughout the table. To do this, select the row first (you can click just to the left of a row to select it), and then drag the column divider. Only cells in the selected row(s) will be affected.

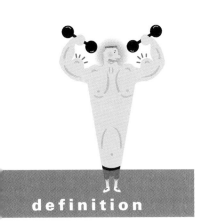

Combining Cells to Make Larger Areas

In some rows of your form, you'll need a few large columns instead of the number of columns you have specified in your table. One way to do this is to select several cells and "merge" them into one. To do so, just select the cells by clicking in the first and dragging through to the last one, and then choose Table | Merge Cells.

definition

Cell: *A portion of a table, formed from the intersection of a column and a row. A cell is the smallest unit in a table.*

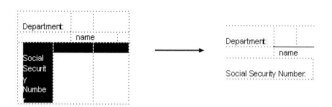

Work your way to the bottom of the form, manipulating the cells until the text areas sort out into the form you envisioned.

ADDING AND DELETING ROWS AND COLUMNS

No matter how good your initial estimates of the numbers of rows and columns needed for your form were, you'll probably need to add or delete a few before you're done. To select a row, click in the margin just to the left of it. To select a column, press ALT and click in the column. To delete a selected row or column, choose Table | Delete Rows or Table | Delete Columns.

Inserting a row or column is also easy. Again, select a row or column. This time, select the row above or the column to the left of the point at which you want to insert the new area. Then click on the Insert Table button on the Standard toolbar. In this context, clicking the button inserts a row or column into the table. To insert a column after the last column of a table, hold down ALT and click to the right of any cell in the last column. Then click on the Insert Table button.

ADDING LINES TO A FORM

In Word, lines are called *borders*, which gives you a hint about how they're applied. You can add borders to any or all sides of most document elements, such as a paragraph or a selection. For your form, you'll generally apply borders to table cells (though you might sometimes apply borders to the text floating inside a cell).

Right-click on one of the toolbars and choose Borders from the menu that pops up. This will bring up the Borders toolbar. Remember to select the cells to which you want to add a border first. Then, to apply a border to a selection, simply click on one of the buttons on the toolbar. Figure 8.3 shows a fill-in-the-blank line being created.

Borders toolbar

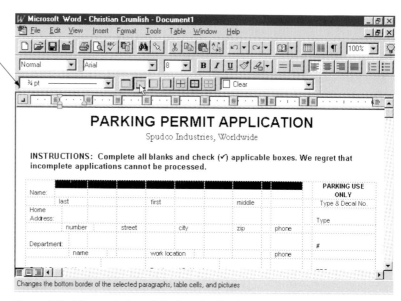

Figure 8.3 A button being clicked on the Borders toolbar to add a line to the bottom of all the selected cells

Sometimes a selection of cells will behave strangely (it may include stray cells or skip needed ones) after you've moved column dividers or merged cells. If this happens, select individual cells in the area and apply the borders one by one.

When you want a different type of line, click on the drop-down list box at the left end of the Borders toolbar and choose which one you want to apply. Again, make sure to select the cells whose borders you want to modify first. If you add a border to a cell or set of cells by mistake, it's easy to remove it. Keep the cells selected (or select them again). Then click on the No Border button (the rightmost one, which shows gridlines but no borders) on the Borders toolbar.

SHADING SELECTED AREAS

What good would a form be without some shaded "for office use only" areas? Shading is also a good way to emphasize the heads of some sections. You add shading from the Borders toolbar, from the drop-down list box at its right end.

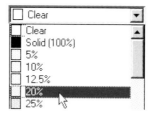

Just select the area you want to shade, and then choose a shading. (The values in the list refer to the percentage of black on white.)

VIEWING A COMPLETED FORM

The best way to judge a form (besides printing it out) is to turn off the dashed gridlines that show the structure of the underlying table. To do so, choose Table | Gridlines. The gridlines will disappear and your form will snap into focus (see Figure 8.4).

Turn off the Borders toolbar when you're done (right-click on it and uncheck Borders). There's little enough room on the screen as it is!

MAKING AN ONSCREEN FORM

Most of you are done with this chapter now and should get out while you can. If you're interested in the slightly more arcane topic of onscreen forms, though, read on.

The purpose of an onscreen form is to save paper and to provide a sort of interactive guidance system that helps the form user fill out the form efficiently and accurately. (Does it really work that way? Beats me. It might take a while to pay off because people will find it unfamiliar at first.) Also, a form of this sort can have protected areas, so that the subject filling out the form can't accidentally overwrite or change the contents of the form.

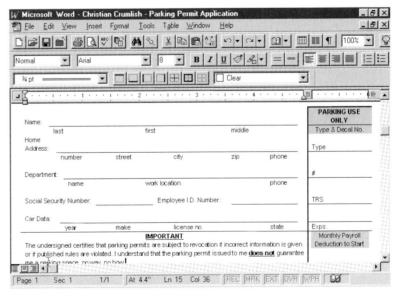

Figure 8.4 The top half of a completed form, *sans* gridlines

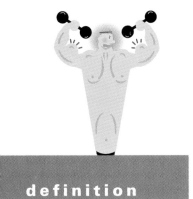

If you're willing to attempt this, start by bringing up the Forms toolbar. Right-click on any toolbar and choose Forms from the menu that pops up. The compact, floating Forms toolbar appears, shown here, with an assortment of cryptic buttons.

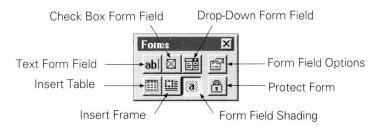

The Forms toolbar has its own copy of the Insert Table button, and you can use it to create fairly wide tables. Just move the toolbar over to the left of your screen. Then click on the Insert Table button and drag across the waffle-patterned grid that appears in order to highlight the number of rows and columns you want. When you release the mouse, the empty table will be in your document. For any area of the form that requires the user to enter text (as opposed to protected areas of the form and those for which a check box or drop-down list would be more appropriate), click in the appropriate cell and then click on the Text Form Field button. A shaded box will appear in the cell.

Inserting Check Boxes

Check boxes give users simple yes or no options, making a form easy to fill out. To insert a check box, click on the Check Box Form Field button. Then, to control whether or not the box is checked to begin with, make sure that your insertion point is on the check box field you created and then click on the Form Field Options button of the toolbar (see Figure 8.5). In the Check Box Form Field Options dialog box that appears, click on Checked in the Default Value area to have the check box checked by default.

To add explanatory text to the form (which won't appear on the form itself), click on the Add Help Text button in the dialog box. When you do, the Form Field Help Text dialog box pops up. Select the Status Bar tab and then type your explanatory text in the box provided. Click on OK. This text will appear in the Word status bar at the bottom of the screen when the user puts the insertion point on the check-box field.

Onscreen form: *A form designed to be viewed and filled out on a computer screen. Once the blanks are filled in, forms of this type can then be printed out, if desired, or they can simply be passed on and stored electronically.*

Form field: *An area in a form designed to hold a specific type of data. Text form fields allow text to be entered, check box form fields allow options to be checked or unchecked, and drop-down form fields allow the user to select from a list of choices.*

The Text Form Field Options dialog box allows you to control the maximum length of the text entry, among other things.

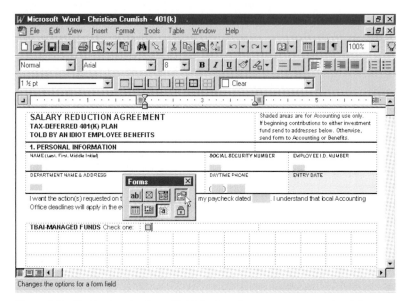

Figure 8.5 Clicking on the Form Field Options button to set up a check box on an onscreen form. Shaded boxes in the form indicate areas for user entry

Inserting Drop-Down List Boxes

To insert a box that can drop down a list of allowable choices for the user, first click on the Drop-Down Form Field button on the Forms toolbar. Then to create the list of user choices, click on the toolbar's Form Field Options button. In the Drop-Down Form Field Options dialog box that appears, type each option in the Items in Drop-Down box, clicking on the Add button after every entry.

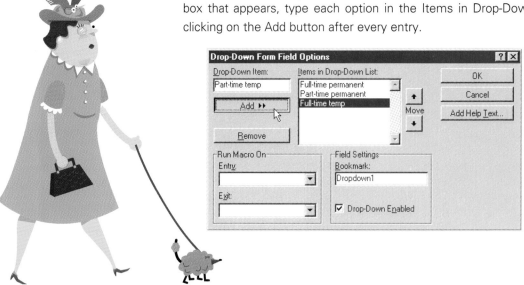

CAUTION

The form template must be saved in the Templates folder if you want it to show up as an option when a user chooses File | New. Be sure that the Save in area of the Save As dialog box is pointed to that folder after you choose Document Template.

Protecting an Onscreen Form

As I mentioned earlier, to make an onscreen form function properly, you have to protect it. Not only does this prevent the people who are filling out the form from accidentally changing the fixed part of it, it also enables all the form field boxes to work the way the form designer intended them to. To protect the form, click on the Protect Form button on the Forms toolbar (or choose Tools | Protect Document).

Saving an Onscreen Form as a Template

If you want to use an onscreen form time and again, it's best to save it is as a template. Then, when you want someone to fill out a copy of the form, you just have them create a new document based on the template. The document will work the way the original form did, and when you save the results, the template will be unaffected.

To save a completed blank form as a template, choose File | Save As. In the Save As dialog box, type a filename for the form and then choose Document Template in the Save as Type drop-down list box. Then click on Save.

USING AN ONSCREEN FORM

When the time comes to use an onscreen form, choose File | New (don't click on the New button on the toolbar, because that will not let you choose a template). In the New dialog box that appears, choose the template for the form, and then click on OK.

Then simply have the user fill out the form. All the interactive elements should work as advertised. When the form has been completed, save it as a normal Word document. You can then print out the entire form with its contents, or, if you prefer, you can print just the entries without the form itself. To do that, choose Tools | Options and click on the Print tab. Check Print Data Only for Forms in the Options for Current Document Only box, and then click on OK.

I hope it was worth all the effort.

PRIORITY!

MEMO:

FIRST CLASS
OVERNIGHT

RUSH!

Preparing a
Mass Mailing

FAST FORWARD

START A MAIL MERGE ➤ *pp 128-129*

1. Start a new document.
2. Choose Tools | Mail Merge.
3. Click on the Create button in the Mail Merge Helper dialog box, and choose Form Letters.
4. In the dialog box that appears, click on the Active Window button.

CREATE A DATA SOURCE ➤ *pp 129-130*

1. Click on the Get Data button in the Mail Merge Helper dialog box, and choose Create Data Source.
2. Add and remove field names as needed in the Create Data Source dialog box.
3. Click on OK.
4. Save your data source.
5. Click on the Edit Data Source button in the dialog box that appears.

ENTER THE DATA IN A DATA SOURCE ➤ *pp 130-131*

1. Create a data source as explained in the previous Fast Forward item.
2. Type the contents of a field in the Data Form dialog box.
3. Press TAB to move to the next field.
4. Repeat steps 2 and 3 until the record is complete.
5. Click on the Add New button to start a new record.
6. Repeat steps 2 through 5 until you've entered all the records.
7. Click on OK when you're done.

ADD A MERGE FIELD TO THE MAIN DOCUMENT ➤ *p 132*

1. Click on the Insert Merge Field button on the Mail Merge toolbar, and choose the field you want to insert.
2. Include normal spacing and punctuation around and between merge fields.
3. Repeat as necessary.

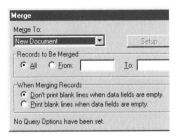

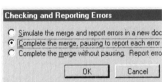

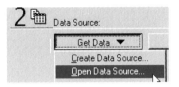

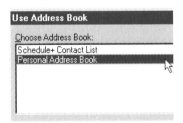

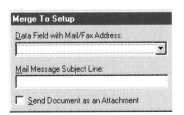

MERGE THE DATA SOURCE
INTO THE MAIN DOCUMENT ➤ *p 132*

1. Prepare a Data Source and a Main Document.
2. Click on the Merge button in the Mail Merge Helper dialog box.
3. Click on the Merge button in the Merge dialog box.

CHECK FOR ERRORS
BEFORE PRINTING ➤ *pp 135-136*

1. In the Merge dialog box, click on the Check Errors button.
2. Choose one of the error-checking options and click on OK.

MERGE A FORM LETTER
WITH AN EXISTING DATA SOURCE ➤ *p 137*

1. Click on the Get Data button in the Mail Merge Helper dialog box, and choose Open Data Source.
2. If the data source is not a Word document, choose All Documents in the Files of type drop-down list box.
3. Choose a data source and click on Open in the Open Data Source dialog box.

MERGE A FORM LETTER
WITH AN ADDRESS BOOK ➤ *p 138*

1. Click on the Get Data button in the Mail Merge Helper dialog box, and choose Use Address Book.
2. Choose the address book you want to use.
3. Click on OK, and OK again, if prompted.
4. Choose a profile, and click on OK.

MERGE TO E-MAIL ADDRESSES ➤ *pp 140-141*

1. Click on the Merge To drop-down list box in the Merge dialog box and choose Electronic Mail.
2. Click on the Setup button.
3. In the Merge To Setup dialog box, choose the merge field from the data source (the address book) that contains the e-mail addresses of the recipients.
4. Type a subject line.
5. Check Send Document as an Attachment if you want the letters to be sent as Word documents and not as plain e-mail text.
6. Click on OK.

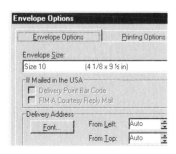

CREATE ENVELOPES FOR A MAILING ➤ *pp 141-143*

The following steps assume you have a main document on the screen and have created a data source.

1. From within the main document, click on the Mail Merge Helper button on the Mail Merge toolbar.
2. Click on the Create button in the Mail Merge Helper dialog box, and choose Envelopes.
3. In the dialog box that appears, click on the New Main Document button.
4. Back in the Mail Merge Helper dialog box, click on the Get Data button and open a data source.
5. In the dialog box that appears, click on the Set Up Main Document button.
6. In the Envelope Options dialog box, choose your envelope type.
7. Click on OK.
8. In the Envelope Address dialog box, click on the Insert Merge Field button and choose merge fields to construct an address.
9. Type punctuation and spaces as needed.
10. Click on OK.

CREATE MAILING LABELS ➤ *pp 143-145*

1. From within the main document, click on the Mail Merge Helper button on the Mail Merge toolbar.
2. In the Mail Merge Helper dialog box, click on the Create button and choose Mailing Labels.
3. In the dialog box that appears, click on the New Main Document button.
4. Back in the Mail Merge Helper dialog box, click on the Get Data button and open a data source.
5. In the dialog box that appears, click on Set Up Main Document.
6. In the Label Options dialog box, choose the labels' manufacturer in the Label Products drop-down list box.
7. Choose the labels' product number in the Product Number list box.
8. Click on OK.
9. In the Create Labels dialog box, click on the Insert Merge Field button and choose merge fields to construct an address.
10. Include punctuation and spaces as needed.
11. Click on OK.

Yes, the dreaded mail merge. Sending a form letter to everyone on a mailing list (or to just some of the people on the list) is probably one of the toughest computery tasks that normal, busy people such as you ever have to do. If it were a little more tricky, you'd be able to palm the job off on some computer jockey. It's one of those procedures that always turns up some ridiculous problem. Something always goes wrong.

If your mailing list already exists in some database program (such as Access, dBASE, or FileMaker Pro), you might be better off doing the mail merge in that program rather than in Word. Granted, the form letter will be a little trickier to put together. (Database programs usually make you think in terms of forms and page layout instead of the nice page and typing metaphors used in Word.) But it will still be easier, I predict. Nevertheless, Word *can* handle outside data sources.

In fact, Word has a pretty helpful automated routine that walks you through the steps of creating a mail merge. As with all such procedures, it gets trickier if you stray from the main path. It can also get a little confusing because there are something like 30 different dialog boxes you might be faced with, depending on exactly what you do. Don't worry—I'll guide you through everything carefully.

WHEN TO MERGE

A mail merge is not the sort of operation to get into lightly. If you need to send the same letter to a relatively small number of people, six or ten or so, you'll probably be better off just creating boilerplate and then making changes to each letter individually. You'll find that only if you have a large number of recipients or a complicated letter will the additional "overhead" of setting up the mail merge be justified. With a mailing list of 30 names or more, mail merge is definitely the way to go.

Another factor to consider is whether you'll be sending letters out to the same set of people again. If you are, the time invested in creating the mailing list will pay off when you need to reuse it.

It might also be worth your while to create a data source in Word if you have other uses for a database of names and addresses, for example, but you don't have a full-fledged database manager program.

WHAT'S INVOLVED IN A MAIL MERGE?

The mail merge process in Word is somewhat flexible, and it's possible to start or continue the process from several different points, but here is the typical sequence of procedures:

1. Start a main document and enter the "dummy" letter into which all the specific information will be poured.
2. Create or open a data source that contains the specific information to be added to each merged document.
3. Finish the main document, inserting references to the information in the data source.
4. Merge the data source with the main document to create a set of merged documents.

STARTING A MAIL MERGE

To kick things off, choose Tools | Mail Merge. The Mail Merge Helper dialog box appears, with instructions in a small area at the top (see Figure 9.1). Click on the Create button and choose Form Letters.

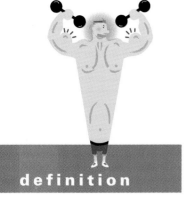

definition

Main document: *In Word's mail merge procedure, the prototype into which all the data from a mailing list is merged to create each specific letter (usually a form letter).*

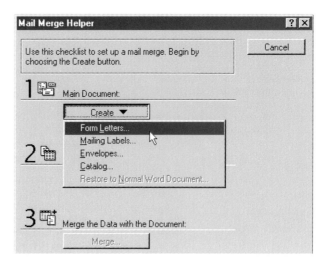

Figure 9.1 The Mail Merge Helper dialog box

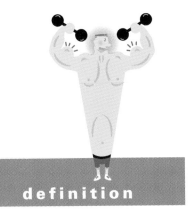

Data source: A document containing data organized into fields and records, as in a database. A record is one complete set of related data (such as a person's name, address, and phone number). A field is an individual category of data (such as addresses).

Word displays a dialog box offering you the choice of either making a form letter (main document) from your current document or starting a new document. If you've just started Word or have already started a blank new document, click on the Active Window button. If the current document is one you don't want to use for this mail merge, click on the New Main Document button.

If you want to base your form letter on an existing letter, open that document first, save a copy of it (use File | Save As) under a different name, and then start the mail merge process. When Word asks which document to use, click on Active Window.

ASSEMBLING A DATA SOURCE

Next you need to make a data source for the merge. This involves establishing the structure of the data source (that is, what information will go into it) and the more tedious job of data entry. (Quick, where's your assistant?)

If you already have a data source, either in the form of a Word document or in a database program, skip ahead to "Merging with an Existing Data Source" later in this chapter. (If the data source is a Word document, it has to be formatted as a data source and not simply as a list of information.)

Creating the Data Source Document

Click on the Get Data button next to step 2 in the Mail Merge Helper dialog box, and choose Create Data Source. The Create Data Source dialog box appears (see Figure 9.2).

Word starts you off with a reasonable list of field names (categories): Title, FirstName, LastName, and so on. You can remove any field name you won't need by highlighting it and clicking on the Remove Field Name button. To add a field name, type it in the Field Name box and click on the Add Field Name button.

Try to make the categories as narrow as possible, so that in the future you can sort or choose from the records based on a specific field (such as the city a person lives in, as opposed to a complete address). One useful field to include is a salutation field, indicating how to address the person at the beginning of a letter.

When you're done, click on OK. Word automatically displays the Save As dialog box so that you can give your data source a name. Type

CAUTION

Only remove field names that you're absolutely sure you won't need. It doesn't cost you much to retain a category, even if it's blank most (or all) of the time. (You can add fields at a later date, but it's a hassle.)

You can edit the main document now instead of doing the data entry. To do so, click on the Edit Main Document button and skip ahead to "Constructing a Form Letter," later in this chapter. (You'll still have to enter the data sometime, though.)

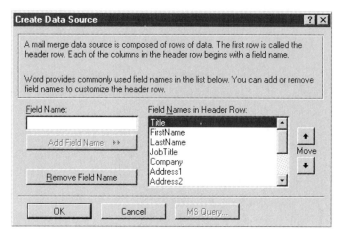

Figure 9.2 The Create Data Source dialog box

a name you'll remember later (perhaps including the word *data*), note where you're saving the document, and click on Save. Don't mix up your data source documents and your main merge documents. Giving them distinctive file names can help keep them straight. You might also want to create a special Merge folder for all your merge-related documents.

Word then notices that your data source has no contents yet and displays a message box asking you whether you want to work on remedying that or jump over to the main document (the form letter). Stay on the data source track for now by clicking on the Edit Data Source button.

Entering the Data

Word next displays the Data Form dialog box (see Figure 9.3). The dialog box is called Data Form because it represents a form you can fill out to enter the records into your data source.

This is that tedious data entry phase I told you about. A great character-building task for someone just starting out in your field, right? The mechanics are easy, though. Just type the person's title (Mr. or Ms., usually), press TAB, type the person's first name, press TAB, and so on. Skip any fields that don't have values by pressing TAB twice. (You can also move from field to field using the left- and right-pointing arrowhead buttons at the bottom of the dialog box, or you can jump forward or back an entire record at a time using the outer two buttons.)

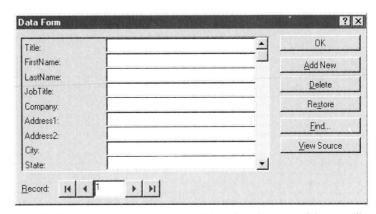

Figure 9.3 The Data Form dialog box, which makes the entry of data...well, convenient, if not exactly fun

It's very easy to click on the OK button when you really meant to skip to the next record. If that happens, the Data Form dialog box will close. To bring it back up, click on the Edit Data Source button in the Mail Merge toolbar of the main document.

When you get to the bottom of the list of fields (the list will scroll as you go), click on the Add New button to enter the next record. Repeat ad infinitum. Click on OK when you're done.

CREATING A FORM LETTER

You'll next be presented with the empty document window of your so-called main document. The window now includes a special Mail Merge toolbar, shown here.

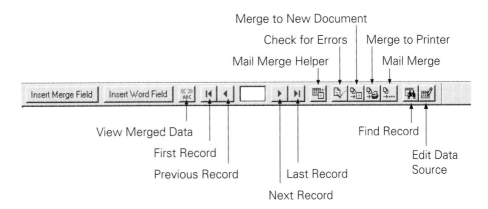

This is a complicated looking toolbar, but you can ignore most of it for now. The buttons from View Merged Data over to Last Record are currently useless to you (and you might never need to touch them). The Mail Merge Helper button is a good one to remember, since it gets you

back to that main dialog box with steps 1, 2, and 3 that sort of guides you through the mail merge process. The next four buttons start the final step, the actual merge, but it's too soon for that. The Find Record button won't come in handy unless you have an enormous data source. The last button, Edit Data Source, is a convenient way to flip over to the data source.

Typing the Normal Text

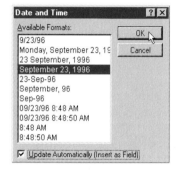

Most of your form letter will be like any other letter or document—plain text. Type or insert your letterhead. To add a date code that will automatically show the date of the mail merge, choose Insert | Date and Time from the main menu bar. In the Date and Time dialog box that appears, choose the format you prefer, click in the Update Automatically (Insert as Field) check box, and then click on OK.

Adding Merge Fields

When the time comes to enter the parts of the form letter that will need to change for each person you're sending the letter to (such as the name and address), click on the Insert Merge Field button on the Mail Merge toolbar and choose the first field you want to insert.

Word will insert the name of each merge field, enclosed in guillemets (<< >>). Remember to include normal spacing and punctuation between and around the merge fields. If you want the resulting text to be formatted in a particular way, choose the merge fields and format as you would normal text. Figure 9.4 shows the beginning of a form letter that includes the merge fields for a recipient's address and the salutation. Write the contents of the letter, including merge fields where appropriate. When you're done, save the form letter.

PERFORMING THE MERGE

When you've got your data source completed and the main document drafted, you're ready for the actual merging of the two documents. Click on the Mail Merge Helper button on the Mail Merge toolbar to start the third act of this drama.

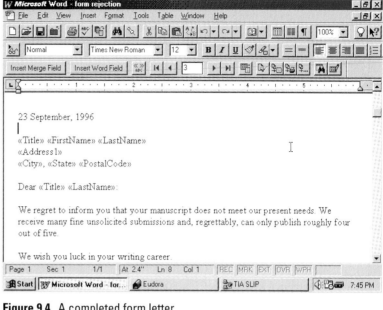

Figure 9.4 A completed form letter

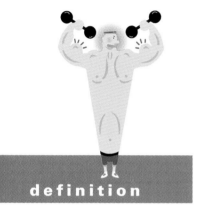

definition

Query: *A request for only those records that meet specified criteria, usually from a database.*

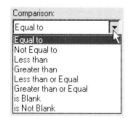

Controlling Which Records Are Included in the Merge

Some form letters don't go to every person on a mailing list. For example, overdue notices might go out only to customers with a number greater than 60 in their InvoiceOverdue merge field. Or you might want to send your letter to only the people on your list who live in Chicago. If you want to send your letter to everyone on your mailing list, skip to the next section.

To be more selective, click on the Query Options button in the step 3 area of the Merge Helper dialog box. Then click on the Filter Records tab. Word displays yet another dialog box full of empty boxes (see Figure 9.5).

Pull down the Field drop-down list and choose the field (or the first of several fields) from the data source that governs who's in and who's out. The Comparison box, shown here, suggests Equal to, but you can also choose any of a number of other types of comparisons by clicking on the drop-down list.

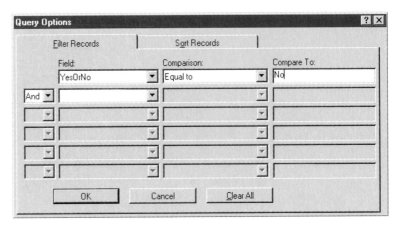

Figure 9.5 The Query Options dialog box

If needed, the Compare To box will then become live, and you can type the value or contents that a field must have, or lack, or be greater than, or whatever.

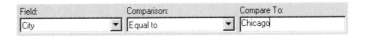

If you want to add more criteria to your filter, repeat the process in the next line. The default conjunction between the criteria is And, but you can change it to Or if you want to combine the results of the two comparisons, rather than further narrowing the results. For example, if you include the criteria "City Equal to Chicago" *And* "InvoiceOverdue Greater Than 60," your letter will be sent only to those recipients who match both criteria. If you include the criteria "City Equal to Chicago" *Or* "City Equal to San Francisco," the letter will go to people in the data source who live in either city.

If your mailing list was entered in no particular order *and* you want your form letters to come out in some order, you can sort the records in the data source. Just click on the Sort Records tab in the Query Options dialog box, and choose up to three different merge fields for the mailing to be sorted on. For each you can choose ascending (A-to-Z for nonnumeric fields) or descending (Z-to-A for nonnumeric fields). Then click on OK. You'll be returned to the Mail Merge Helper dialog box.

If you've put off entering the data for your data source, you must do so now. Click on the Edit button under step 2 in the Mail Merge Helper dialog box, and choose the data source name (it should be the only choice). Then jump back to "Entering the Data."

Why would you need to sort on more than one field? Well, you could do so as a further way of sorting when two records match in the first sort field—a kind of tie-breaker. For example, you might want to sort records based first on City, then on LastName, and finally on FirstName, to make sure that even people with the same last name are sorted properly by first name.

Clearing a Query

Once you've established the criteria for a query, those criteria will be used to filter your records for subsequent merges until you clear them. To do so, click on the Clear All button in the Query Options dialog box.

Producing the Form Letters

Now that you've got all your ducks in a row, click on the Merge button in step 3 of the Mail Merge Helper dialog box. This brings up the Merge dialog box (see Figure 9.6).

Generally, you'll want to merge your form letters into a new document. Your other options— in the Merge To list box— are to merge directly to the printer or to e-mail. However, you can take a moment now to save yourself some grief later and check if anything's gone wrong in the process (though, honestly, if you've stuck close to the guidelines, everything ought to be fine).

Checking for Errors Before Printing

When you're ready to actually perform your merge, you can stage a dry run to check for errors. In the Merge dialog box, click on the Check

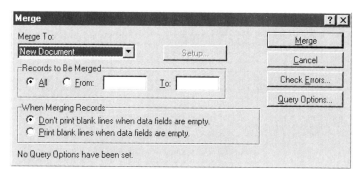

Figure 9.6 The final Merge dialog box

Errors button. Word then displays a dialog box with three radio buttons for the following options: simulate the merge and report any errors it encounters, perform the merge but pause to report errors as it goes, or perform the merge and report errors at the end. (The simulated merge does not produce a merged document or send anything to the printer.)

Choose an option and click on OK. (The default is the second option, but I recommend the third. If you're merging directly to the printer, as explained later in the chapter, the first option is the safest bet.) This returns you to the Merge dialog box, in which you can click on the Merge button to start the merge process.

Back to the Merge

Go ahead and click on the Merge button to make Word complete the task. Word creates a new document that contains all the resulting letters, each one based on the form letter but with actual information from the data source merged in, record by record. Each letter is separated from the previous letter by a section break that also functions as a page break.

A BASIC MAIL MERGE step by step

1. Start a main document by clicking on the Create button and choosing Form Letter. Then click the Edit button and choose the document.

2. Create or open a data source by clicking on the Get Data button and choosing Create Data Source or Open Data Source. Then set up the data source if it's new, or click on the Edit button to edit an existing data source.

3. Click on the Edit button that appears to finish the main document.

4. Finally, click on the Merge button.

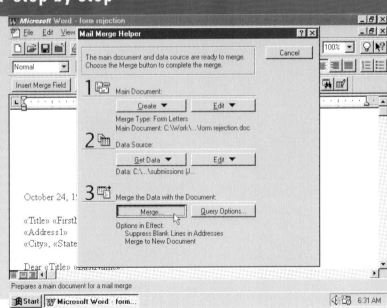

By now mail merge may seem impossibly complicated, but it's not so hard, really. The procedure's been boiled down to just a few steps in that can't-miss blue box at the bottom of the previous page. (To begin choose Tools | Mail Merge to bring up the Mail Merge Helper dialog box.)

WHAT TO DO WITH MERGED DOCUMENTS

OK, now you have umpteen documents back-to-back, each very similar. What do you do? Usually, you'll just want to print them. There's no real need to save the results when they're so repetitive, take up so much disk space, and can be re-created at the drop of a hat.

But before you print, you should inspect the results to make sure they look OK. This is the main reason for not printing them directly while merging. If there's anything wrong with the resulting merged documents, close the file without saving it and make corrections to the main document, the data source, or the query used to generate the merge.

DIVERSIONS FROM THE STRAIGHT AND NARROW

I've just outlined the most straightforward approach to mail merge, but you can actually perform the steps in many different orders, and some situations require slightly different procedures. I'll run through the most common variations now.

Merging with an Existing Data Source

If your data source already exists, you still need to create a main document to begin with, as explained in "Starting a Mail Merge." Then click on the Get Data button in the step 2 area of the Mail Merge Helper dialog box, and choose Open Data Source.

The Open Data Source dialog box (which looks very much like the normal Open dialog box) appears. Browse through the folders, if necessary, to find the data source document, and select it. If your data source is not a Word document, click on the Files of type drop-down list box and choose All Files. Then click on Open.

Now you have to put together your form letter, so skip back to "Constructing a Form Letter" for instructions.

CAUTION

If there's something wrong with your main document, do not correct each letter manually! It might be tempting to do this and avoid the hassle of running another mail merge, but trust me, you're better off redoing the merge.

For more on finding files from within Word, see Chapter 7.

CAUTION

Be sure to filter the addresses in your address book so that only specific people get the form letter (unless you really want to send it to everyone in the book). Filtering is explained in "Controlling Which Records Are Included in the Merge."

definition

***Header:** When speaking of data sources, a header is the row of field titles that names each of the elements of each record.*

Merging with an Address Book

If you have a working address book in Windows that is tied in to Microsoft Exchange or some other work group software, you can use the addresses stored there (or some subset of them) as your data source.

You still need to create a main document to begin with, as explained in "Starting a Mail Merge." Then click on the Get Data button in the step 2 area of the Mail Merge Helper dialog box, and choose Use Address Book. The Use Address Book dialog box will appear, asking you to choose which address book to use.

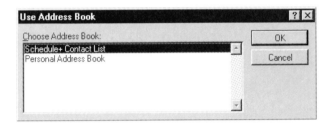

Choose the address book you want to use, such as your Personal Address Book, and then click on OK. If Word then laboriously asks you to confirm that you really, really want to use this address book, click on OK again.

The next little dialog box you have to get past is the Choose Profile box. Most likely the suggested default will be correct and you can click on OK. It depends on how your computer and possibly your network is set up. If you're not sure what to do, ask whoever maintains the shared computer resources where you work.

Now you have to put together your form letter, so skip back to "Constructing a Form Letter" for instructions.

Using a Separate Header Source

Some data sources lack header information and require that you use or set up a separate header source file that contains only the names of the merge fields to be used in your merge. If you are saddled with this type of data source, after you've created the main document, click on the Get Data button in the step 2 area of the Mail Merge Helper dialog box and choose Header Options. This will bring up the Header Options dialog box.

If a header source document already exists, click on the Open button and open it in the Open Header Source dialog box that appears. If a header source document does not already exist, click on the Create button and create one on the fly. The procedure is essentially the same as that for creating a data source (but without the painful data entry), as explained in "Creating the Data Source Document."

Next you have to put together your form letter, so skip back to "Constructing a Form Letter" for instructions.

Editing a Data Source Manually

Tables are explained in Chapter 12.

Although it's nice to use the data form to edit your records because it insulates you from the nitty-gritty mechanics of the mail merge, you *can* open the data source document directly and edit it by hand as you would any document. To get to the data source document, click on the View Source button in the Data Form dialog box that was shown in Figure 9.3.

The data source document, an example of which is shown in Figure 9.7, is basically a table, but don't worry about its appearance. Unlike a table that was created to display information, this one exists purely to keep information straight. Therefore, the column widths do not matter and it affects nothing if the data in the table cells is awkwardly word-wrapped. (Normal table gridlines will appear unless you turned them off yourself previously.) The data source also has its own special toolbar.

The most important buttons on the toolbar are Data Form, which takes you back to the familiar Data Form dialog box; Manage Fields, which lets you add, delete, and rearrange fields; and Mail Merge Main Document, which switches you back to your form letter.

habits & strategies

If you run into memory problems while performing a mail merge, you should try merging directly to your printer (after proof-reading your main document very carefully). This approach will often get around the memory problem.

Merging Directly to a Printer

I don't recommend merging directly to a printer. It's easy enough to print a merge document, and if you merge directly to a printer you won't have the opportunity to audit the results and perhaps make changes without wasting a lot of paper. Nevertheless, if you're determined to do it, click on the Merge To drop-down list box in the Merge dialog box and choose Printer. Then click on the Merge button.

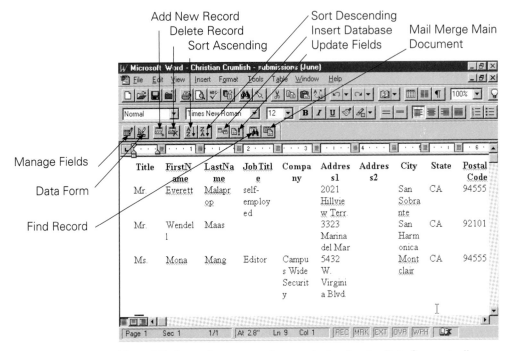

Figure 9.7 A raw data source document, showing the Data Source toolbar

Merging to E-Mail Addresses

It's possible to send out a mailing via e-mail if you have valid e-mail addresses for all the recipients. This is similar to using an address book as your data source (see "Merging with an Address Book," earlier in this chapter). To send the merged mailing electronically, click on the Merge To drop-down list box in the Merge dialog box and choose Electronic Mail. The Setup button in the Merge dialog box will become active. Click on it to display the Merge To Setup dialog box, and choose the merge field from the data source (the address book) that contains the e-mail addresses of the recipients in the Data Field with Mail/Fax Address list box.

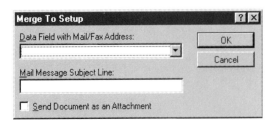

Type a subject line for the e-mail messages in the Mail Message Subject Line box, and check Send Document as an Attachment to have the merged letters attached to e-mail as Word documents. If you don't check this option, the contents of the merged letters will be sent as plain e-mail. Then click on OK. Back in the Merge dialog box, click on the Merge button.

RETURNING TO A PARTIALLY COMPLETED MAIL MERGE

This chapter explains how to perform a mail merge as one continuous series of dialog boxes and choices. In reality, it's a long and sometimes arduous process that often involves a lot of data entry somewhere in the middle, and it's possible that it will take several days to get it together. If so, be sure to save all your documents before quitting Word.

When you return to the mail merge the next day, open the main document. Then click on the Mail Merge Helper button on the Mail Merge toolbar. This will return you to where you left off. If you start with any other document and choose Tools | Mail Merge, you'll be starting a completely new merge, and you don't want that.

CREATING ENVELOPES FOR YOUR MAILING

Once you've successfully merged your form letter with your mailing list, you still need to mail the resulting letters (that is, unless you're using electronic mail). From within the main document, click on the Mail Merge Helper button. Click on the Create button in the step 1 area, and choose Envelopes.

Word will display a dialog box giving you the option of opening a new document or turning the current one into an envelope document. Click on the New Main Document button. Then click on the Get Data button in the Mail Merge Helper dialog box and choose Open Data Source. Choose a document (the same data source you used for the form letters) in the Open Data Source dialog box and click on Open. When the next dialog box appears, click on Set Up Main Document.

habits & strategies

Word will pick up your return address from its User Info data. If you want to use a different address, choose Tools | Options, and click on the User Info tab. Then enter your name and address, and click on OK. Be sure to change it back later if necessary.

Choosing an Envelope Type

In the Envelope Options dialog box that appears (see Figure 9.8), choose your envelope type. Most of the time, you'll be using a Size 10 envelope (4 1/8 by 9 1/2 inches), also called a No. 10 envelope, and won't have to change a thing. If you're using some other envelope type, click on the Envelope Size drop-down list box and choose the correct type.

Word can usually figure out the orientation for feeding your envelopes to your printer, even if the printer doesn't have an envelope feeder.

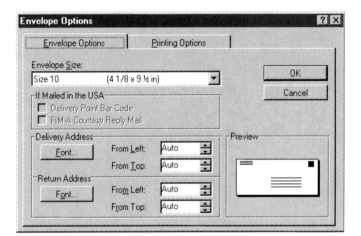

Figure 9.8 The Envelope Options dialog box

Indicating How the Envelopes Will Be Fed into the Printer

If your printer requires you to feed your envelopes in some unusual way (that is, if your printer doesn't have an attached envelope feeder and you have to insert the envelope right down the middle), click on the Printing Options tab of the Envelope Options dialog box.

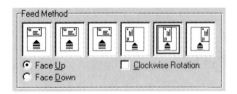

From the choices illustrated in the dialog box, click on the envelope orientation that matches the way your printer works. In the Feed

From drop-down list box, choose a method of feeding the envelopes into the printer.

Merging the Envelopes

When you're ready to perform the merge, click on OK in the Envelope Options dialog box. The Envelope Address dialog box will appear (see Figure 9.9). Click on its Insert Merge Field button and choose merge fields from the data source to assemble an address. (Don't forget to enter spaces and line breaks as well.) Then click on OK.

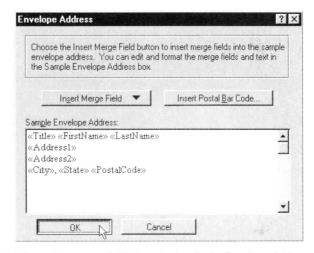

Figure 9.9 Inserting merge fields into the box in the Envelope Address dialog box to construct an address

Now complete the merge as you would a normal mail merge. Word will produce an output document consisting of all the envelopes and show them to you in page layout view (see Figure 9.10). The envelopes are separated by page breaks. If they look OK, print them.

CREATING LABELS FOR YOUR MAILING

An alternative to printing envelopes is to print mailing labels and then stick them onto envelopes. This is helpful if you have the labels and lack a convenient way to print envelopes. From within your main document, click on the Mail Merge Helper button. In the Mail Merge Helper dialog box, click on the Create button in the step 1 area, and choose Mailing Labels.

habits & strategies

If you've already been working on another type of main document, Word offers to change the current document type or create a new main document. If you choose New Main Document, click on Get Data and set up the data source as before.

143

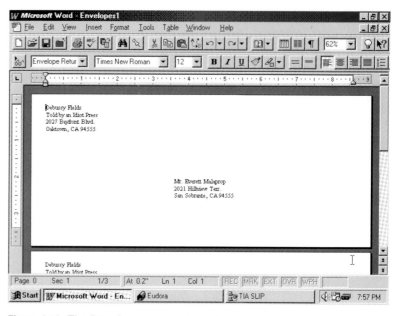

Figure 9.10 The first of many merged envelopes

The Label Options dialog box will appear. Look at the packaging your mailing labels come in and note the manufacturer (it's Avery, nine times out of ten) and the product number. Then choose the manufacturer in the Label Products drop-down list box and choose the product number in the Product Number list box. Then click on OK and skip ahead to "Setting Up the Address."

Dealing with Nonstandard Labels

If your label type is not listed, or if your labels are made by some fly-by-night company, choose Custom Laser from the top of the Label Products list in the Label Options dialog box. Then click on the Details button. A Custom Laser Information dialog box for the label type you started with will appear, showing a detailed diagram of the label type with all the pertinent measurements pointed out.

You'll have to measure your labels if all the information isn't on the packaging. Enter the actual figures for your labels (you will see the diagram change in response to the numbers you enter), and then click on OK.

If you need to print a label for a single document, see Chapter 11.

Setting Up the Address

Once you've specified your labels, the Create Labels dialog box appears (which looks very similar to the Envelope Address dialog box shown in Figure 9.9). Use the Insert Merge Field button to choose merge fields from the data source and assemble the address to go on the labels. Don't forget to include spaces, punctuation, and line breaks as necessary. Then click on OK.

Completing the Merge

Then proceed with the merge as usual. Word will produce an output document showing the merged labels (see Figure 9.11). If everything looks OK, go ahead and print them.

Well, you've made it through probably the most challenging and difficult procedure you'll ever have to do with Word! Congratulations.

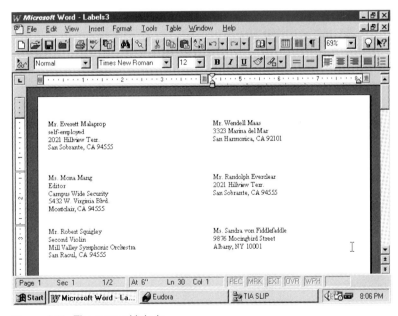

Figure 9.11 The merged labels

MAIL

Sharing Documents and Keeping Track of Changes

147

FAST FORWARD

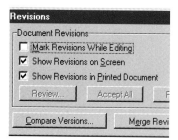

PROTECT A DOCUMENT ➤ *p 150*

1. Choose Tools | Protect Document. This will bring up the Protect Document dialog box.
2. Choose Revisions or Annotations.
3. Type a password if you want. (Be sure to remember it!)
4. Click on OK.

TURN ON REVISION MARKING ➤ *p 151*

1. Double-click in the MRK box in the status bar to bring up the Revisions dialog box.
2. Check Mark Revisions While Editing.
3. Click on OK.

REVIEW REVISIONS ➤ *p 152*

1. Double-click in the MRK box in the status bar to bring up the Revisions dialog box.
2. Do *one* of the following:
   - Click on Accept All and then on Yes in the dialog box that pops up.
   - Click on Reject All and then on Yes.
   - Click on Review.
3. If you clicked on Review, click on Find Next After Accept/Reject.
4. Click on the Find button that has the right-pointing arrow.
5. Review each revision as Word identifies it, clicking on either Accept or Reject as appropriate.
6. Click on OK when you get to the end of the document.

a lot of hard [CC1]work, we'

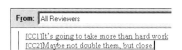

From: All Reviewers

[CC1]It's going to take a lot mor

From: All Reviewers

[CC1]It's going to take more than hard work
[CC2]Maybe not double them, but close.

Routing Slip

From: Christian Crumlish

To:

Address... | Remove

Subject:
Routing: Draft Agenda.doc

The document below has a routing slip.
choose Send from the Word File menu

Draft Agenda.doc

ADD A NOTE TO A DOCUMENT ➤ *pp 153-154*

1. Position the insertion point.
2. Choose Insert | Annotation.
3. Type the text of your note.
4. Click on Close.

REVIEW ANNOTATIONS ➤ *p 154*

1. Choose View | Annotations.
2. Choose All Reviewers or an individual's name in the From drop-down list box at the top of the Annotations window.
3. To incorporate suggested wording from an annotation, use cut and paste as you would with normal text.

ATTACH A ROUTING SLIP ➤ *pp 154-157*

1. Choose File | Add Routing Slip.
2. Click on Address to start adding names to your routing slip.
3. Select names in the Address Book dialog box, clicking on To after you select each one.
4. Click on OK.
5. Write a message in the Message Text box.
6. Click on Route to route the document right away or Add Slip to route it later.

REVIEW A DOCUMENT ROUTED TO YOU ➤ *p 157*

1. Open the e-mail message containing the document.
2. Read the message text.
3. Double-click on the embedded Word document icon.
4. Review the document and make changes or suggestions as needed.
5. Choose File | Send.
6. Click on OK.

Computers and networks are supposed to allow people to work together seamlessly. As we all know, this utopian ideal is still far from a reality. However, Word has several features that allow a group of people to collaborate on a document by circulating successive drafts and keeping track of changes and who has said what. Think of it as a paper trail without the paper.

Each of these procedures—revision marking, attaching annotations, and routing—can be done separately. For example, you can give someone a copy of a draft document by handing them a disk (instead of routing a file via e-mail) and still keep that person's revisions distinct from the original text.

PROTECTING A DOCUMENT

Creating and protecting online forms is explained in Chapter 8.

When you've drafted a document and are getting ready to solicit comments from your colleagues, you can take the precaution of *protecting* the document. If you protect the document for *revisions*, any changes that anyone makes to the document from that point on will be marked as revisions (as explained in the next section). If you protect the document for *annotations*, no one will be able to make changes directly to the document or to anyone else's annotations, but anyone will be able to add annotations. (Annotations are explained later in this chapter.) Read on and learn more about both revisions and annotations before you decide which type of protection to choose.

To protect your document, choose Tools | Protect Document. This will bring up the Protect Document dialog box. Click on Annotations if you want to protect the document for annotations and not for revisions, and click on Revisions if you want to protect the document for revisions and not for annotations. (If you want to protect for both, you have to go through this procedure twice.) If you're really concerned about security, you can type a password. Make sure you remember it! (Capitalization counts.) Then click on OK.

MARKING REVISIONS

The purpose of using revision marks is to make it easy to tell what text was changed in a document. Deleted text is struck through but left visible. Added text is underlined. Both are colored. Also, a vertical line appears in the left margin next to any line that has revisions. Word assigns a different color to each contributor.

Turning On Revision Marking

You won't need to turn on revision marking if you or someone else has already protected the document for revisions.

If you want your changes to a document to be marked as changes, choose Tools | Revisions before you start editing. You can also double-click in the MRK box in the status bar which will bring up the Revisions dialog box.

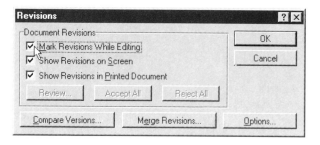

In the Revisions dialog box, click on Mark Revisions While Editing. (Make sure Show Revisions on Screen is checked or your revisions will appear on screen as normal changes, without any marks.) Then click on OK.

Making Changes

After revision marking has been turned on, edit the document as you normally would. For example, to change a phrase, first highlight it.

so with a little luck, we'll be

Then type over it. Instead of seeing the old text replaced by the new text, as usual, you'll see that the old text is struck through and the new is underlined, and both are in color.

| so with a <u>lot of hard work</u><s>little luck</s>, we'll be

CAUTION

If you accidentally started editing before turning on revision marking, you will not be able to see the changes you have done so far as revisions. Undo the changes and turn on revision marking. Then go back and redo the changes.

Reviewing the Revisions

At some point, when all the shouting has died down, you'll want to accept or reject the changes or suggestions that your co-workers have made. First, save the document, in case you want to change your mind later. Next, double-click in the MRK box in the status bar to bring the Revisions dialog box up again. If you've already looked the changes over and want to incorporate them all, go ahead and click on the Accept All button. (Sometimes it's easier to read an edited document if you first hide the revision marks. To do so, uncheck the Show Revisions on Screen check box in the Revisions dialog box. Word will still track changes.) If all the suggested changes were worthless and you prefer your original pristine prose, click on the Reject All button. Either way, Word will ask you to confirm your choice. Click on Yes, unless you have a sudden attack of doubt.

If you're somewhere in between these two frames of mind, click on the Review button. Word will show you the revisions, one at a time, along with the Review Revisions dialog box. The following step-by-step explanation walks you through this procedure.

REVIEWING REVISION MARKS step by step

1. In the Revisions dialog box, click on Find Next After Accept/Reject.

2. Click on the Find button that has the right-pointing arrow.

3. Review each revision as Word identifies it, clicking on either Accept or Reject as appropriate. (The dialog box will tell you who made the revision and the date it was made.)

4. Click on OK in the dialog box that appears when you get to the end of the document.

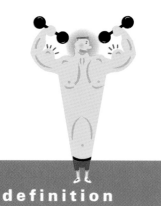

Annotation: *A note added to a Word document and anchored to a specific place in the text. Annotations will not print unless you specifically choose them on the Print tab of the Options dialog box.*

Your annotations will appear colored and underlined in the Annotations pane if you also happen to be showing revision marks. You don't need to have revision marking turned on to use annotations, though.

ANNOTATING A DOCUMENT

Another way that others can kibitz—I mean, help you with suggestions—is by adding annotations. Annotations are the electronic equivalent of those sticky yellow notes with which people would otherwise decorate your manuscript. They are marked in the text with bracketed initials (which you won't see at all unless you click on the Show/Hide ¶ button on the Standard toolbar), and they can be read in their own window at the bottom of the screen.

Adding a Note

To add a note to a document, place the insertion point in the relevant place and choose Insert | Annotation. The Annotations window will open at the bottom of the screen and a highlighted, bracketed marker will appear in the document where the insertion point was (see Figure 10.1). The marker will contain your initials (from the User Info tab of the Options dialog box) and a number. In the Annotations window, the same bracketed initials and number will appear at the beginning of the annotation, which looks much like a footnote. Type the text of your note. When you are done, click on Close at the top of the Annotations window.

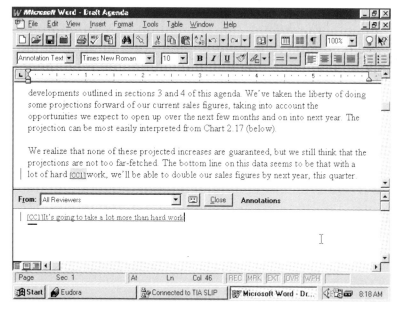

Figure 10.1 The Annotations pane shows the text of annotations preceded by the bracketed initials of each annotation's author and sequential numbering of each note

To add another note, move the insertion point to the next relevant place and choose Insert | Annotation again. The same window will open with a new note started. The initial marker will show up again, with the number incremented by one to show that this is the second note. Type the note text and click on Close again.

Reviewing Annotations

To review the annotations in a document, choose View | Annotations. This will open the Annotations window at the bottom of the screen without inserting a new one. To see all the notes made by various people, choose All Reviewers in the From drop-down list box at the top of the Annotations window. To see just one person's notes, choose that person's name from the same list.

If you want to incorporate suggested wording from an annotation into the document, you can cut and paste it (or drag and drop it) as you would normal text.

SHORTCUT

If the Show/Hide ¶ button on the Standard toolbar is "pushed in," the initials for each annotation will appear in the text. Double-clicking on the initials will open the Annotations window.

ROUTING A DOCUMENT TO A SERIES OF REVIEWERS

Although you can put a document onto a disk and simply walk it over to someone (using the proverbial "sneakernet"), if you have a network connection with your co-workers (or if you can reach them via an online service such as The Microsoft Network), you can send your document electronically to a list of people, using a routing slip. The document can be automatically passed from person to person and finally back to you, or you can have each person get his or her own copy simultaneously and then send it back to you. It might take longer to route the document from person to person, but if you choose that method you will have the advantage of getting everyone's comments in the same document.

Attaching a Routing Slip

To route a document to a list of people, choose File | Add Routing Slip. The Routing Slip dialog box will appear (see Figure 10.2).

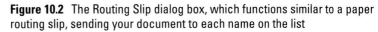

Figure 10.2 The Routing Slip dialog box, which functions similar to a paper routing slip, sending your document to each name on the list

You'll most likely want to use the Personal Address Book option in the Show Names from the drop-down list.

Adding Names to the Routing List

Click on Address to start adding names to your routing slip. This will bring up the Address Book dialog box (see Figure 10.3).

If you have more than one address book available, choose the one you want in the Show Names from the drop-down list box at the top of the dialog box. Select the first person you want to route the document to and click on the To button. Repeat this process as many times as you need to. When you're done, click on OK.

Back in the Routing Slip dialog box, you can change the order of the names by highlighting the one you want to move and clicking on the up or down Move arrow button.

Writing the Message to Accompany the Document

Word will suggest a subject line for the e-mail cover message that will accompany the document, but you can select it and change it if you like. Type a message in the Message Text box.

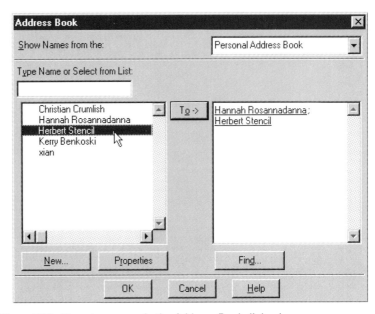

Figure 10.3 Choosing names in the Address Book dialog box

*I recommend One After Another,
of the Route to Recipient
choices, unless you're on a tight
schedule and are worried that
the document will get bogged
down along the way.*

Deciding How the Document Will Be Routed

In the Route to Recipients area, choose whether you want the document to be sent to each person on the list successively or a seperate copy sent to everyone at once.

You should also consider making the following choices in the Routing Slip dialog box before you send the document on its way:

- If you leave the Return When Done box checked, the last person to get the document will be prompted to return it to you.
- If you keep the Track Status box checked, you can be notified by e-mail every time the document is sent along to the next person on the list.
- The Protect For list box on the bottom right is equivalent to the Protect Document dialog box shown at the beginning of this chapter. The Revisions choice is probably your best bet. This guarantees that changes made by the reviewers will be displayed with revision marking.

If you later decide to make changes to the routing slip before sending the document, you can choose File | Edit Routing Slip to return to the Routing Slip dialog box.

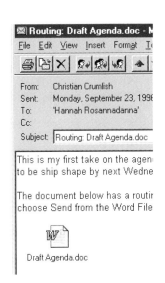

Sending the Document

If the document is ready to go, click on the Route button in the Routing Slip dialog box. If you intend to work on the document a little more before routing it, click on the Add Slip button. Either way, the Routing Slip dialog box will disappear.

If you attached the routing slip without sending (for example, to edit the document further before sending), you can send the document on its way by choosing File | Send. Word will ask you to confirm that you want to route the document with the routing slip and not just send a copy of it to a new person.

Reviewing a Document That Was Routed to You

If someone places your name on a routing slip for a document, the document will be sent to you as an attachment to e-mail. When you are notified that your mail has arrived, open the message as you normally would.

Double-click on the embedded document icon to open and review the routed document. After you've made your revisions and/or added your comments, send the document along its merry way by choosing File | Send. Word will ask you if you want the document sent to the next person on the routing list (or, if you were the last, to the original sender). Click on OK to route the document along.

GETTING BEYOND PAPER

If you and your co-workers can take advantage of these Word features, you can share a huge amount of written work without constantly printing out copies of documents, each with minor variations. Chapter 11 will show you some other alternatives to printing, such as sending documents via e-mail (as was touched on in this chapter) or fax. The rest of the book deals with specialized types of documents—plain or fancy reports, newsletters, and other publications, and World Wide Web pages.

CAFÉ

MAIL

Alternatives to Printing
and Printing Alternatives

FAST FORWARD

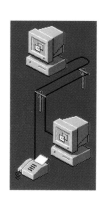

SEND A DOCUMENT VIA E-MAIL ➤ *pp 162-163*

1. Choose File | Send.
2. Type the recipient's address (or click on To and choose one from your address book) and press TAB.
3. Add names to the Cc list the same way, if you want and press TAB.
4. Type a subject line and press TAB.
5. Type a message to accompany the document.
6. Click on the Send button.

FAX A DOCUMENT ➤ *pp 163-165*

1. Choose File | Print.
2. Click on the Name drop-down list box at the top of the dialog box and choose your fax from the list of printers that drops down.
3. Click on OK.
4. If you're not working on a laptop or notebook computer, in the Compose New Fax dialog box, check the I'm not using a portable computer, so don't show this to me again box, and then click on the Next button.
5. Type the name of the person you're sending the fax to or click on the Address Book button to choose a name from the Address Book dialog box, and then click on Next.
6. Choose a cover page option, and then click on Next.
7. Type a subject line for the fax.
8. Press TAB.
9. Type a brief note.
10. Click on Next.
11. Click on Finish.

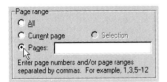

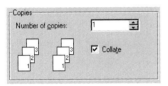

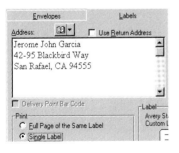

PRINT ONLY THE CURRENT PAGE ➤ *p 166*

1. Choose File | Print.
2. In the Page range area, choose Current page.
3. Click on OK.

PRINT A PAGE RANGE ➤ *p 166*

1. Choose File | Print.
2. In the Pages box of the Page range area, type the page numbers you want to print.
3. Click on OK.

PRINT MULTIPLE COPIES
OF A DOCUMENT OR SET OF PAGES ➤ *pp 166-167*

1. Choose File | Print.
2. Type the number of copies you want in the Number of copies box.
3. Click on OK.

PRINT AN ENVELOPE ➤ *pp 167-169*

1. Choose Tools | Envelopes and Labels.
2. If the Labels tab is in front, click on the Envelopes tab.
3. Correct the addressee or return address, if necessary.
4. To print the envelope directly, click on the Print button. To have the envelope attached to the beginning of the document, click on the Add to Document button.

PRINT A MAILING LABEL ➤ *pp 169-171*

1. Choose Tools | Envelopes and Labels.
2. Click on the Labels tab if it is not already in front.
3. Confirm the address.
4. If you want to print a single label instead of a whole page full of labels, click on Single Label in the Print area.
5. To choose a label type, click on the Options button.
6. Choose a label type in the Product Number list box, or choose Custom Laser if your label type is not listed.
7. If your label type is not listed, click on the Details button, type in the measurements of your labels, and click on OK.
8. Click on OK to close the Label Options dialog box.
9. Click on the Print button.

If you use Word and your computer as a typewriter, you'll probably want to print out your documents at some point. Nowadays, though, more and more work is being done from start to finish online, and other ways of distributing documents are becoming popular. One way to get your writing to others is to e-mail it to them. You'll save a lot of paper in your office if you and your co-workers are on a network. Yet another alternative to printing is faxing. Why print out a document and pay a courier to deliver it when you can fax it?

Still, these alternatives to printing do not completely obviate the need to print documents the traditional way. Furthermore, there are a couple of printing tricks you ought to know about as well, besides simply printing an entire document at the press of a button. We'll get to that at the end of this chapter, along with how to print envelopes and mailing labels for traditional correspondence.

E-MAILING A DOCUMENT

If your computer is on a network or has dial-up access to a network, you can send copies of your document to others via e-mail. (The Word document will be attached to an e-mail message; it won't provide the text contents of the message.) To do so, choose File | Send. Word will drop you into a new message window for whatever e-mail application you use. Figure 11.1 shows the type of window you'll see if your e-mail system is Microsoft Exchange.

Adding Recipients

Type the address of the recipient in the To box or click on the To button to open your address book. In the Address Book dialog box, choose a recipient and click on the To button to add her to your list. You can send your document to more than one person by repeating this process. When you're done, click on OK.

To route a copy of your document to several different recipients to elicit their comments and feedback, you should attach a routing slip, as explained in Chapter 10.

Depending on what e-mail program you use, some of these details might differ, but the general instructions should still be just about right.

habits & strategies

If the recipient has never before received a document via e-mail, you might want to tell them that they can go ahead and double-click on the Word document icon to open the document you've sent.

CAUTION

As with printing, before you try to send your document, be sure to save it. You never know what might go wrong.

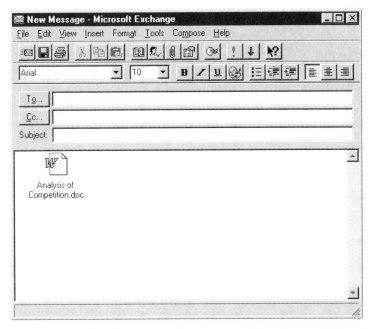

Figure 11.1 Word launching an e-mail program and dropping an embedded copy of the document into it

If you want to send a copy to anyone besides the main recipient, click on the Cc button. You'll see the Address Book dialog box again. Choose an additional recipient or recipients, and then click on OK again.

Press TAB to put the insertion point in the Subject box, and type an informative subject line. This is all your recipient will see at first in her inbox.

Writing a Message to Accompany the Document

Press TAB again and type an explanatory message. You can format the message using the toolbar, and even add color for emphasis if you like (see Figure 11.2). When you're done, click on the Send button.

FAXING A DOCUMENT

You need a fax modem to fax a document directly from your computer. You might be able to do it over a network, but you'll need advice from your local computer guru to make sure it will work. From

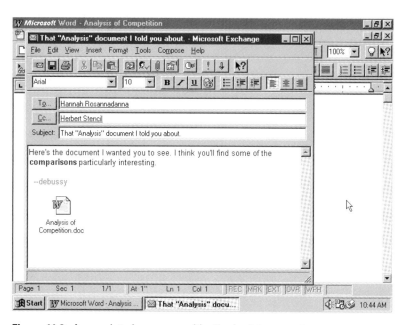

Figure 11.2 A completed message with attached document

Word's point of view, faxing a document is not much different from printing it. You just use the Print dialog box to change the printer to your built-in fax, and then proceed as usual. Word sends the document to the fax modem (or internal card), and the Windows Fax Wizard takes over, walking you through the necessary steps.

Choosing the Fax as a Printer

To begin, choose File | Print. This brings up the Print dialog box. Click on the Name drop-down list box at the top of the dialog box and choose your fax from the list of printers that drops down.

After you have chosen your fax, click on OK. A Windows dialog box called Compose New Fax will appear. If you're not working on a laptop or notebook computer, check the I'm not using a portable computer, so don't show this to me again box.

Enter the Recipients

Now, click on the Next button. The Compose New Fax dialog box will change (see Figure 11.3), allowing you to enter the name of the recipient or recipients. Type the name of the person you're sending the

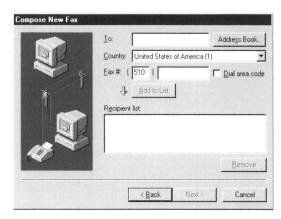

Figure 11.3 Enter your recipient's name or address in the second Compose New Fax dialog box

document to, or click on the Address Book button to choose a name from the Address Book dialog box, as outlined earlier in this chapter. Then click on the Add to List button. Repeat to add additional recipients. When you're done, click on Next.

Choose a Cover Page

The dialog box will change again, this time asking you what kind of cover page, if any, you want to send with your fax. A cover page is usually a good idea, unless you're sending something very short, such as a one-page document. Choose a cover page option or choose No. Your list of cover page options may differ from mine.

If you want to have the fax sent at night or at some other off-peak time, click on the Options button and then either click on Discount rates or click on the Set button, choose a time, and click on OK. Then click on OK to return to the Compose New Fax dialog box. When you have made your cover page choice and other choices, click on Next.

Include an Explanatory Note

The dialog box now displays the Subject and Note boxes. Type a subject line for the fax and then a brief note for the cover page, explaining what the document is. Click on Next one final time, and then click on the Finish button. Your document will now be faxed (or queued up to fax at a later time).

SPECIAL PRINTING OPTIONS

If you want to print your document the old-fashioned way, on a printer, but you don't want to print the whole thing or you want to print more than one copy, don't click on the Print button on the Standard toolbar. Instead, choose File | Print. This will bring up the Print dialog box (see Figure 11.4).

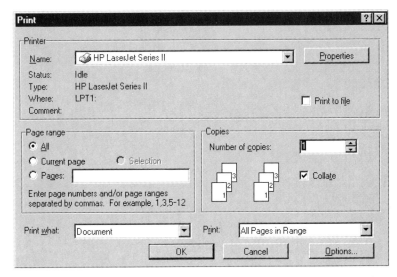

Figure 11.4 The Print dialog box, in which you can tell Word the portion of a document to print and the number of copies to print

The dialog box may look confusing, but its pretty easy to operate:

- To print only the page that the insertion point is on, choose Current Page.
- To print several pages or a range of pages, type the numbers in the Pages box. Separate noncontiguous page numbers with commas. You can indicate a range of pages by typing the beginning and ending page numbers and putting a hyphen between them. You can also combine these two formats—requesting, for example, that Word print pages 2,5,7-9,15.
- To print more than one copy of the document (or the selected pages), enter or choose a different number in the Number of copies box in the Copies area. Uncheck Collate

if you want the pages grouped together. (The illustration on the dialog box will change to show you the results of collating or not collating.)

When you've chosen all the options you want, click on OK.

PRINTING ENVELOPES AND MAILING LABELS

To print envelopes or labels for an entire mail merge run, see Chapter 9.

After you have written a letter or composed some other form of correspondence, if you're not going to fax it or send it by e-mail or use smoke signals, you're going to need to put it in an envelope. To address said envelope, you can either print on it directly (assuming that your printer can do that without chewing up the envelope) or you can print the recipient's address on a mailing label and stick it on the envelope.

Either way, Word has established a nicely automated procedure to take the pain out of positioning the text and fitting the address into the right space. First, let's do an envelope.

Printing an Envelope

Choose Tools | Envelopes and Labels. The Envelopes and Labels dialog box will appear (see Figure 11.5). If the Labels tab is in front, click on the Envelopes tab. If it guesses wrong or nabs *your* address by

SHORTCUT

To use an address from your address book, click on the Insert Address button above either of the address boxes in the Envelopes and Labels dialog box.

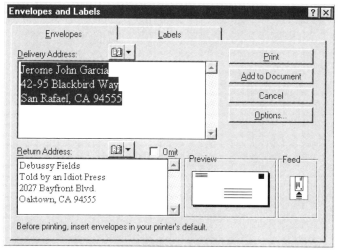

Figure 11.5 The Envelopes tab of the Envelopes and Labels dialog box

habits & strategies

If you have trouble feeding an envelope into your printer, click on the Printing Options tab in the Envelope Options dialog box. Then try a different orientation for the envelope, or switch from manual feed to another option in the Feed From box.

mistake, just type the address yourself (or copy it from the document and paste it into the window). Figure 11.5 also shows the return address, which Word gets from the User Info tab of the Options dialog box (Tools | Options).

To format the text on the envelope or choose a different envelope size, click on the Options button. This brings up the Envelope Options dialog box (see Figure 11.6).

The Envelope Options tab should be in front. (Click on it if it isn't.) You can choose from the following options in this dialog box:

- To choose a type of envelope other than the ubiquitous No. 10, click in the Envelope Size drop-down list box.
- To insert a postal bar code to make it easier for the U.S. Postal Service to sort your mail, check Delivery Point Bar Code.
- To format either of the addresses, click on the Font button in the Delivery Address or Return Address area, choose the character formatting you want, and click on OK.
- To adjust the position of either address, enter a positive or negative number or use the tiny arrow buttons to jump by 0.1" increments in the From Left or From Top box in the Delivery Address or Return Address area.

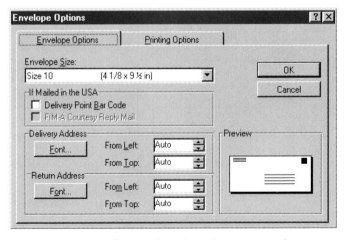

Figure 11.6 The Envelope Options dialog box, where you can choose a different envelope size, add a postal bar code, or format either of the addresses

When you've made all your choices, click on OK. Back in the Envelopes and Labels dialog box, click on the Print button to print the envelope immediately, or click on the Add to Document button to have the envelope added (in its own section, with its own page size and so on) at the beginning of the document. Figure 11.7 shows an envelope attached to a letter in page layout view.

Figure 11.7 An envelope that has been added to a document

Printing a Label

Choose Tools | Envelopes and Labels. The Envelopes and Labels dialog box will appear (see Figure 11.8). Click on the Labels tab if it is not already in front. If Word thinks the first few lines at the top of your letter look like an address, it will place those lines in the Address box as a suggestion. If it does not identify an address, the box will be blank. In this case, simply type the address yourself (or copy it from the document and paste it into the window).

The Labels tab lets you choose from the following options:

- To include a return address, check Use Return Address. (This will only work on labels that are big enough.) The

Address box will then show your address from the User Info tab of the Options dialog box.

- To print just a single label, click on Single Label in the Print area. If you don't want to print on the label in the top left corner, enter or click your way to another position in the Row and Column boxes in the Print area.

- To choose a label type, click on the Options button. This brings up the Label Options dialog box (explained next).

The Label Options dialog box allows you to make specific selections with respect to the type of labels you are using. Word can print to just about any type and size of label you're likely to run across.

If your labels are not made by Avery, click in the Label Products drop-down list box and look for your brand. If it's not there, leave Avery Standard selected. Choose a label type in the Product Number list box, or choose Custom Laser if your label type is not listed.

If the packaging does not specify the dimensions, get out a ruler and measure each of the items specified in the Preview window.

If your label type is not listed, click on the Details button. This brings up the Custom Laser Information dialog box (see Figure 11.9). Type in the measurements of your labels. As you enter the new numbers, the preview illustration will adjust to reflect your changes. When you're done, click on OK.

When you're finished with the Label Options dialog box, click on OK. Then, when you're finished with the Envelopes and Labels dialog

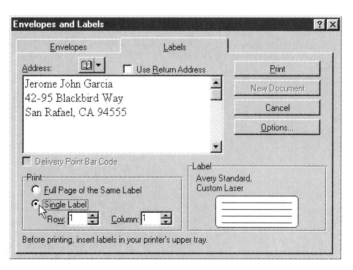

Figure 11.8 The Labels tab of the Envelopes and Labels dialog box

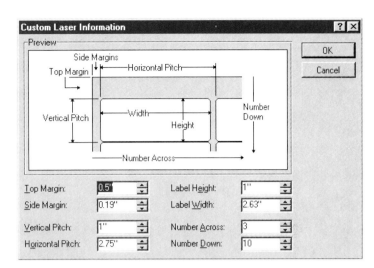

Figure 11.9 Entering the measurements of labels in the Custom Laser Information dialog box

box, click on the Print button (and get ready to feed your labels into the printer). Word will print your label.

MOVING RIGHT ALONG

Ideally, some day in the future, we can stop printing out documents on paper completely and just beam images and text directly to each other's goggles. For now, though, you've got the essentials covered. The last four chapters in this book deal with special types of documents, from reports and newsletters to World Wide Web pages.

PRIORITY!

Fashioning Deluxe Reports

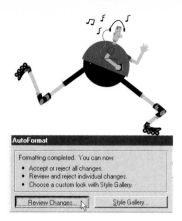

FAST FORWARD

AUTOFORMAT A DOCUMENT ➤ *pp 180, 182-183*

1. Save the document (press CTRL-S).
2. Select the part of the document you want to AutoFormat (or make no selection to AutoFormat the whole thing).
3. Choose Format | AutoFormat (or press CTRL-K to skip the review stage and the rest of these steps). A small AutoFormat dialog box appears, offering to format your document.
4. Click on OK. Word formats your document and displays a different AutoFormat dialog box.
5. Click on Reject All if you don't like any of the changes. (If you choose Reject All, you're now done with AutoFormat.)
6. Click on the Review Changes button to sign off on the changes one by one.
7. Check the Find Next after Reject check box.
8. Click on the Find button with the right-pointing arrow (unless Word has already found the first change automatically).
9. To turn down a change, click on Reject.
10. To see the next change, click on the Find button with the right-pointing arrow.
11. Repeat steps 9 and 10 until you get to the end of the document.
12. Click on Cancel.

CHOOSE A DOCUMENT DESIGN FROM THE STYLE GALLERY ➤ *pp 183-184*

1. Choose Format | Style Gallery.
2. Choose one of the listed templates.
3. Choose to display either a preview of your document, a made-up example document, or a listing of the styles in the template.
4. Scroll through the Preview box and look at the design.
5. Repeat steps 2 through 4 until you find a design you like (or until you give up).
6. Click on OK to choose a style, or click on Cancel to bag it.

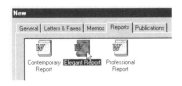

START A DOCUMENT BASED ON A TEMPLATE ➤ *pp 184-185*

1. Choose File | New.
2. Choose the tab in the New dialog box that pertains to the type of document you're creating.
3. Choose a template.
4. Click on OK.

DEFINE A NEW STYLE ➤ *pp 186-188*

1. Choose Format | Style.
2. Click on the New button.
3. Type a name in the Name box.
4. Choose Character or Paragraph in the Style Type box to indicate the kind of formatting you want to apply.
5. If you want to base the new style on an existing style, click on the Based On drop-down list box and choose the existing style.
6. When you apply a style to a paragraph, Word will apply either that style or the Normal style to the paragraph that will follow. If you don't want this to happen, click on the Style for Following Paragraph drop-down list box and choose the style you want to apply to the following paragraph.
7. Click on the Format button, and a choose the type of formatting you want to apply from the menu that drops down.
8. Choose the formatting you want from whichever dialog box appears, and click on OK.
9. Repeat steps 7 and 8 until you've completely formatted your style.
10. Check the Add to Template check box if you want your new style to be available to all new documents that will be based on the current template.
11. Click on OK.
12. To apply the style to the current paragraph, click on Apply.
13. Click on Close.

EDIT A STYLE ➤ *p 188*

1. Choose Format | Style.
2. Choose Styles in Use in the List drop-down list box.
3. Choose the style you want to edit.
4. Click on the Modify button.
5. Follow steps 4 through 13 from the previous Fast Forward item.

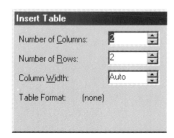

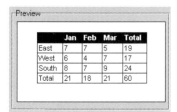

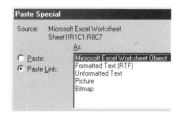

Idiot's backlist are suitable for r
; sense of mak   **backrest**
yperlinked tab.   **backlash**
ll-fledged mult   **blacklist**

                        Ignore All
                        Add
TLES   Spelling...

CREATE A TABLE ➤ *p 190*

1. Choose Table | Insert Table.
2. Type the number of columns, and press TAB.
3. Type the number of rows, and then click on OK.
4. To start filling in the table, type the contents of the first cell and then press TAB.
5. Move across each row by pressing TAB or using the arrow keys.
6. Press TAB in the last cell of the last row of the table to add a new row.

AUTOFORMAT A TABLE ➤ *p 192*

1. Right-click anywhere in the table and choose Table AutoFormat.
2. Check the AutoFit check box.
3. Choose the types of formats you want to apply in the Formats to Apply area.
4. In the Apply Special Formats To area, choose the special rows and columns that should be acknowledged in the table's design.
5. Click on OK.

LINK DATA FROM ANOTHER PROGRAM INTO THE CURRENT DOCUMENT ➤ *pp 193-196*

1. Start both the other program and Word, and open the Word document.
2. From the other program, select the portion of the document that you want to link to your Word document.
3. Right-click, and from the menu that appears, choose Copy.
4. Switch to Word.
5. Position the insertion point at the location to which you want to paste the link.
6. Choose Edit | Paste Special.
7. Choose a format for the link.
8. Choose Paste Link.
9. Click on OK.

CHECK SPELLING ➤ *pp 197-199*

1. Right-click on any word that is underlined with a squiggly red line.
2. Make one of four choices:
   - If the word is correct as is, click on Add on the menu that pops up.

- If the word is spelled inorrectly and the pop-up menu offers the correct spelling as one of the choices, choose the correct spelling.
- For unusual words that are spelled correctly, but that you don't want to add to your dictionary, simply choose Ignore All. That word will not be queried for the rest of your Word session.
- If Word doesn't suggest the correct spelling but you know what it is, just retype the word yourself.

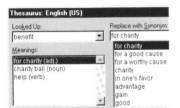

LOOK UP A BETTER WORD IN THE THESAURUS ➤ *pp 200-201*

1. Place the insertion point on a word you'd like to improve.
2. Press SHIFT-F7.
3. Choose a meaning in the Meanings box.
4. Choose a word from the Replace with Synonym box on the right.
5. Double-click on a word in the Replace with Synonym box (or choose it and click on the Look Up button) to look up further synonyms for that word.
6. Repeat as often as you like.
7. When you find the word you want, click on Replace.

**habits &
strategies**

*Before you start working with
the appearance of a formal
document, you should write
a first draft and review it,
making any necessary
corrections and improvements.
Only when the content is fairly
stable and finalized are you
ready to polish it.*

When you need to prepare a formal document, perhaps to hand out at a meeting or to fulfill a request from your boss, you have to pay some attention to the impression that the document will make. How is it formatted? How does it come across visually? Does it communicate as well as it should? Are there any embarrassing errors? In an ideal world, it wouldn't matter how your document *looks*. Only the contents—your brilliant words—would matter. Like it or not, though, the more "superficial" issues of appearance do matter, not to mention the more substantial issues of presentation and formatting.

These matters of presentation take some time, so they're not worth bothering with in the early phases of the development of a report. As you get closer to the moment of truth, however, you will have to devote time to your document's appearance, no matter how busy you are. You can't skip combing your hair, can you?

In this chapter, I'll tell you how to spruce up your report's appearance, how to add special elements such as tables that communicate more visually than text, and how to use Word's automatic proofreading tools to check for errors and problems. Don't just sit down and read this whole chapter from start to finish. Instead, jump ahead to the specific tricks you need to make your report shine, and then move on. (In other words, treat this chapter as a reference.)

HOW TO LOOK YOUR BEST

By now you've probably played around a little with fonts, character formatting (such as boldface and italics), and formatting that affects entire paragraphs (such as indentation, spacing, and alignment). After a quick review of those hands-on formatting tools, I'll show you how to let Word format your document for you, how to choose a predesigned template to establish the look of your document, and how to create your own styles from scratch.

♪ ♪

*Font and paragraph formatting were
introduced in Chapter 3.*

A Review of Basic Formatting

Let's begin with a quick recap of the formatting basics.

Choosing Fonts, Sizes, and Character Formatting

To choose a font (typeface), a size, and character formatting such as bold, italic, underline, and small caps, right-click on the word or selection in question and choose Font. This brings up the Font dialog box (see Figure 12.1). As you choose or experiment with various options for font, font style, size, and so on, the Preview area in the bottom right corner shows how your choices will look. When you're done, click on OK.

SHORTCUT

Press ALT-0-F to bring up the Font dialog box directly.

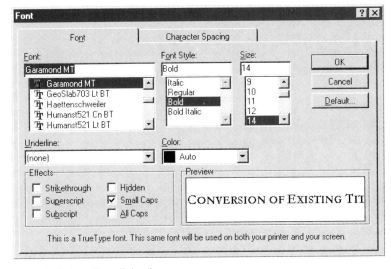

Figure 12.1 The Font dialog box

Apply character formatting in layers. First, choose a font for body text. A font with serifs is considered easiest to read. Then format headings, captions, words that require emphasis, etc. In dressing up your documents, it's the subtle use of character formatting that signals your style, not unlike the glimpse of an elegant tie or tasteful earrings.

definition

Serifs: Small "tails" jutting out from the tops or bottoms of letters that make text easier to read.

Choosing Indents, Spacing, and Alignment

To indent a paragraph, change the spacing, or choose a paragraph alignment, first place the insertion point in the paragraph (or select the paragraphs if you want to do more than one at a time), and then right-click and choose Paragraph from the menu that appears. This brings up the Paragraph dialog box (see Figure 12.2). By the way, as long as your selection starts in the first paragraph and ends in the last one, you can format any number of contiguous paragraphs at once.

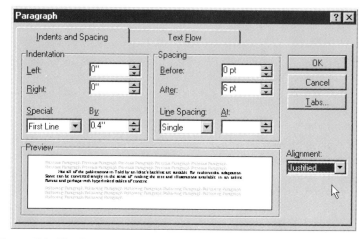

Figure 12.2 The Paragraph dialog box

SHORTCUT

Press ALT-O-P or double-click on an indent marker on the Ruler to bring up the Paragraph dialog box.

As you choose or experiment with various choices for indentation, spacing, and alignment, the Preview area in the bottom portion shows how your choices will look. When you're done, click on OK.

Formatting with Keyboard Shortcuts

Perhaps the fastest way to apply formatting to individual words, paragraphs, or entire selections is by using shortcut keys on text that you have selected. Table 12.1 shows the most useful shortcut keys for formatting.

Letting Word AutoFormat Your Report

In Chapter 3 you saw how Word offers to format your document automatically as you type (and how you can turn off this feature if you find it intrusive). That same "interactive" helping hand can be invoked more selectively when you're done composing and ready to consider the format of your document. Remember, always save your document first before you let the computer have a go at formatting it. Sure, you can reject the changes that Word makes—you can even undo them—but you never know what can happen. It's better to be safe and save.

Desired Result	Keyboard Shortcut
Change the current font in the Formatting toolbar	CTRL-SHIFT-F
Change the current font size in the Formatting toolbar	CTRL-SHIFT-P
Increase the font size by a preset increment	CTRL-SHIFT->
Decrease the font size by a preset increment	CTRL-SHIFT->
Increase the font size by 1 point	CTRL-]
Decrease the font size by 1 point	CTRL-[
Change the case of letters (all caps, all lowercase, initial caps)	SHIFT-F3
Change all letters to caps	CTRL-SHIFT-A
Format letters as small caps	CTRL-SHIFT-K
Apply or remove boldfacing	CTRL-B
Apply or remove italics	CTRL-I
Apply or remove underlining	CTRL-U
Apply or remove underlining for single words, not the spaces between them	CTRL-SHIFT-W
Apply or remove double underlining	CTRL-SHIFT-D
Apply or remove subscripting	CTRL-=
Apply or remove superscripting	CTRL-SHIFT-=
Apply or remove hidden text designation	CTRL-SHIFT-H
Remove formatting (restore plain text)	CTRL-Spacebar or CTRL-SHIFT-Z
Format text in single-spaced lines	CTRL-1
Format text in double-spaced lines	CTRL-2
Format text in 1.5-line spacing	CTRL-5
Add or remove one line of space preceding the paragraph	CTRL-0 (zero)
Center a paragraph	CTRL-E
Justify a paragraph	CTRL-J
Left-align a paragraph	CTRL-L
Right-align a paragraph	CTRL-R
Indent a paragraph from the left margin	CTRL-M
Remove a paragraph indent	CTRL-SHIFT-M
Create a hanging indent	CTRL-T
Remove a hanging indent	CTRL-SHIFT-T
Remove paragraph formatting	CTRL-Q

Table 12.1 Shortcut Keys for Applying Formatting

SHORTCUT

You can press CTRL-K to tell Word to AutoFormat your document without further ado. Word will just go ahead and do it. Press CTRL-Z (Undo) if you don't like the results.

To format a specific portion of a document, select that portion first. To format the entire document, do not make any selection. Begin the AutoFormatting process by choosing Format | AutoFormat. (If you did not change your toolbars as I recommended in Chapter 2, you can also click on the AutoFormat button on the Formatting toolbar.) Then click on OK (to start the AutoFormatting right away) or Options (to control what will be formatted) in the first AutoFormat dialog box.

Controlling AutoFormat Options

If you want to control what will be formatted by AutoFormat, click on Options in the first AutoFormat dialog box. This brings up the Options dialog box with the AutoFormat tab in front (see Figure 12.3).

In the Apply area of the dialog box, choose the document elements you want Word to format. Your choices are headings, (numbered) lists, bulleted lists, and plain paragraphs.

In the Replace area, choose the substitutions you want Word to make—curly quotation marks for straight ("" and '' instead of " and' '); superscripted ordinal number endings, such as 1st, 2nd, 3rd, 4th, and so on; fractions, such as ½ and ¼ and symbols, such as ©. By default, all four Replace options are checked, so you'll only have to alter a setting if you *don't* want Word to make the change.

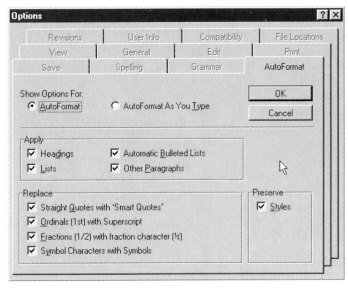

Figure 12.3 The AutoFormat tab of the Options dialog box

Uncheck Styles in the Preserve area if you want to allow Word to assign new or different styles to elements of your document. Then click on OK to return to the AutoFormat dialog box. Click on OK and Word will format your document.

Reviewing Changes

If you've changed your mind about the AutoFormat or don't like the results as far as you can see, click on the Reject All button.

When Word is done formatting your document, it pops up a dialog box giving you the options of accepting all changes, rejecting all changes, or reviewing the changes one by one. I recommend reviewing the changes. It's a good idea to see what Word has done to your report. Click on the Review Changes button. The Review AutoFormat Changes dialog box will appear.

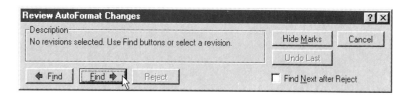

Check the Find Next after Reject check box to save yourself from having to click on Find every time after you reject a change. If Word does not automatically find the first change, click on the Find button with the right-pointing arrow. A description of the change will appear in the Description area. At this point, you can do one of several things:

- Click on the Reject button to veto a change.
- If you're happy with a change, click on the Find button with the right-pointing arrow again to go to the next one.
- To reverse your response to the most recent change, click on the Undo Last button.

Proceed through your document until you've reviewed all the changes. When you are done, click on the Cancel button.

Using the Style Gallery

You have to run through the AutoFormat process once (even if you reject all the changes) before the Style Gallery button will appear in the AutoFormat dialog box.

Another convenient way to format a document all at once is to choose a template from the Style Gallery, which is a set of predesigned document formats. To see the choices, click on the Style Gallery button in the AutoFormat dialog box. (Alternatively, you can get to the Style Gallery at any time by choosing Format | Style Gallery.)

In the Style Gallery dialog box (shown in Figure 12.4), you can choose from any of the existing templates provided with Word. There are three report designs: Contemporary Report, Elegant Report, and Professional Report. (The titles are subjective.) In the Preview area in the bottom-left corner of the dialog box, you can choose to see the styles of the chosen template imposed on your document, used with an example document, or laid out one style after another.

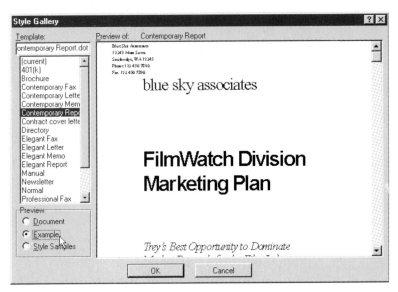

Figure 12.4 The Style Gallery dialog box

Try a few templates on for size. If you like one, choose it and click on OK. If you don't like any, click on Cancel.

Rejecting All After All

If you're not happy with any of the results of the AutoFormat, click on the Reject All button in the AutoFormat dialog box. You're under no obligation to actually like the way your computer wants to format the document. It's just following some rules that may or may not make good aesthetic sense in this case.

Starting a New Document
Based on a Template

The Style Gallery mentioned in the previous section is really just a way of previewing the various templates that come with Word (or that

Styles are explained in more detail in the next section, "Establishing Consistent Styles." Templates were introduced in Chapter 4.

can be developed by users), each with its own preformatted styles. To design a report based on one of the templates, just start a document by choosing File | New (don't click on the New button on the Standard toolbar). The New dialog box will appear (see Figure 12.5). Click on the Reports tab (or one of the others, of course, if the document you're working on is not a report). Choose a report template and then click on OK.

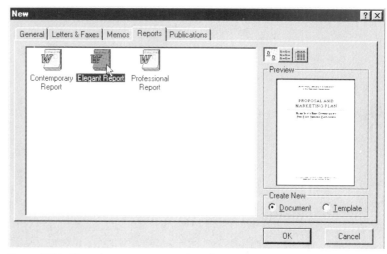

Figure 12.5 Choosing a report template from the Reports tab of the New dialog box

By the way, if you make your own templates, save them in the proper folder (the Templates folder, or one of its subfolders, in the MSOffice folder) and they'll show up in the New dialog box along with the supplied templates.

Establishing Consistent Styles

Both AutoFormat and the templates use *styles* to format documents. The Blank Document (Normal.dot) template comes with a number of built-in styles, such as formatting for heading levels, but you can also create your own. In Chapter 5 you learned how to create a style by using text you already formatted. You can also create styles from scratch (or change the existing styles in the Style Gallery). When your boss finally agrees that his favorite sans serif font is an eyesore in body text, you can choose the font you've always wanted to use by simply changing the style you used for the body text, *assuming that you did set up such a style*. To create a style, bring up the Style dialog box by choosing Format | Style.

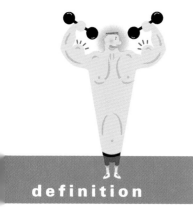

definition

Style: *In Word, a collection of character or paragraph formatting information that can be applied all at once to any selection. If a style is changed, all the text that has been formatted with that style will change automatically.*

For headings that look better than the plain Blank Document styles provided in the template, but that are still visible in Outline view (see Chapter 13), edit the existing heading styles—don't create a new, parallel set of heading styles.

Defining a New Style

To create a new style, first choose User-Defined Styles from the List drop-down list box in the bottom-left corner of the Style dialog box. (This should really be a *tab* to be consistent with other dialog boxes, by the way.) Then click on the New button. This brings up the New Style dialog box, shown in Figure 12.6.

You don't have to choose User-Defined Styles to define a new style, but it makes it easier to see which styles are the new ones.

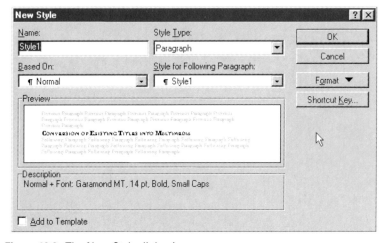

Figure 12.6 The New Style dialog box

Before you can create your new style, you need to give Word some information so that it can prepare and save your new style correctly. The following steps will get you started.

1. Type a name for your new style in the Name box.
2. Choose Character or Paragraph in the Style Type box (depending on the kind of formatting you want to apply). Character styles can contain only character formatting, whereas Paragraph styles can contain both character and paragraph formatting.
3. If you want to base the new style on an existing one, click on the Based On drop-down list and choose the existing style.

habits & strategies

Many specialized types of document elements, such as headings and captions, should be followed by the base paragraph style (which is often the Normal style).

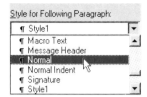

4. When you apply a style to a paragraph, Word will apply either that style or the Normal style to the paragraph that will follow. If you want the style of the paragraph following your new style to be formatted with a style *other than* the one suggested by Word, click on the Style for Following Paragraph drop-down list and choose the style you want to apply to the following paragraph.

Now you're ready to do the dirty work. The next few paragraphs will take you through all the procedures needed to actually create a new style.

Format the Style   Here's where you apply the formatting you want to your style. Click on the Format button and a menu will drop down. From this menu, choose the type of formatting you want to apply, and then the appropriate dialog box will appear (Font, Paragraph, and so on). Choose the formatting you want and click on OK. Repeat this process as often as necessary to choose font and size, add enhancements such as bold or italics, change the line spacing, add borders or paragraph numbering, and so on. I'll stop being so specific now. We all know what formatting is, right?

Assign a Shortcut Key to Your Style   If you want to assign a shortcut key combination to your style so that you can apply it easily in the future (as long as you remember the shortcut), click on the Shortcut Key button. This brings up the Customize dialog box with the Keyboard tab showing (see Figure 12.7).

Press a likely key combination. The keys will appear in the Press New Shortcut Key dialog box. If that particular combination has already been assigned to some other action, that action will appear in the Currently Assigned To area below the box. Good luck finding an unused key combination! My advice is to try CTRL-SHIFT-something. (You can override an underused shortcut if you want.) When you're happy with your choice, click on Assign.

Use Your New Style for Other Documents   To add your new style to the current template, check Add to Template in the bottom-left corner of the New Style dialog box. If you don't add your new style to the template, it will exist only in your current document and will be unavailable to future documents.

CAUTION

If you've changed some of the basic styles that come with Word (such as Heading 1), you probably don't want to add your edited styles to the Blank Document template, unless you really want to change those styles for all documents in the future.

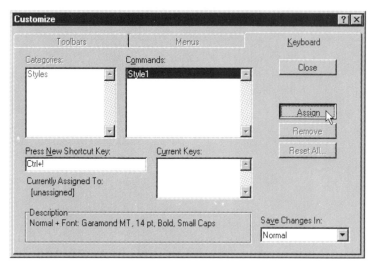

Figure 12.7 Assigning a keyboard shortcut in the Customize dialog box

Apply that Style When you are done creating your new style, you can apply it immediately to the text your insertion point is in by clicking on the Apply button. If you don't want to apply the style right now, click on the Close button.

Editing (Changing the Format of) an Existing Style

To edit an existing style, first choose Styles in Use in the List box in the bottom-left corner of the Style dialog box. Choose the Style you want to change in the Styles list and then click on the Modify button.

This brings up the Modify Style dialog box, which looks just like the New Style dialog box (shown in Figure 12.6). From here on, the procedure is just like that for creating a new style, except that some formatting choices have already been added to the style. (These, however, can be overridden.) If you leave Add to Template unchecked, the style will be modified only in the current document. See the previous section for more details.

Adding Any Style to Any Template

You can add a style you're creating or editing to the current template just by checking Add to Template in the dialog box. To add a style that's already in existence to a template, click on the Organizer button in the Style dialog box. This brings up the Organizer dialog box with the Styles tab in front (see Figure 12.8)

CAUTION

You can't change a paragraph style to a character style.

The filename of the Blank Document template is Normal.dot, but to make matters more confusing, the Organizer dialog box refers to it as the Global Template.

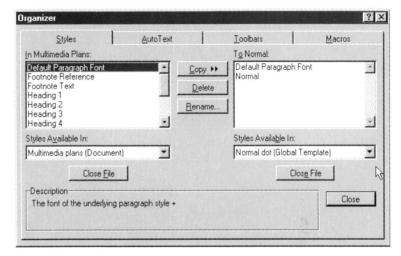

Figure 12.8 The Organizer dialog box

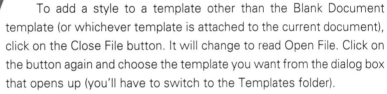

To add a style to a template other than the Blank Document template (or whichever template is attached to the current document), click on the Close File button. It will change to read Open File. Click on the button again and choose the template you want from the dialog box that opens up (you'll have to switch to the Templates folder).

Choose a style in the list box on the left side of the dialog box, and then click on the Copy button to copy the style to the template named on To line on the right side. When you are done, click on Close.

Using Keyboard Shortcuts for Styles

The following table shows some keyboard shortcuts for use with styles.

Desired Result	Keyboard Shortcut
Choose a style in the Formatting toolbar	CTRL-SHIFT-S
Apply the Normal style	CTRL-SHIFT-N
Apply the Heading 1 style	ALT-CTRL-1
Apply the Heading *n* style	ALT-CTRL-*n*
Apply the List style	CTRL-SHIFT-L

SPECIAL REPORT ELEMENTS

Some arguments can be won with a picture, or a clear diagram, or a chart, or some persuasive numbers. The power to frame information is as valuable these days as it ever was. Although nobody likes gratuitous or confusing tables or charts, judicious use of such elements can help a report punch through the tedium of fat columns of gray "focus group results." This section explains how to insert tables, as well as more complicated objects, such as spreadsheets, charts, and pictures, into your document.

Adding Tables to Documents

A table can often help you get right to the point and can be useful for clarifying numerical information.

Inserting a Table

There are two ways to insert a table, via the toolbar button or a menu:

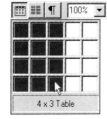

- For small tables, use the Insert Table button on the Standard toolbar. Click on it and drag across the grid that drops down to indicate the number of rows and columns you'll want. (You can always add or subtract rows later.) Word will insert an empty dotted-line grid into your document. This is the table, ready to be filled in.
- You can also insert a new table by choosing Table | Insert Table. This brings up the Insert Table dialog box. Type a number for the number of columns, press TAB, type a number for the number of rows, and then click on OK.

If you've got preexisting text, such as an aborted attempt to create a table using tabs, you can turn it into a table. Select the text, and then choose Table | Convert Text to Table. In the small dialog box that pops up, indicate the character that should be treated as a cell divider (comma, tab, or paragraph mark, for example), and click on OK. You can also just select your text and then click on the Insert Table button on the Standard toolbar. Most converted tables will come out a little screwy. If you can play with the table a bit to get it into shape, fine. If it looks too messed up, press CTRL-Z to undo the conversion and then try to straighten out the source text, perhaps by inserting tabs or commas, before trying again.

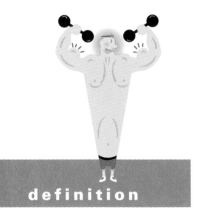

definition

Cell: *A square representing the intersection of a column and a row in a table. Each cell has a paragraph mark and can be formatted separately. (Entire rows and columns can also be formatted at once.)*

If you want to do more complicated mathematics in tables, you might be better off using a real spreadsheet program and then linking the information into your document (as explained later in this chapter).

Entering Text into an Empty Table

After you insert a table, the insertion point will be in the first cell. Type the contents of the cell and then press TAB. The insertion point will jump to the next cell over in the same row. The following rules of movement apply to tables:

- You can move across each row, and down to the next row if you are in the last cell of a row, by pressing TAB.
- You can also get around in a table by using the standard arrow keys.
- If you press TAB in the last cell of the last row of a table, a new row will be added automatically.

Doing Simple Sums in a Table

Probably the most common mathematical operation that's performed in tables is summing (totaling) the numbers in a column or row. To do this in a Word table, you will need to add a formula to it. First place the insertion point in the cell where you want the total to appear. Then choose Table | Formula. This brings up the Formula dialog box.

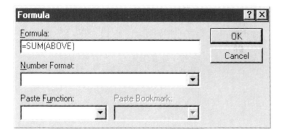

Word can usually make a pretty good guess about what you're trying to do, and it will probably suggest the formula =SUM(ABOVE) or =SUM(LEFT), depending on whether you're summing up a column or a row. If Word does not suggest either of these formulas, you can type the one you want yourself. Then click on OK.

Formatting the Table

When you've finished entering the text into a table, you should think about how you want the table to look. (You can wait, of course, until you format the rest of the document.)

Using AutoFormat   To apply a predesigned format to your table, right-click anywhere in the table and choose Table AutoFormat from the menu that appears. This brings up the Table AutoFormat dialog box (see Figure 12.9).

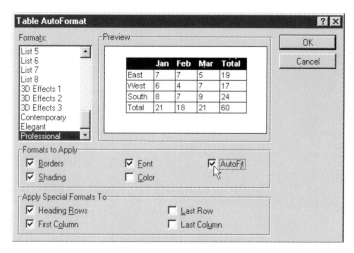

Figure 12.9   Choosing a format in the Table AutoFormat dialog box

Word can adjust the column widths for you so that the text fits as neatly as possible (to avoid crowded cells). If you want this to happen during the AutoFormat, check AutoFit. Decide whether you want Word to apply borders, shadings, fonts, and/or colors. If the first or last row or column should get special treatment, check the appropriate options in the Apply Special Formats To area. Then click on OK. If you don't like the results, press CTRL-Z to undo the formatting.

Formatting by Hand   Of course, you can format your table by hand as well. Start with general formatting, such as font and size. First select the entire table and apply whatever formats you want. Then select specific areas of the table, such as the top row or the rightmost column, to give any such areas distinctive formatting. Finally, format specific cells, if necessary. Tables have some special selection shortcuts:

- To select the whole table, choose Table | Select Table.
- To select an entire row, click in the left margin next to the row.

Don't confuse borders with gridlines. The dotted gridlines that surround a table on your screen (unless you turn them off) are there to make the table easier to work with, but they don't print out.

- To select an entire column, hold down ALT and click on the column, or point to the top gridline and click when the pointer changes to a downward-pointing arrow.

To add lines and shading to your table, first right-click in any toolbar and choose Borders from the menu that pops up. This brings up the Borders toolbar. Now select entire rows or columns, groups of cells, or individual cells and then click on the various buttons in the toolbar to apply lines to the top, bottom, side, or all exterior edges of a selection.

Linking Data from Another Program to Your Document

Windows 95 makes it easier for programs to share information (which I'll call data or info for short). This means that part or all of one document can be copied or linked into another. When this works well, it can make your computer seem a little bit more cooperative and can sometimes mean the difference between sanity and its alternative. (Most Microsoft products, such as the rest of the Microsoft Office suite, handle OLE (which stands for Object Linking and Embedding) very well now. I'm not flacking for Microsoft; it's just part of the company's strategy that their applications help the user think in terms of the document and not the programs.)

If you've got info you've already created in another program, or if you want to add to your document some data that would be easier to put together in another program, you can have that source material poking right into a Word document. You don't have to redo anything. For existing info, it's almost as simple as copying and pasting between the two programs. (Oops, I'm drawing your attention to the *programs* again.)

Once you've linked data from another program to a Word document, don't delete, move, or rename the source, or your links will be broken. If you must delete, move, or rename the source, you'll have to remake the links in the Word document.

Link: *To insert data from one program (the source) into a document in another program, creating a connection that allows the insertion to be updated automatically when the source is updated.*

Embed: *To insert data from one program (the source) into a document in another program without maintaining a connection to the source. When the source is updated, the data in the destination document will not be updated.*

Linking with Copy and Paste

To copy data from another program into Word, simply select the data in that other program, right-click, and choose Copy. Then switch back to Word, place the insertion point where you want the copy to appear, right-click, and choose Paste. The pasted data becomes plain old Word data and no longer "remembers" the program it was created in. To link or embed an object (one that will "remember" where it came from), the first half of these instructions are the same. When you switch back to the Word document, though, instead of right-clicking and choosing Paste, choose Edit | Paste Special.

The Paste Special dialog box will appear (see Figure 12.10). It will identify the source of the document (such as Microsoft Excel) and offer you several choices for the format of the data you're about to paste. (Word refers to the data from another program as an *object*.) To use OLE, you have to choose the original format of the object (the program in which it was created). Then you can do one of two things:

- Check Paste to *embed* the data. Double-clicking on the object in the document will start up its original program.
- Check Paste Link to *link* the object to its source.

Finally, click on OK.

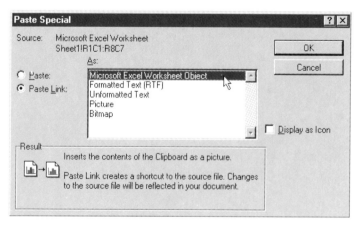

Figure 12.10 Choosing to embed or link an object in the Paste Special dialog box

Linking by Inserting an Object

While in Word, you can create a new object in another program or insert an existing object that belongs to another program, as long as you also have that program installed on your computer. To do so, start by choosing Insert | Object. This brings up the Object dialog box. Make sure that the Create New tab is in front.

Choose an object type in the Object Type list box, and then click on OK. In my example, shown in Figure 12.11, the object appears as an Excel worksheet. You can enter data into it as you would with any worksheet. When you move the insertion point back to the main Word document, the worksheet will look more like a simple table, as shown in Figure 12.12.

Double-click on the object to bring back the controls of the program it was made in. To delete an object, click on it to select it, and then press DELETE.

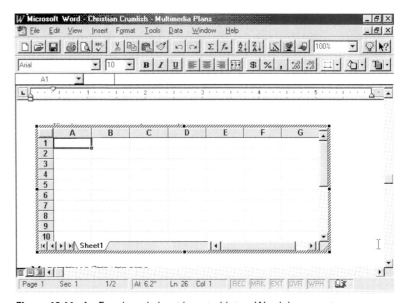

Figure 12.11 An Excel worksheet inserted into a Word document

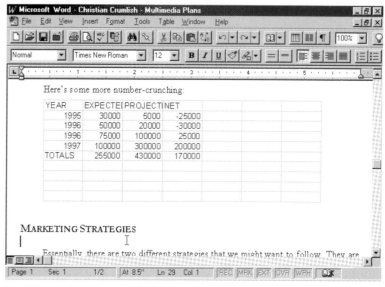

Figure 12.12 The Excel worksheet unselected

SERIOUS PROOFREADING AND POLISH

The last thing to do before presenting your work in a formal report is to proofread those pages carefully. Yes, this can involve printing the document out (double-spacing it first if it's not too long) and scanning it with your eyes. Word can help too, by checking your spelling, grammar, and suggesting alternatives to improve on repetitive or otherwise problematic word choices.

Using the Spelling Options

As you've probably discovered by now, Word performs automatic spell checking all the time, putting a squiggly red line under every suspect word.

upgrade note

Word's old tried-and-true spell checker, with a full-fledged dialog box and advanced spelling options, is still available. I'll cover it as well as the new automatic spell checker in Word for Windows 95 in this section.

Automatic Spell Checking

I've covered this elsewhere in the book, but I'll repeat it here for your convenience. If you don't want Word to query you about words it doesn't recognize, you can turn off automatic spell checking (or at least keep it hidden). To do so, choose Tools | Options and click on the Spelling tab (see Figure 12.13). To keep those red squiggles off the screen, check the Hide Spelling Errors in Current Document check box (or uncheck Automatic Spell Checking—the result is the same). Isn't it just like a computer program to call the words it doesn't recognize *errors*? Then click on OK.

If you *do* want to correct errors as you go, either retype any squiggly-underlined word or right-click on the suspect word and choose an option from the menu that pops up. If the word is correct, you can add it to the spell checker's dictionary so that it will check out OK in the future. To do this, choose Add. If the word is spelled incorrectly and the pop-up menu offers the correct spelling as one of the choices, choose the correct spelling.

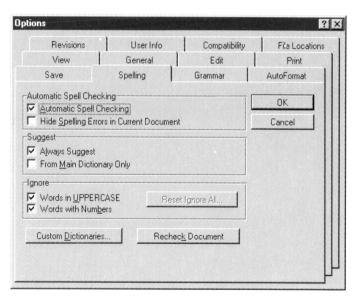

Figure 12.13 The spelling options in the Options dialog box

If Word queries an unusual word that is spelled correctly but that you don't want to add to the dictionary, you can simply choose Ignore All to prevent Word from querying it for the rest of the Word session. You can always choose Spelling at the bottom of the menu to bring up the traditional spell checking dialog box. If Word doesn't suggest the correct spelling, but you know what it is, just retype the word yourself. In fact, that's always an option. The red squiggle will disappear if you correct a word manually and Word recognizes the corrected version.

"Traditional" Spell Checking

The easiest way to bring up the traditional Spelling dialog box is to click on the Spelling button on the Standard toolbar. Word will start checking your document at the insertion point unless part of the document is selected, in which case it will check only the selection. Word scans your document or selection for the first unfamiliar word it can find, and the Spelling dialog box appears with the questionable word in the Not in Dictionary box at the top (see Figure 12.14).

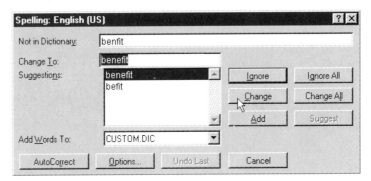

Figure 12.14 The Spelling dialog box

The Spelling dialog box is very flexible and offers you many possible options. From this box, you can

- Correct the word manually by retyping it in the Change To box and clicking on Change.
- Accept Word's first suggestion by clicking on Change (or, in the case of duplicate words, Delete).
- Choose a different suggestion and click on Change.
- Skip this word this time by clicking on Ignore.

- Skip all instances of this word from now on (in this session) by clicking on Ignore All.
- Add this word to the dictionary by clicking on Add.
- Change every instance of this word to the word in the Change To box by clicking on Change All.
- Go to the Spelling tab of the Options dialog box by clicking on the Options button.
- Undo (and take a second crack at) your last decision by clicking on Undo Last.
- Click on Cancel (or Close, which is what the button changes to after you've done something) to quit at any time.
- Click on AutoCorrect to add the unfamiliar word and the correct word as a pair to the AutoCorrect list so that the misspelling will be corrected automatically from now on. This option is the one remaining advantage of the Spelling dialog box over the automatic spell checking feature.

When Word has scoured your entire document or selection, it tells you it's done. Click on OK to end your spell checking session.

Using the Grammar Checker

If you're like most people, you're still a little suspicious of computers that claim to be able to read sentences and check grammar. It's true that computers don't really *understand* your sentences. Instead, they analyze them in a more-or-less mathematical way, by looking for certain key words and constructions. Grammar checking can be time-consuming, so in that sense it's not really for busy people, especially when you consider the amount of time you have to spend tailoring the types of rules you want to apply and ignoring bogus corrections. (When I used the expression "shrink to fit," the grammar checker suggested I substitute "counselor" or "therapist" for "shrink.")

On the other hand, if you occasionally mix up "its" and "it's"; "their," "there," and "they're"; "effect" and "affect"; and so on, you might appreciate having an impersonal proofreader look over your important documents.

Performing a grammar check automatically causes a spelling check to start as well, so you'll sometimes be presented with the Spelling dialog box. Respond to potential spelling errors as outlined in the previous section.

SHORTCUT

Press SHIFT-F7 to start the thesaurus.

Finding the Perfect Word in the Thesaurus

It's natural to sometimes get into a rut while writing and start using the same word over and over. Sometimes this is OK. If it's correct jargon, you might as well just keep using it. It can be distracting when you realize that a writer is varying the vocabulary to avoid repeating a word. Then again, sometimes a word just gets stuck in your forebrain and comes out in many different contexts, robbing your ideas of their nuances.

Word comes with a built-in thesaurus that makes it easy to choose any word and look for words with similar meanings. Place the insertion point in the word you want to improve and choose Tools | Thesaurus. This brings up the Thesaurus dialog box.

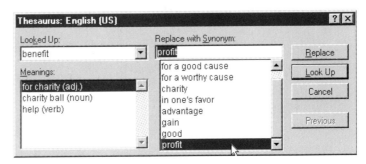

You can undo the replacement by pressing CTRL-Z.

The Meanings box shows different possible definitions of the word you're working on. Choose another meaning if the first one is not the one you were thinking of. This dialog box will sometimes offer you a Related Words option, which will let you choose another form of the word related to the original word (such as "illustrate" for "illustration").

A list of possibilities will appear in the Replace with Synonym box on the right. You can double-click on a word in the Replace with Synonym box (or select it and click on the Look Up button) to look up further synonyms for that word. Continue this process for as long as you like. To review the words you've looked up so far, click on the

Looked Up box (the one in the upper left). You can also retrace the history of your looked-up words one by one with the Previous button. When you have found the word you want, select it and click on Replace to replace the original word with the suggestion. The dialog box will close. You can click on Cancel at any time to quit the thesaurus without replacing a word.

By the way, you can also type a new word in the Replace with Synonym box and click on the Look Up button to have Word look up synonyms for the new word.

Making the Report Fit the Pages Neatly

The last thing to do before printing is to check the document page by page for bad breaks. Consider forcing a new page before a large table to make sure that it doesn't break over the next page. (Press CTRL-ENTER to insert a page break.)

If you did not change your toolbars the way I recommended in Chapter 2, you can choose File | Print Preview and then click on the Shrink to Fit button on the Print Preview toolbar.

If your document ends with an almost empty page, save the document and then click on the Shrink to Fit button on the Standard toolbar to squeeze the last page's text onto the previous page. You might want to recheck all the page breaks again after this. If the reformatting causes some unacceptable problems, press CTRL-Z to undo the change.

HEAVY-DUTY PROJECTS

Now that you've been let in on all the shortcuts and tricks for formatting splendid-looking documents, the rest of the book is devoted to complicated projects: extra-long documents, publications literally suitable for the public, and putting up a page on the World Wide Web.

CHAPTER 13

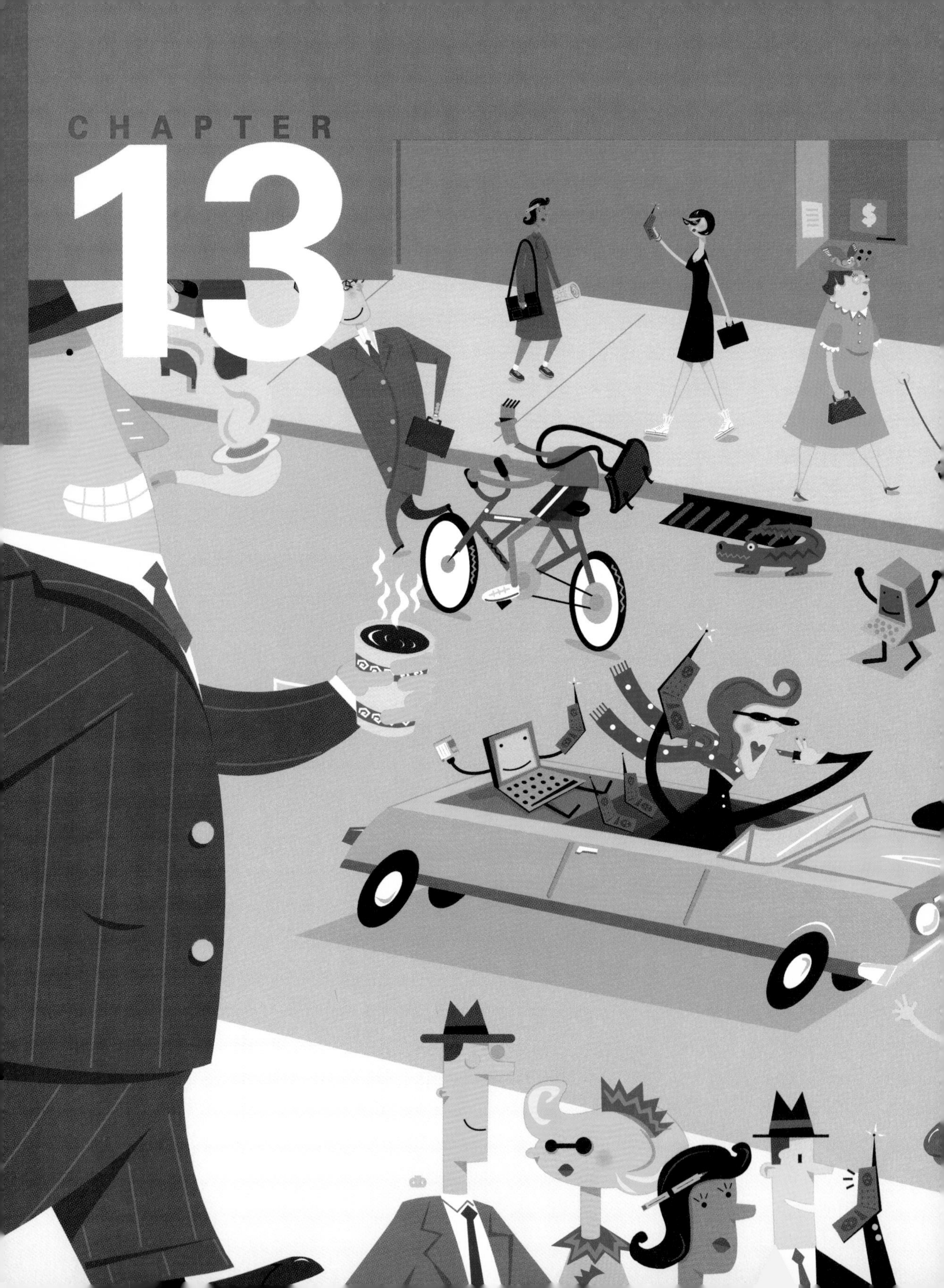

Maintaining Very Large Documents

FAST FORWARD

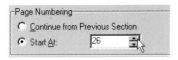

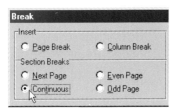

PLACE A BOOKMARK ➤ *pp 207-208*
1. Place the insertion point or make a selection.
2. Choose Edit | Bookmark.
3. Type a name for your bookmark.
4. Click on the Add button.

GO TO A BOOKMARK ➤ *p 208*
1. Press F5.
2. Choose Bookmark in the Go to What area of the Go To dialog box.
3. Choose a bookmark from the Enter Bookmark Name drop-down list box.
4. Click on the Go To button or press ENTER.

RESTART PAGE NUMBERING ➤ *p 210*
1. Choose Insert | Page Numbers.
2. Click on the Format button.
3. Click on Start At in the Page Numbering area and enter a new number (or increment the old number by clicking on the tiny arrow buttons).
4. Click on OK.

INSERT A SECTION BREAK ➤ *pp 210-211*
1. Position the insertion point where you want the new section to begin.
2. Choose Insert | Break.
3. In the Break dialog box that appears, you can do one of several things:
   - If you want the section after the break to start on a new page, choose Next Page. The break will force a new page to start.
   - If you want the new section to start right where the insertion point is, choose Continuous. There'll be no page break.
   - If you want the new section to start on the next even or odd page, choose Even Page or Odd Page.
4. Click on OK.

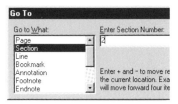

GO TO A SECTION ➤ *pp 211-212*

1. Press F5.
2. Click on Section in the Go to What box in the Go To dialog box that appears.
3. Either type a section number and press ENTER, or click on the Next or Previous button as many times as necessary to get to the section you want.
4. Click on Close.

SWITCH TO OUTLINE VIEW ➤ *p 214*

- Choose View | Outline.
- Click on the Outline View button to the left of the horizontal scroll bar.

EDIT AN OUTLINE ➤ *p 215*

With your document in outline view, you can use the Outlining toolbar to do the following things:

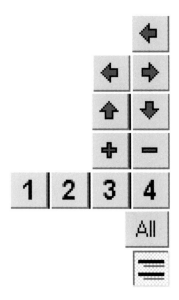

- To turn regular text into a heading, click on the Promote button.
- Use the Promote and Demote buttons to change the levels of individual heads or of entire selections.
- Click on Move Up or Move Down to change the placement (not the heading level) of a selection.
- Click on Expand or Collapse to show or hide all the headings subordinate to a selection.
- Use the Show Heading *n* buttons to show the headings that are at all levels up to and including the number of the button you click.
- Click on Show All to instantly expand the entire outline.
- Click on Show First Line Only to hide everything after the first line of each paragraph. This creates a sort of mini-outline of each text section.

CREATE A SUBDOCUMENT ➤ *p 221*

1. Choose View | Master Document or click on the Master Document View button on the Outlining toolbar.
2. Create an outline of your document (if you haven't done so already).
3. Select the heading that begins the part you want to designate as a subdocument.
4. Click on the Create Subdocument button.

EDIT A SUBDOCUMENT ➤ *pp 221-222*

A subdocument will appear surrounded by a dotted rectangle with a subdocument icon in the top-left corner. To edit the subdocument in its own window, separate from the master document, double-click on the subdocument icon.

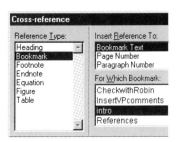

INSERT A CROSS-REFERENCE ➤ *pp 223-224*

1. Place the insertion point where you want the reference to go.
2. Type the regular portion of the reference, such as "See Chapter."
3. Choose Insert | Cross-reference.
4. Choose the type of document element you want to refer to in the Reference Type box of the Cross-reference dialog box.
5. In the Insert Reference To box, choose the aspect of the element you want to refer to (the text, the number of the page it's on, the heading or paragraph number, the text of the caption, or whatever).
6. In the For Which box, choose the specific heading, bookmark, or other element you want the cross-reference to refer to.
7. Click on the Insert button.

INSERT A TABLE OF CONTENTS ➤ *p 225*

1. Place the insertion point at the beginning of the document.
2. Choose Insert | Index and Tables.
3. Click on the Table of Contents tab.
4. Choose a format from the Formats box.
5. Make sure the number in the Show Levels box reflects the number of heading levels you want to have appear in the table of contents. If it does not, choose a different number.
6. If you want a different type of leader (the dots or other characters between the heading text and the page number), choose one in the Tab Leader drop-down list box.
7. Click on OK.

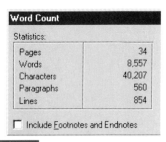

COUNT THE WORDS IN A DOCUMENT ➤ *p 227*

1. Choose Tools | Word Count.
2. Note the total number of words.
3. Click on Close.

If you never have to spin out a document that is longer than ten pages or so, you can skip this chapter until you need information on one of the topics it covers. Eventually, though, most of us will have to put together a very long report, a dissertation, or some other magnum opus.

Big documents come with their own special problems. They take a long time to load up into your word processing program. You sometimes have to wait for other people to complete their work on one section before you can make changes to your section. A large document can even be harder to move around in, because it's no longer simply a matter of jumping to the top or bottom of the document and then hitting PAGEUP or PAGEDOWN a couple of times. Large documents sometimes require specialized page numbers, chapter numbers, section numbers, and so on. A really long document can be difficult for readers to manage without a table of contents. In this chapter, I'll show you the easiest way to deal with all of these issues.

GETTING AROUND IN A LARGE DOCUMENT

In Chapter 3, I showed you how to use the Find and Go To buttons (or Edit | Find and F5, respectively) to navigate documents. These two methods become even more useful as the document gets longer. Go To, especially, can help you zero in on defined parts of documents very rapidly. Besides being able to take you directly to a new page or section (see "Subdividing a Document into Sections," later in this chapter), Go To can also take you to locations you define with bookmarks.

Placing a Bookmark

It's easy to drop a bookmark into any part of your document. A bookmark can correspond to a specific place (the location of the insertion point when you created the bookmark) or to a selection. After placing the insertion point or selecting the text you want to mark, choose Edit | Bookmark. The Bookmark dialog box appears.

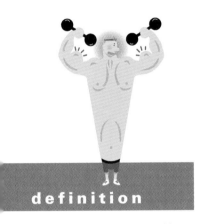

definition

Bookmark: A code inserted into a document that marks an exact location so that the user can return to it at any point, much like a real bookmark placed in a book to mark a specific page.

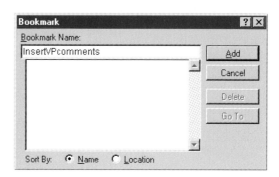

The box is empty at first, because no bookmarks have been defined. Type a name for your bookmark. Choose something that will help you remember what it refers to. (The length doesn't really matter, because you'll usually be picking the name from a list box; however, bookmark names cannot have any spaces in them.) Then click on the Add button.

To see the bookmarks that have been inserted in your document, choose Tools | Options, click on the View tab, check Bookmarks, and click on OK. To hide them again, repeat the steps.

Going to a Bookmark

To go to a bookmark, either click on the Go To button on the Standard toolbar (if you arranged your toolbars the way I suggested in Chapter 2) or press F5. In the Go To dialog box that appears, choose Bookmark in the Go to What box. Then choose a bookmark from the Enter Bookmark Name drop-down list box. Then click on the Go To button or press ENTER.

SHORTCUT

You can also double-click anywhere on the left side of the status bar to bring up the Go To dialog box.

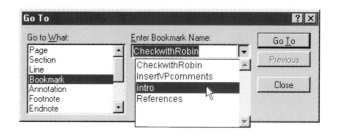

ORGANIZING LONG DOCUMENTS

One of the most difficult aspects of working with long documents is keeping the various subsections organized, numbered, and formatted properly. There are several different, equally valid approaches to doing this, each of which are more appropriate for some projects and less so for others.

The least complicated method is to keep each separate section of a document in its own file and manually change the page numbering for each portion as necessary. If you don't expect to make too many changes (think carefully, now), and if you'd rather do a little handwork than master some word processing geekery, this is the best way to go.

If you want to keep your whole document in one file but you want to apply different formatting or page characteristics (such as margins, headers and footers, orientation, and so on) to different portions of the document, you should create sections.

For more complicated documents, you should learn to work in outline view. This enables you to look at overall structure down to the level of detail you need. It also makes rearranging portions of a document easy. For the longest and most complicated documents, you should invest a little more time and learn how to work with a master document and subdocuments. This actually gives you most of the convenience of keeping the documents separate while providing the automated numbering and other advantages available within a single document.

Combining Separate Documents into a Printed Whole

As I just mentioned, the tricky part about keeping portions of your document in separate files is making sure that the page numbering does not start over again at 1 in each portion. The solution to this is buried down there in dialog boxes, but it's really not too hard to do. Assuming that you've already inserted page numbers in each separate file, note the final page number of the first portion of the document. If you want

habits & strategies

Don't worry about page numbering until you're almost done with a document—it's not worth it to keep renumbering the sections every time a change adds or takes away a page. Think of page numbering as one of the final steps before printing.

the next section to start on an odd page, and the first document ends on an odd one, then you'll have to insert a blank page (by pressing CTRL-ENTER) at the end of the first document.

Now open the second document. Choose Insert | Page Numbers. The Page Numbers dialog box will appear. Click on the Format button to get to a new dialog box, Page Number Format.

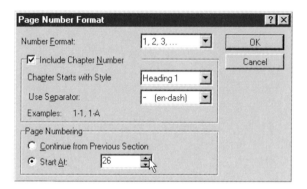

Here, click on Start At in the Page Numbering area and enter the new page number (or increment the old number by clicking on the tiny arrow buttons). Then click on OK. Repeat for subsequent documents in the sequence.

Subdividing a Document into Sections

Some formatting that applies to documents at the page level (such as formatting for margins; vertical alignment; headers and footers; columns; and paper size, type, and orientation) can just as easily be applied separately to sections within a document. Normally, the page formatting choices you make (or the defaults that are in effect) govern the entire document. But you can apply different page formatting to different parts of a document by dividing the document into *sections*. For example, a report with a title page, introductory text, and then text arranged in columns would require three sections. To create separate sections, you insert section breaks.

Inserting a Section Break

Position the insertion point where you want the new section to begin. Then choose Insert | Break. The Break dialog box will appear.

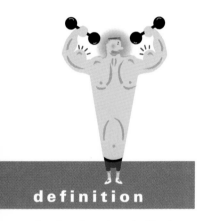

definition

Section: *A portion of a Word document with its own page formatting (stored in the section break at its end). Each section can be set up differently from other sections in the document. Not to be confused with* selection.

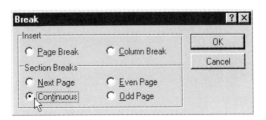

This box offers you several choices:

- If you want the section after the break to start on a new page, choose Next Page. The break will force a new page to start. If you want the new section to start right where the insertion point is, choose Continuous. There'll be no page break.
- If you want the new section to start on the next even or odd page, choose Even Page or Odd Page.

Then click on OK. A section break will appear in your document.

....End of Section..

Now you can format the two sections (the one before and the one after the break) separately. If you ever forget which section the insertion point is currently in, look in the status bar: the second item from the left shows the current section.

Removing a Section Break

To remove a section break, simply select it and press DELETE. Or, if the insertion point is located just below it, press Backspace. Remember, all the formatting that applies at the section level (mostly page formatting) is stored in that break. Deleting a break, therefore, is a little like deleting a paragraph mark. The section before and the section after the break become a single section, which takes on the formatting of the latter.

Going to a Section

To go directly to a section, click on the Go To button, press F5, or double-click in the left side of the status bar. In the Go To dialog box that appears, click on Section in the Go to What box and then either type a section number and press ENTER or press the Next or Previous

CAUTION

When you delete a section break, the section before the break will take on the page formatting of the section that follows.

habits & strategies

You can copy and paste a section break to apply the formatting of an existing section to a new one. The section preceding the newly created break will get the formatting of the original section.

button as many times as necessary to get to the section you want. When you're there, click on Close.

Formatting a Section

Most of the formatting that is applied to complete sections is page formatting. You'll notice that once you have established sections in your document, all your page formatting choices will include the option of applying the formatting to the current section only or to the entire document.

To format a section, choose File | Page Setup. This brings up the Page Setup dialog box, which is shown in Figure 13.1. Choose a tab. After making your choices, take a look at the Apply To drop-down list at the bottom of the box. Each tab of the dialog box has a list like this, but the items in it vary depending on the state of the document (and on whether you made a selection before opening the dialog box). Click on the box if you want to choose a different option. When you are done with the first tab, choose the other tabs and make your choices on them too. When you're done with this dialog box, click on OK.

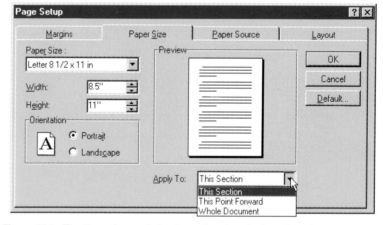

Figure 13.1 The Page Setup dialog box, showing the box that gives you control over whether your changes will affect the current section or the entire document

Using Headers and Footers in Sections

Once you've got separate sections in your document, you can specify all sorts of variations in features (such as footnote and endnote numbering, page numbering, and so on) to have them remain consistent from one section to the next or take on new values with a new section. Usually, the defaults Word chooses for you will work fine and you can ignore these options, but at times you might want to override the defaults. One case in point is headers and footers: you might sometimes want a header or footer to reflect the current section.

To create a header or footer that differs from the one in the previous section, place the insertion point in the section you want to change and choose View | Header and Footer. Word will switch into page layout view, highlight the header, and place the Header and Footer toolbar on the screen. By default, the Same as Previous button will be "pushed in." This button makes the header (or footer) take on the same text and numbering choices as the previous header (or footer). This is usually what you'll want. If you want a header to change with a new section (to reflect a new chapter name, for example), click on the button to deactivate it.

habits & strategies

If you want page numbering to be continuous despite changing headers or footers, click in the second section, choose Insert | Page Numbers, click on Format, click on Continue from Previous Section, and then click on OK. Repeat for each section.

The two buttons to the left of the Same as Previous button (Show Previous and Show Next) jump you to the previous or next section to inspect the headers (or footers) there.

Organizing Your Document By Outlining It

Mention the idea of making an outline and just about everybody groans. It seems like extra work, doesn't it? Sure, it might help you get your thoughts sorted out and allow you to anticipate problems you might encounter further down the road, but there's still something onerous about having to make an outline. Word, however, has done a pretty good job of integrating outlines seamlessly into the document creation process.

In fact, although you might picture an outline as a document separate from your actual manuscript, Word's approach to outlines is to simply offer you an *outline view* of your original manuscript. The outline view is a way of focusing in on the headings and subheadings of a document, allowing you to hide and ignore the contents.

Chapter 12 shows how to edit styles.

Word's outlining feature works only if you use the preset heading styles (Heading 1, Heading 2, and so on). You can edit these styles to make them look different, if that's what you're after.

Outlining an Existing Document

Even if you haven't been using the preset heading styles, you can outline an existing document just by jumping into outline view and then assigning levels to its headings. To do so, choose View | Outline or click on the Outline View button at the left end of the horizontal scroll bar.

Your document will be presented as a series of indented headings, each of which is preceded by a plus sign if it contains subheadings or a minus sign if it does not (see Figure 13.2).

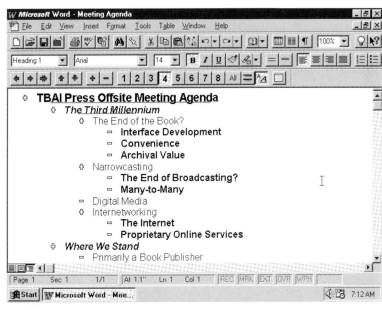

Figure 13.2 A document in outline view, with the first four heading levels shown

Regular text paragraphs will appear preceded by hollow squares. If you have not yet created any headings, your entire document will appear this way.

If your document does not use the preset heading styles, you can now select paragraphs (specifically, the short lines of text you want to use as headings) and assign them to heading levels. You can do this either by using any of the traditional methods of choosing styles (such as choosing one from the drop-down Style list box in the Formatting toolbar) or with the help of the Outlining toolbar, as explained in the following section. Be sure to use the preset styles called Heading 1, Heading 2, and so on.

Working in Outline View and Using the Outlining Toolbar

In outline view, you can control the level of detail you'll see in your document. The main instrument you use to do this is the Outlining toolbar. Table 13.1 describes the action of each toolbar button.

Button	Description	Action
⇦	Promote	Promotes the level of an individual heading or an entire selection by one; turns regular text into a heading
⇨	Demote	Demotes the level of an individual heading or an entire selection by one
⇨⇨	Demote to Body Text	Demotes the level of an individual heading or an entire selection to body text
⬆	Move Up	Changes the placement (not the heading level) of a selection
⬇	Move Down	Changes the placement (not the heading level) of a selection
✚	Expand	Shows all the headings subordinate to a selection
➖	Collapse	Hides all the headings subordinate to a selection
1	Show Heading *n*	Shows the headings that are at levels up to and including the number of the button you click
All	Show All	Instantly expands the entire outline, including body text
☰	Show First Line Only	Hides everything after the first line of each paragraph, creating a sort of mini-outline of each text section
^A𝐴	Show Formatting	Hides or shows the formatting of the entire document

Table 13.1 The Outlining Toolbar

Creating an Outline from Scratch

To start typing an outline before you've created a document (good for you!), first switch into outline view as explained earlier. Then type the first heading. Word will automatically assign the Heading 1 style to this heading. When you press ENTER, Word will give the new line the same heading style as the previous line.

□ **TBAI Press Offsite Meeting Agenda**
□ **The Third Millennium**

You can then click on the Demote button (before or after typing the new heading, as long as the insertion point is still on that line) to make it subordinate to the previous one. When you press ENTER again, the next line will get the same style as the second line.

✥ **TBAI Press Offsite Meeting Agenda**
　　□ *The Third Millennium*
　　□
　　—

Continue typing headings and promoting or demoting them as you go. You can enter regular text at any time by clicking on the Demote to Body Text button.

Expanding or Collapsing an Outline

As you work on an outlined document, you'll want to see different levels of detail at different times. The primary benefit of outlining is this ability to choose between a view that shows only the first level headings, one that shows the entire structure, and ones that show anything in between. At its most collapsed level, the outline view shows just first-level headings. At its most expanded, it shows the entire document, though you can reduce each text paragraph to a single line.

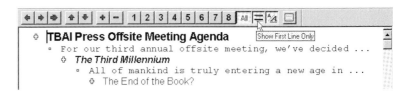

To see an outline collapsed down to just a few headings, click on the Show Heading button that corresponds to the number of the lowest level of heading you want to see (see Figure 13.3). The dotted gray lines that you might see under some headings represent collapsed headings and/or body text.

You can also select an individual heading and then expand or collapse the selection by clicking on the Expand or Collapse button on

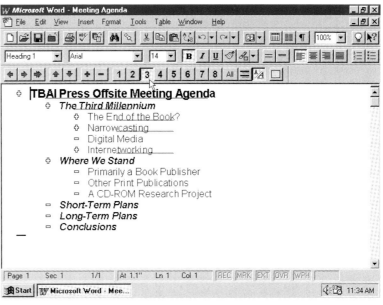

Figure 13.3 An outline collapsed to three heading levels

habits & strategies

Whenever you need to enter large blocks of text, consider switching back to normal view to do so, since it will seem more familiar and, well, normal. Then switch again to outline view to continue working on the organization of the document.

the Outlining toolbar. Alternatively, you can double-click on any plus sign to expand (or collapse) the entire outline "family" subordinate to it.

Although you can select text in the normal way in outline view, clicking on the hollow plus sign to the left of a heading will select the heading and its entire "family" of subordinate headings.

Rearranging an Outline

Another convenience of outlining is the ease with which you can rearrange the items in the outline, changing their order and altering the structure until you arrive at the best possible organization.

SHORTCUT

You don't have to select a heading first if you plan to drag it by its plus (or minus) sign.

Moving Headings To move a heading or heading family from one place to another in an outline (in other words, to reorder the headings), first make your selection. Then either click on the Move Up or the Move Down button in the Outlining toolbar or click on the plus or minus sign icon for the selection and drag it up or down. When you click on Move Up or Move Down, the selected head will move up or down one position in your outline. When you use the drag-and-drop method, the pointer will change to a four-headed arrow. A dotted horizontal line with an arrowhead on it will move up and down as you move the mouse, showing the potential destinations for the selection as you drag.

When you release the mouse button, the headings will move.

SHORTCUT

You can also demote a heading by pressing TAB or promote a heading by pressing SHIFT-TAB when the insertion point is in the line.

Promoting and Demoting Headings To promote or demote a heading or heading family, first make your selection. Then either click on the Promote or Demote button in the Outlining toolbar or click on the plus or minus sign icon for the selection and drag it left or right. If you use the drag-and-drop method, a dotted vertical line with a box hanging off it to the left will move left or right as you move the mouse, showing the levels you're dragging to. When you release the mouse button, the headings will move.

If you move, promote, or demote a heading with a collapsed "family" below it, all the headings subordinate to it will also be moved, promoted, or demoted to the same extent. When the family is expanded, however, only the parent heading will move.

Numbering the Headings

To number your headings automatically, choose Format | Heading Numbering. (You don't have to be in outline view to do this.) The Heading Numbering dialog box will appear (see Figure 13.4). Choose a numbering style from the examples (or click on the Modify button to customize one of the styles), and then click on OK.

habits & strategies

You have to apply heading numbering first before you can include chapter numbers with page numbers.

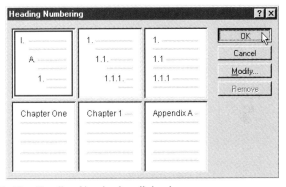

Figure 13.4 The Heading Numbering dialog box

Incorporating Chapter Numbers with Page Numbers

If a heading level in your document represents the beginning of a chapter or other major organizational division, you may want to include the chapter number as part of the page number. (For example, page 2-5 is page 5 of Chapter 2.) To do this, choose Insert | Page Numbers. In the Page Numbers dialog box that appears, click on the Format button, to bring up the Page Number Format dialog box.

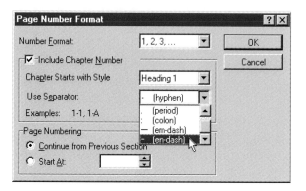

Check Include Chapter Number. Then choose the style that represents the beginning of each new chapter. (The default is Heading 1, and that's usually what you'll want to use.) Finally, choose the type of separator (hyphen, period, colon, etc.) that you'd like to have appear between the chapter and page numbers.

Using Master Documents

If you are working with a very large document, perhaps one that has been created by several different authors in collaboration, and you're willing and able to invest a little extra time into structuring it, you can set up what's called a *master document*.

Once you have done this, each of the *subdocuments* in the master document can be worked on separately and then reintegrated into the master document at any point. Any numbered elements, including page numbers, headings, captions, and tables, will increment correctly from subdocument to subdocument, saving you the hassle of micromanaging the sort of details that computers keep better track of anyway.

You can turn an existing document into a master document, designating portions of the original document as subdocuments. You can also create a new master document from existing subdocuments. To create or work on a master document, choose View | Master Document or click on the Master Document View button on the Outlining toolbar (see Table 13.1).

Master document view is a close variation of outline view. The document appears with outlining marks and the Outlining toolbar appears, along with the Master Document toolbar, shown here.

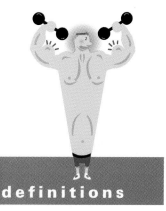

Master document: *A document that contains several subdocuments, each of which can be treated as a separate document.*

Subdocument: *One of the component documents of a master document.*

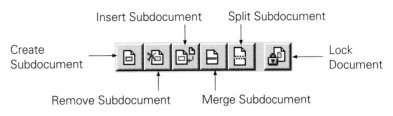

The outline will automatically be set to show all levels, regardless of the level you were viewing previously, but you can just click on a Show Heading button again to return to the overview you want.

upgrade note

The master document feature has changed in functionality since earlier versions of Word. It is now almost an offshoot of the outlining feature, but it is much easier to use. Now, for the most part, you either click on toolbar buttons or double-click on icons to manipulate subdocuments.

Creating Subdocuments from an Existing Outline

After entering master document view, create an outline of your document (if one does not already exist) or work on the existing outline. To designate a portion of the outline as a subdocument, select the heading (or headings) involved and click on the Create Subdocument button. The part you turned into a subdocument will appear surrounded by a dotted rectangle with a subdocument icon in the top-left corner (see Figure 13.5).

Repeat the process to create as many subdocuments as you want in the master document. When you're done, choose File | Save As, type a name for the master document, and click on the Save button. Word will save the master document under the name you typed, and it will save each of the subdocuments under a name based on the first words in the heading.

Editing a Subdocument

You can open a subdocument directly, as you would a normal document, and work on it that way, or you can open a subdocument from

In normal view, subdocuments are separated by section breaks.

CAUTION

If you want to change the name of a subdocument, open it from within the master document, or the master won't recognize the new document. Also, keep all the components of a master document together in the same folder.

Elements such as a title page or even introductory text can be part of the master document, since the master document is itself a normal document, separate from the inserted subdocuments. However, elements such as headers and footers, tables of contents, and indexes must all be part of the master document (not a subdocument) to apply consistently to the whole.

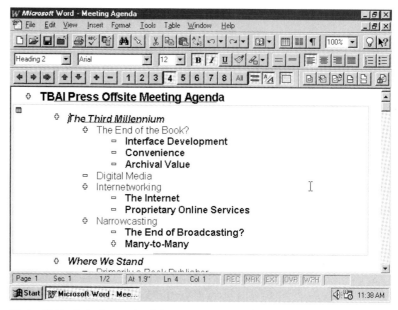

Figure 13.5 A designated subdocument, surrounded by a dotted box and marked with a subdocument icon in its upper-left corner

within a master document. To do the latter, just double-click on the subdocument icon in the top-left corner of the subdocument area. Word will open the subdocument in normal view. (The master document will still be open.)

Inserting Existing Documents into a Master Document

You can also build a master document from existing documents. To do so, start a new document and enter master document view. On the Master Document toolbar, click on the Insert Subdocument button. An Insert Subdocument dialog box (a clone of the Open dialog box) will appear. Choose the document you want to insert and click on the Open button. Repeat this process as often as you need to.

Read this next paragraph over again. Once you've inserted a subdocument, it's linked into the master document. When you make changes to it in one place, it changes in the other as well. If you want to delete some of the text of the subdocument from the master document without actually cutting from the original subdocument, you have to first put the insertion point in the subdocument portion of the master document and click the Remove Subdocument button. The Remove Subdocument button does not actually remove any text from your document; it just disassociates the text of the subdocument within the master document from the external subdocument file. In making this change it also removes the subdocument rectangle and subdocument icon from the master document, leaving the text that was within the rectangle. After this, you can change the text without affecting the original subdocument.

TRICKS FOR LONG DOCUMENTS

Some Word features are really only useful for long documents. In this section I'll show you how to create cross-references and tables of contents, and how to count the words in a document.

For very long documents, cross-references are essential tools that help you organize the information. How many of the projects you work on do you think can be adequately explained in a simple, linear fashion? If you had to explain complex information to someone in conversation, you'd probably jump forward and back, make asides, and occasionally say "Don't worry, I'll get to that." In a long document, you similarly want to be able to point a reader further ahead or back to pertinent information or to acknowledge a link between separate parts of the overall work. Cross-references serve that very purpose.

A table of contents is a more straightforward tool, but it is nonetheless valuable for a long document. It allows readers to go directly to the section of the work that they need. It also helps, much as an outline does, to convey a sense of the overall structure of a document.

Finally, you'll sometimes need to adhere to a maximum word count, or stay close to a specific range, or simply know the number of words in the document so you can note it on the title page. Naturally, Word can count the words in your document automatically.

Cross-References

Word can maintain automated cross-references to many different types of document elements. The cross-references are automated in the sense that if they specify the page number of the referenced text, for example, and the page number changes, the reference will change as well. A cross-reference can also contain the exact wording of a heading or caption and will reflect changes to the text automatically.

To insert a cross-reference, place the insertion point where you want the reference to go. Then type the regular portion of the reference, such as "For more about Antilles mule-frogs, see" or "See page". Then choose Insert | Cross-reference. The Cross-reference dialog box appears.

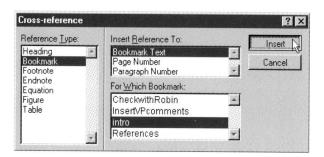

Choose the type of document element you want to refer to in the Reference Type box on the left. In the Insert Reference To box, choose the aspect of the element you want to refer to (the number of the page it's on, the heading or paragraph number, the text of the caption, or whatever). In the For Which box, choose the specific heading, bookmark, or other element you want the cross-reference to refer to. Finally, click on the Insert button, and the cross-reference will appear in your document. Finish the sentence or edit the spaces around the inserted reference to make everything fit smoothly.

Tables of Contents

If you have an existing outline (based on the preset heading levels) or even a consistent set of headings of your own, making a table of contents (also known as a TOC) from the headings is no problem.

upgrade note

Tables of contents have gotten easier to create with later versions of Word. You can still insert table markings and assemble your table of contents from them, but the default method is now to base table of contents levels on heading styles, which is easier and integrates more naturally with outlining.

habits & strategies

Check the Preview area in the middle of the dialog box to see how each table of contents format looks.

Creating a Table of Contents

Place the insertion point at the very beginning of the document. Then choose Insert | Index and Tables. Click on the Table of Contents tab in the Index and Tables dialog box that appears (see Figure 13.6). Choose a Format from the Formats box at left. Enter a number in the Show Levels box below the Preview area if you want a different number of heading levels to appear in the table of contents. Choose a different type of leader (the dots or other characters between the heading text and the page number) in the Tab Leader drop-down list box, if you prefer.

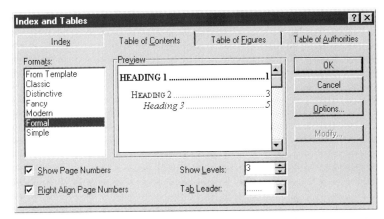

Figure 13.6 Choosing a format and the number of heading levels for a table of contents

Using Different Styles for the Table of Contents

To base your table of contents on a different hierarchy of headings, click on the Options button in the Index and Tables dialog box. This brings up the Table of Contents Options dialog box (see Figure 13.7). Check all the styles you want to have correspond to a level in the table of contents, and then enter a number in the TOC Level box across from it. Scroll through the list to see all the available styles. When you're done, click on OK.

Inserting the TOC

When you're done in the Index and Tables dialog box, click on OK. Word will insert your table of contents at the beginning of the document, with a hard page break separating it from the rest of the document (see Figure 13.8).

225

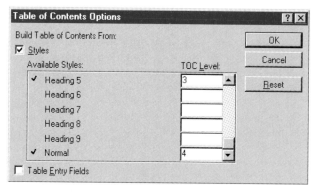

Figure 13.7   The Table of Contents Options box

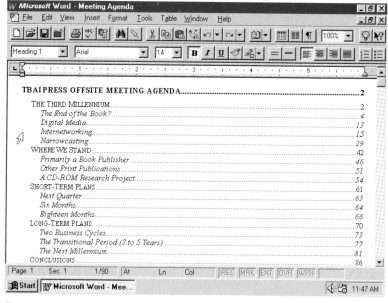

Figure 13.8   A table of contents based on the first three heading levels

Updating a TOC

If you end up revising a document after making a TOC (and believe me, you will), you can update the TOC by clicking anywhere in it and pressing F9. (Pressing F9 updates fields, and the TOC is made up of fields—not that you really need to know that.)

Counting the Words

Word considers any character or characters before a space, period, comma, or other punctuation to be a word. To count the words in your document, choose Tools | Word Count. This brings up the Word Count dialog box.

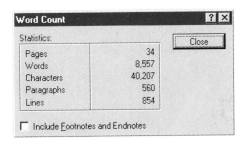

It will take a moment (or two, depending on your computer) for Word to complete the count, and then grayed out numbers will be replaced with solid numbers reflecting the current totals.

Copy down any numbers you may need to refer to. (There's no way to copy and paste them directly!) Then click on Close.

YOU'RE GETTING GOOD AT THIS

If you're putting together documents with the techniques described in this chapter, you've really mastered Word, perhaps more than you realize. The only frontiers left to you are the kinds of documents that require such a high degree of organization, design, and creativity that they are called publications. Chapter 14 will show you the ropes of traditional desktop publishing projects, such as newsletters, and Chapter 15 enables you to publish on the World Wide Web.

MAIL

Cranking Out a Newsletter

SpudCo

Volume 23, Issue 12   The Latest

Potato Harvest B

by Julienne Freis

Just when our business most needed a kick in the pants, the

say pototto, I say tomato and you say tomotto, potato, pototto, tomato,

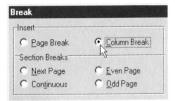

FAST FORWARD

DESIGN A DOCUMENT
FROM THE TOP DOWN ➤ *pp 234-236*

- Begin planning the document by first considering the broadest issues (such as page layout) and then progressing to the narrowest (such as fonts and character spacing).
- Use section breaks to keep various parts of the newsletter separate.
- Establish styles for the various design elements.
- Make a template from the first issue and use it to create later issues.

MAKE A BANNER ➤ *p 237*

1. Choose a font and a large size.
2. Type the text of the banner.
3. Put a dateline below the banner to display the issue number, a slogan or some other information about the newsletter, and the date of publication. (To do this, start a new line, choose fonts and sizes for the text, and add borders to the top and bottom of the line.)
4. Choose Insert | Break.
5. Click on Continuous in the Break dialog box.
6. Click on OK.

DIVIDE THE PAGE INTO COLUMNS ➤ *pp 238-239*

1. Place the insertion point at the beginning of the portion of the document in which you want columns (or select text to be made into columns).
2. Click on the Columns button on the Standard toolbar.
3. Drag the mouse across the box that drops down until the number of columns that you want are selected.

INSERT A COLUMN BREAK ➤ *p 239*

First, position the insertion point where you want the new column to start. Then

- Choose Insert | Break, click on Column Break, and click on OK, *or*
- Position the insertion point and press CTRL-SHIFT-ENTER.

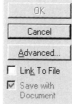

PUT BORDERS ON A SELECTION ➤ *pp 239-240*

1. Right-click on any toolbar and choose Borders from the menu that pops up.
2. Select the portion of your newsletter around which you want to add a border or lines.
3. Choose a line weight from the Line Style drop-down list.
4. Click on one of the buttons in the middle of the Borders toolbar to place a border or individual lines around the selection or to remove borders from the selection.

INSERT A FRAME ➤ *pp 240-241*

1. Choose Insert | Frame.
2. Click on Yes when Word asks you if you want to switch to page layout view.
3. Click on the page at the point where you want the top-left corner of the frame to appear.
4. Drag the opposite corner of the dotted rectangle that appears to create a frame of the appropriate size.

INSERT A PICTURE ➤ *p 242*

1. Choose Insert | Picture.
2. Find the folder that contains your pictures.
3. Choose a picture to insert.
- To make the picture a link, check the Link to File box.
- If you check Link to File, uncheck Save with Document to reduce the size of the Word document by not saving the picture file inside the Word document.
4. Click on OK.

FORMAT A FRAME ➤ *p 243*

1. Select the frame.
2. Choose Format | Frame.
3. Make the choices you want in the Frame dialog box that appears.
- If you don't want text to wrap around the frame, choose None in the Text Wrapping area.
- To set an exact size for the frame, fiddle with the numbers in the Size area.

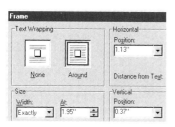

> "It's like the
> potatoes are
> just walking out
> of the ground
> this year"

And like it or not, we must remember that you say potato and I say pototto, I say tomato and you say tomotto, potato, pototto, tomato, tomotto, let's call the whole thing off.

- To establish the frame in a position relative to the upper-left corner of the page or to a specific paragraph, play around with the settings in the Horizontal and Vertical areas.
- Enter numbers in the Distance from Text boxes in the Horizontal and Vertical areas to define a "gutter" of space around the frame.
- To remove a frame, click on the Remove Frame button.

4. When you're done, click on OK.

CREATE A PULL QUOTE ➤ *p 244*

1. Insert a frame.
2. Copy the text you want to pull out, and paste it into the frame.
3. Format the text.
4. Use the Borders toolbar to put lines above and below or around the frame.
5. Play around with the shape and size of the pull quote frame to make it fit nicely and to make sure the text flows well around it.

MAKE A DROP CAP ➤ *pp 244-245*

1. Place the insertion point where you want the drop cap to be inserted.
2. Choose Format | Drop Cap.
3. In the Drop Cap box that appears, make the style choices you want.

- Choose the type of drop cap.
- Choose a font if you want one that is different from the rest of the text.
- In the Lines to Drop box, choose the number of lines to wrap around the drop cap (3 is the default).

4. Click on OK.
5. Click elsewhere to see the result.

SHORTCUT

Check your version of Word for any newsletter templates listed on the Publications tab of the New dialog box. You might be able to use one of them and forgo the design work entirely.

definition

Desktop publishing: *Producing a formal document for public consumption with the use of desktop computer equipment. Desktop publishing is the equivalent of what used to be called typesetting.*

Sounds like fun, at first, doesn't it? A newsletter! You get to play journalist for a day. It's always nice to produce something solid (until you look closely and find the typos). Well, OK, it can be fun at times. But putting together a newsletter can also become a time-wasting boondoggle.

Face it, Word is not a page layout program. Sure, it has all kinds of fiendishly clever bells and whistles, all of which help to jazz up a document, but since it's not a page layout program, nothing can float freely on the page. Everything's attached to everything else. Take one element out of the sequence and it's like pulling a loose thread on a sweater. Also, most of the design elements, such as columns, lines, and so on, are attached to paragraphs or sections. When you move the breaks, some of the formatting moves with them, often with disastrous results.

Probably the most important advice I can give you is to try not to get too fancy with your publication. As the marketing people say, "Keep it simple, stupid." If your layout gets profoundly confused, click on the Show/Hide ¶ button on the Standard toolbar. That should help you keep track of which paragraphs contain which formatting elements.

If I haven't scared you off yet, give me one more try. If you're serious about putting out a newsletter (especially if you want to publish it on a regular basis), consider buying Aldus PageMaker. It's fairly easy to learn and use, and it's infinitely more flexible than Word. If you're really ambitious, think about getting a professional desktop publishing program, such as QuarkXPress.

If you're determined to go ahead with this (that is, if you have no choice), try to bear in mind that desktop publishing is not the same as typing. It's important that you use more elegant characters (such as curly quotation marks instead of inch marks and long dashes instead of double dashes). You have to be more concerned with line spacing to make sure that columns of text fit smoothly and align properly on the page. In general, there's a finer level of attention to detail that you must apply to the finished product.

definition

Landscape: *A page orientation in which the height of the page is shorter than the width. (The opposite is called* portrait *orientation.)*

TOP-DOWN DESIGN

One way to keep the design of your publication under control is to start with the broadest elements, such as the overall shape and makeup of the page, and work your way down to specific paragraph styles and then font choices and other details.

The first thing you should do with your new document is establish a page setup. To do so, choose File | Page Setup to bring up the Page Setup dialog box. Click on the Margins tab to set up fairly small margins at the top, bottom, left, and right sides of your page. The smaller the margins, the more room there will be for your text.

Next, click on the Paper Size tab and either choose a paper size from the Paper Size drop-down list box or type custom measurements in the Width and Height boxes (see Figure 14.1). If you want to change the orientation of your pages, click on Landscape (or Portrait) in the Orientation area.

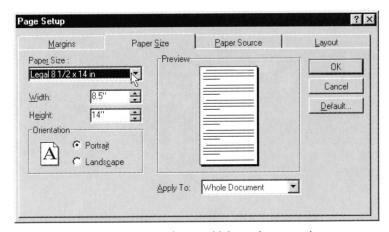

Figure 14.1 Choosing the paper size on which to print a newsletter

Finally, click on the Layout tab. This is where you decide about the placement of headers and footers. The typical newsletter includes no header or footer on the first page, and often has headers that mirror each other on the following odd and even pages. To set up your newsletter this way, check both the Different Odd and Even box and the Different First Page box in the Headers and Footers area. When you're done with all the tabs in this dialog box, click on OK.

Assembling Individual Pages with Sections

Chapter 13 explains all about sections and working with section breaks.

After you've set up your basic page, you should start thinking about page layout. Most of the time, you'll need to use section breaks to allow you to easily assemble disparate elements (such as columns of text that are placed before or after text that runs all the way across the page) and to create a special page (such as a landscape page with a schedule on it) that has a design that varies from that of the rest of the pages.

Using Styles to Keep a Consistent Design

Chapter 12 explains the ins and outs of styles.

One of the best ways to establish an effective, recognizable design is to set up various paragraph styles for each of the design elements in the document. Some of design elements you should think about include

- Headlines (various kinds)
- Bylines
- Body text
- The first paragraph of each article
- Captions
- Pull quotes

Sometimes you'll want to override a style for a specific instance of an element. If you do, be sure to change just the specific selection and not the style itself, or your whole document will spring loose.

Laying Out an Entire Publication

See "Breaking Up the Gray," later in this chapter, for tips on how to insert and work with frames.

Desktop publishing instruction manuals often devote a lot of time to showing you how to assemble a single, beautiful page, but in reality publications are composed of 4, 8, 16, or more pages. Once you have most of your publication's text typed in and formatted, you'll want to step back and look at the layout of the whole thing.

If you want to get an overview of your entire document so that you can work with the layout, switch to page layout view and then click on the Zoom Control button in the Standard toolbar and choose a small

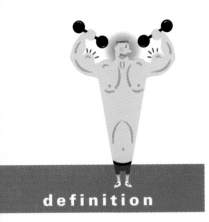

definition

Frame: A moveable box inserted into a Word document. A frame can contain text, art, or just about anything that can go onto a Word page. By default, text will flow around a frame.

percentage. You'll be able to see the entire page, or a significant portion of it in a miniature image.

One thing you'll have to deal with at this level is continuations. When it comes time to continue an article from one page to another, you'll wish you had a real desktop publishing program. There's no better approach, really, than cutting part of the article from one page and pasting it onto another, positioned either in a frame or between two section breaks.

Another layout task you'll sometimes have to perform is over-riding the default line spacing for certain articles in order to make them fit the available space. To do this, select the entire stretch you want to change and choose Format | Paragraph. Enter a specific amount of spacing in the Line Spacing box and click on OK. You may have to tweak your entry a little to get everything to fit.

Cloning Your First Issue

Once you've completed the first issue of your newsletter, you'll want to make a template from it so you don't have to reinvent the wheel when it's time to start work on Issue 2. Choose File | Save As, and choose Document Template in the Save as Type box. Choose the Publications folder to keep everything well organized. Type a name for the template, and then click on the Save button.

Then clear out all the nonessential text in the template copy. Leave your banner art. If you have a box on the first page that says "Inside", keep the box and the title but erase the specific contents from that issue. Keep your headers and other reusable elements, but delete the rest of the text. Then save the template again. This template will contain all the styles you designed for the first issue, keeping them available for reuse. You are, in effect, using the original document that contains the first issue as a guide to laying out subsequent issues.

ESSENTIAL NEWSLETTER TRICKS

OK, enough general guidelines and pieties. The rest of this chapter will explain the exact procedures necessary for assembling a handsome newsletter.

If you have a company logo or other logo you want to include in the banner, choose Insert | Picture, choose the logo, and click on OK.

Making a Banner on the First Page

Start the first page of your newsletter with a banner. (Those unfamiliar with journalism often refer to a banner as a *masthead*, but technically a masthead is a staff listing, usually placed somewhere inside the publication.) Choose a font and a large size and type the text of the banner. You'll probably have to experiment with different sizes and fonts until you get the banner to look just right.

To play around with the spacing between characters, try the Character Spacing tab in the Font dialog box. The Kerning for Fonts box can be especially useful for making sure the internal spacing of capitalized words in large fonts looks good. For example, kerning can help prevent the word *bravo* from looking like BRA VO. You can do this just as easily with a regular paragraph as well. See "Lines and Borders," later in this chapter, for a review of how to add lines and borders to paragraphs, frames, and other things.

You'll probably want a dateline below the banner to display the issue number, a slogan or some other information about the newsletter, and the date of publication. One easy way to produce such a thing is to insert a single-row table (with one or a few columns, depending on the information you want on your dateline) and add border lines to the top and bottom of the table. Another way to create a dateline is to space out the elements by putting a centered tab in the middle and a right-aligned tab at the right end of the dateline to align the contents (see Figure 14.2).

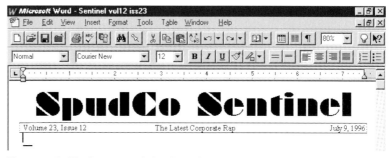

Figure 14.2 The banner and dateline of a newsletter

Don't choose one of the other options—if you do, the following text will start at the top of a new page.

After the dateline, you should insert a section break so you can establish the columns for your articles (without forcing the banner into columns as well). Choose Insert | Break. This brings up the Break dialog box. Click on continuous in the Section Breaks area. Then click on OK.

If you want a sidebar or artwork or anything else to break up the flow of columns, you'll need to insert frames. See "Breaking Up the Gray," later in this chapter.

Dividing the Page into Columns

Columns (also called *snaking columns*, because of the way text slithers down the page and then jumps up to the top at the beginning of each new column) are the mainstay of newsletter design. In the simplest use of columns, a single article will snake across a single page. In more complicated layouts, you'll need to establish section breaks before and after any stretch of columns.

Inserting Columns

If you've just inserted your first section break, the insertion point will be in the right place for you to start inserting columns. (If you've since moved the cursor, move it back to the point immediately after the break.) The easiest way to insert columns is to click on the Columns button on the Standard toolbar and drag the mouse across the box that drops down until the number of columns that you want are selected.

If you want to exert more detailed control over the spacing between columns, or if you want to have a line separate each column, choose Format | Columns. This brings up the Columns dialog box (see Figure 14.3). In this box, you can choose from the preset column configurations in the top of the box or enter the specific details you want in the lower areas. The following list details some of the things you can do from here. When you're done, click on OK.

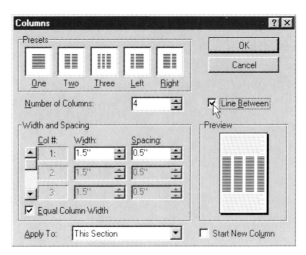

Figure 14.3 The Columns dialog box

- If you want one, two, or three columns of the same width or a pair of columns different widths, choose one of the Presets options.
- To specify a number of columns, enter a number or click on the arrows to get to the number you want in the number of Columns box.
- To control the width of the columns and/or the spacing you want after them (the numbers are interrelated, so changing one affects the others), enter new numbers in the Width and Spacing area.
- If you want your columns to be unequal in width, uncheck the Equal Column Width check box and enter different width amounts for each individual column. If your section has more than three columns, a scroll bar will appear that lets you get to the measurements for the other columns.
- Make sure the Apply To box specifies This Section.
- If you want a vertical line to appear between each column, check Line Between, over on the right.

Inserting a Column Break

Any time you want to force a new column to start, you need to insert a column break. Why would you want to do this? Mainly for layout purposes, such as to even out several columns. The Columns dialog box has a check box labeled Start New Column. (If you check it, also choose This Point Forward in the Apply To drop-down list box, or you'll apply your columns to the entire document.) Checking it is one way to insert a column break. You can also choose Insert | Break and click on Column Break in the Break dialog box. Then click on OK.

Lines and Borders

Except for the lines between columns, you place lines and borders by making selections and choosing options in the Borders toolbar. (You can also choose Format | Borders and Shading and choose options from a full-fledged dialog box, but I think you'll find the Borders toolbar to be sufficient for most needs.) To bring up the toolbar, right-click on any toolbar and choose Borders from the menu that pops up.

By the way, some document elements, such as frames, let you set border options in their individual formatting dialog boxes, but the

SHORTCUT

To start a new column, you can also position the insertion point and then press CTRL-SHIFT-ENTER.

When selecting, make sure you get ahold of the right thing. Many document elements can have borders, and some of them can exist inside each other. For example, a paragraph inside a table cell can have a border around it, and so can the cell itself.

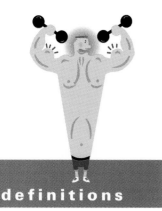

definitions

Pull quote: *A quotation from an article repeated in larger type or in a box or other special setting.*

Sidebar: *A small article related to a main article, often boxed and appearing to the side of the main article.*

easiest approach is to use the same method with all your elements (the Borders toolbar).

Select the portion of your newsletter around which you want to add a border or lines. Choose a line weight from the Line Style drop-down list.

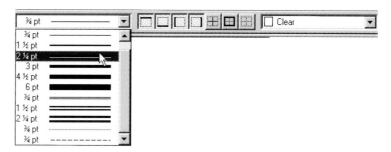

Then click on one of the seven buttons in the middle of the Borders toolbar to place a border or individual lines around the selection or to remove borders from the selection. Experiment with different combinations of line weights, perhaps trying double-lines or dashed lines.

Breaking Up the Gray

Once you've got your rows upon rows of columns, the next priority in laying out a page is to break up the unending sheet of gray. Break it up with what? With a picture, a chart, a pull quote, or whatever you want. All of these elements can be inserted in a frame. Using a frame is also just about the only way to lay out two separate articles (or an article and a sidebar) on the same page.

Inserting a Frame

When you insert a frame, it includes a thin (1-point) border, but that border can be changed or removed as easily as any border. To insert a frame, choose Insert | Frame.

Word will pop up a message box warning you that it has to switch to page layout view to allow you to place the frame. Click on Yes. You'll be switched to page layout view. Click on the page at the point where you want the top-left corner of the frame to appear, and drag the opposite corner of the dotted rectangle that appears to create a frame of the appropriate size (see Figure 14.4).

You'll still be able to resize or reposition the frame later. Figure 14.5 shows part of the front page of a newsletter displaying a main article in the regular text area and another article in a frame in the rightmost column.

*If you've already written or
assembled the contents you plan
to put in a frame, you can select
the contents and then choose
Insert | Frame. A frame will be
inserted around the text.*

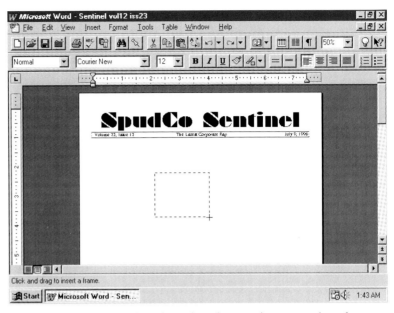

Figure 14.4 Clicking and dragging a dotted rectangle representing a frame to be inserted

Figure 14.5 The article in the right-most column is inside a frame

Inserting objects in general is covered in Chapter 12.

habits & strategies

To save disk space by not storing a copy of a linked picture inside the Word document, uncheck Save with Document.

Inserting a Picture

You can insert a picture or any other object that was created in another program into your newsletter without first creating a frame. (Some people do prefer to create a frame first and then insert the picture into it, though, either because they find it easier to move and resize the picture this way or because they want the extra control over things like text flow and distance from text that the use of frames allows.)

To insert a picture, choose Insert | Picture. The Insert Picture dialog box appears (see Figure 14.6). Find the folder that contains your pictures, and then choose a picture to insert. It will appear in the Preview half of the dialog box. To make the picture link to the Word document (instead of embedding it wholesale into the document), click on Link to File. A linked picture will be updated if the source picture is changed. When you're done, click on OK.

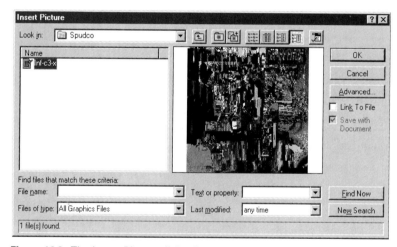

Figure 14.6 The Insert Picture dialog box

Pictures will slow you down a little when you're scrolling around in your document. Every time Word needs to display a new picture, it has to import the image from the original file (if you've linked to an external picture). To hide the pictures and make your document easier to navigate, at least until you need to edit the pictures directly, choose Tools | Options and click on the View tab. Check Picture Placeholders in the Show area. Then click on OK. Your document will show empty boxes in place of the pictures.

Formatting a Frame

To select a frame, click on it. To move it, click on it and drag it. Go slowly, so your computer can keep up with you. To resize a frame, select it, click on one of the tiny black handles at the sides or corners, and drag it to a new position. (To keep the frame's proportions (height to width) consistent when resizing, click and drag a corner instead of a side.)

To format a frame by the numbers, select it and then choose Format | Frame. (You can also right-click on a frame and choose Format Frame from the shortcut menu that pops up to format it.) This brings up the Frame dialog box (see Figure 14.7). This box gives you several choices:

SHORTCUT

You can also delete a frame by clicking on it to select it and then pressing DELETE.

- If you don't want text to wrap around the frame, choose None in the Text Wrapping area.
- To set an exact size for the frame, fiddle with the numbers in the Size area.
- To establish the frame in a position relative to the upper-left corner of the page or to a paragraph, play around with the settings in the Horizontal and Vertical areas.
- Enter numbers in the Distance from Text boxes in the Horizontal and Vertical areas to define a "gutter" of space around the frame.
- To remove a frame, click on the Remove Frame button.

When you're done, click on OK.

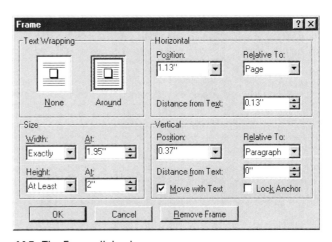

Figure 14.7 The Frame dialog box

**habits &
strategies**

*A column can become too
narrow when it has to flow
around a pull quote or other
framed object, and hyphenation
problems can become severe.
If you have lines with serious
gaps, consider hyphenating
the section.*

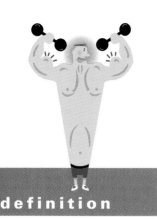

definition

Drop cap: *A large first letter at
the beginning of a paragraph.*

Creating a Pull Quote

To create a pull quote, first insert a frame. Then copy the text you want
to pull out, and paste it into the frame. Apply any formatting you want
to the text (including font, size, character formatting, alignment, and
spacing). Then turn on the Borders toolbar and clear the lines from the
frame. If you want, apply your own lines above and below or around
the frame. Finally, play around with the shape and size of the pull quote
to make it fit nicely and to make sure the text flows well around it (see
Figure 14.8).

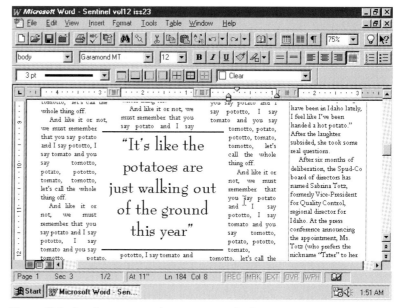

Figure 14.8 A pull quote sprucing up a page nicely

Making a Drop Cap

You can use a drop cap as a design element. Drop caps are handy
for certain types of stories, such as essays or columns, or to indicate
the beginning of a new section of an article. To insert a drop cap, place
the insertion point at the beginning of the paragraph and choose
Format | Drop Cap. This brings up the Drop Cap dialog box, where you
can make your style choices.

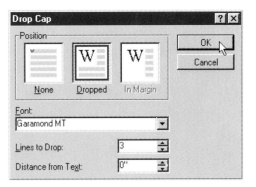

- Choose the type of drop cap you want.
- Choose a font if you want one that is different from the rest of the text.
- In the Lines to Drop box, choose the number of lines to wrap around the drop cap (3 is the default).

When you're done, click on OK. The first letter of the paragraph will be formatted as a drop cap, which will appear in text as a selected frame. Click elsewhere to see the result.

A nd like it or not, we must remember that you say potato and I say pototto, I say tomato and you say tomotto, potato, pototto, tomato, tomotto, let's call the whole thing off.

upgrade note

Although it was possible in the past to create a drop cap manually (by inserting a frame, resizing the character, and cleaning up the spacing), it's automatic as of version 6.0 of Word.

GOOD LUCK

A newsletter is a big job. Get other people to help you! The last chapter in this book will show you how to create the newest kind of publication, a site (or "page") on the World Wide Web.

Designing World Wide Web Documents

- Downloading Internet Assistant

- Converting existing documents to Web documents

- Browsing the Web from within Word

- Creating Web documents from scratch

- Getting help for Internet Assistant

Internet Assistant **now!**

FAST FORWARD

DOWNLOAD INTERNET ASSISTANT ➤ *pp 251-252*

1. Create a temporary folder on your hard disk (if you don't already have one).
2. Point your Web browser at Microsoft's download page for Internet Assistant, http://www.microsoft.com/msoffice/ freestuf/MSWord/download/ia/ia95/chcklist.htm. (If that page doesn't work, go to the main Microsoft page, http://www.microsoft.com/, and then follow the links for Software, Microsoft Office, and Internet Assistant.)
3. Click on download Internet Assistant now.
4. Save the wordia2 (or wordia2b) file in a temporary folder on your hard disk.
5. Double-click on wordia2 (or wordia2b) to begin the installation of Internet Assistant.

CONVERT AN EXISTING DOCUMENT TO A WEB DOCUMENT ➤ *pp 252-254*

1. Open the source document.
2. Choose File | Templates.
3. Type **html**, check Automatically Update Document Styles, and click on OK.
4. Assign headings (with the usual preset styles).
5. Insert hyperlinks (by clicking on the Hyperlink button, selecting a local or Web document to link to, and pressing ENTER).
6. Click on the Title button, type a title for the Web page, and press ENTER.
7. Save the file as an HTML document.

Your First Web Docum

With Internet Assistant, you can use Microsoft Wor
(HTML) documents. HTML is the standard for doc
Web. You can create documents for the Web eithe
creating a new file based on the HTML template in

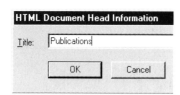

BROWSE THE WEB FROM
WITHIN WORD ➤ *pp 256-260*

Choose File | Browse Web. Then,

- Follow hyperlinks.
- Enter Web addresses directly by clicking on the URL button (type the address in the dialog box that appears and press ENTER).
- Retrace your path by pressing the Go Back, Go Forward, and History buttons.
- Add Web documents to your Favorite Places list by clicking on Add Favorite.
- Visit your favorite Web sites by clicking on Open Favorite.

CREATE A WEB DOCUMENT
FROM SCRATCH ➤ *pp 260-262*

1. Choose File | New.
2. Choose the HTML template and click on OK.
3. Use Save As to save the new document right away.
4. Assign headings (using styles).
5. Insert hyperlinks (by clicking on the Hyperlink button, selecting a local or Web document to link to, and pressing ENTER).
6. Click on the Title button, type a title for the Web page in the HTML Document Head Information dialog box that appears, and press ENTER.

Page: *The Web term for a document. Also* Web page, *sometimes* home page.

Link: *The Web term for a clickable, highlighted word or image that connects the reader to another document, to another part of the same document, or to another kind of file entirely, such as a graphic or sound file.*

Web browser: *A program used to connect to Web sites, display Web pages, and jump from link to link.*

Web site: *A set of interrelated Web pages, usually all stored on the same network computer or Web server. The contents of a Web site usually comprise a coherent whole, functioning as a publication or information center.*

The fastest-growing part of the Internet today is the World Wide Web, an international network of interconnected documents and Internet sites containing archived information. The next thing you know, your company is going to be establishing a presence on the Web (if it hasn't already), and then your department will need to start putting information out there for the benefit of customers, colleagues, or clients.

Up to now, creating Web documents has been a matter of learning how to insert HTML (hypertext markup language) codes, called *tags*, into plain text documents. Documents with existing formatting would have had to be completely reformatted with HTML tags. Now Microsoft offers a free Word add-in called Internet Assistant (IA) that automatically translates between Word formatting and HTML markup.

You edit and format your document using familar commands and shortcuts, and when you save the document, Internet Assistant converts the formatting to HTML. When you open an .htm document in Word for editing, Internet Assistant automatically converts its HTML formatting to Word formatting, until you save again.

Internet Assistant not only makes it as easy to create Web documents as it is to create normal Word documents, but also turns Word into a decent Web browser, allowing you to test the pages and links you create.

PLANNING A WEB SITE

Before you start plunging in and converting existing documents to Web pages or creating a set of interlinked Web documents from scratch, take some time to think through the organization of your proposed Web site. You'll want to create a home page to serve as the "front door" and central hub of all related documents. You'll also want to organize your documents into a logical system of folders so that you or others can easily fix errors and make changes to the site. Setting up the documents for the first time is only half the job. The other half is maintaining the complex set of Web pages as the information within them evolves.

CAUTION

You won't be able to browse the Web from Word unless you have a direct Internet connection, either via a network or by way of dial-up PPP or SLIP access. You can still create Web pages for a local network, though, even without direct Internet access.

One final thing: To make a Web site visible and available to the Internet at large (as opposed to simply within the confines of a local network), you'll need access to a Web server, a computer running software that serves Web pages when requested by Web browsers. Your employer or Internet service provider may offer access to a server. You'll have to ask technical support.

DOWNLOADING AND INSTALLING INTERNET ASSISTANT

You need to have access to the Internet in the first place to be able to download Internet Assistant. First, create a temporary folder on your hard disk (if you don't already have one). Either point your Web browser at http://www.microsoft.com/msoffice/freestuf/MSWord/download/ia/ia95/chcklist.htm or work your way there by first connecting to the Microsoft Web site (http://www.microsoft.com/) and then choosing Software, Microsoft Office, then Internet Assistant. Read as much or as little of the information as you want along the way. (If you're trying to wend your way to the download page for Internet Assistant, keep your eyes peeled for shortcuts from any of the pages that you reach; you may save yourself two or three hops.)

upgrade note

There was an Internet Assistant 1.0 for Word 6 for Windows, but it does not work with Word for Windows 95. You must download the Windows 95 version of Internet Assistant.

On the download page (chcklist.htm), click on the download Internet Assistant now link. Your Web browser should ask you if you want to save the file. Save the file to a temporary folder. (Be sure to indicate that you want to save the file as "source" and not as an HTML file. Some Web browsers will assume that you want to save documents as HTML files unless they are told otherwise.)

To install Internet Assistant, double-click on the icon shown here. Confirm that you do, in fact, want to install IA (Internet Assistant).

After getting itself together, the Setup program will get started with some preliminary chat. Click on Continue. Setup will then poke around for a while. Then it will show you the license agreement. Read it, click on Continue, read more, click on Continue again, and then read the rest and click on Accept. After all those preliminaries, click on the big Complete button to really start the installation.

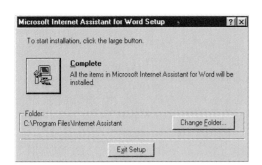

After expanding and copying various files, the Setup program will tell you that the installation was completed successfully. Click on OK.

Internet Assistant is an *add-in* for Word. It places a key part of itself in Word's Startup folder so that it is loaded automatically whenever you start Word. Now that you've installed this add-in, you'll find that new menu and toolbar items will appear. I will explain these as they come up.

CONVERTING DOCUMENTS TO WEB DOCUMENTS

Often when a company or academic department decides that it is time to make information available via the World Wide Web, it proceeds to do so by converting reams of existing documents into Web documents (also called HTML documents). Up to now, this has always been tricky, but with IA it is fairly straightforward.

Once they have been converted and made available on the Web, your documents will no longer look exactly as they do in Word. Each Web browser out there (and there are hundreds) displays the various HTML elements differently. The important thing is to make sure that the relationships between the parts of the document and the levels of the headings make sense so that any reader with any browser will get a sensibly organized document.

Some Things that Don't Convert

Not all of Word's features have Web equivalents, so some formatting and other embellishments will disappear when you convert. Word features that will disappear include

- Annotations
- Borders and shading
- Captions
- Embedded objects, such as equations, graphics, clip art, Word Art, and MS Draw objects
- Fields (although the result will appear in the converted document)
- Footnotes and endnotes
- Frames
- Headers and footers
- Indented paragraphs in any paragraph style other than numbered or bulleted lists
- Index entries
- Page breaks and section breaks
- Revision marks
- Superscripts and some other character formatting
- Tabs in most paragraph styles
- Table of contents entries

Attaching the HTML Template

Start by opening your original document the usual way. Then choose File | Templates. (Notice the new Open URL and Browse Web commands on the File menu, both of which I will explain later in this chapter.) In the Templates and Add-ins dialog box that pops up (see Figure 15.1), type html in the Document Template box. Make sure Automatically Update Document Styles is checked. (Notice the WIAHTM32 add-in listed in the lower box—that's the part of the Internet Assistant that's changing your menus and toolbars.)

Saving the HTML Document

Next, save the document under a new name so that you don't accidentally eradicate your original Word document. Choose File | Save As. Make sure that HTML Document is chosen in the Save File as Type

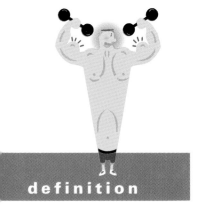

definition

URL: *Web address. It stands for universal resource locator.*

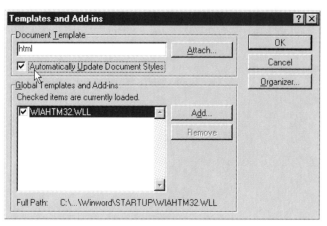

Figure 15.1 Attaching the HTML template

Don't click on the Save button, press CTRL-S, or choose File | Save!

See Chapters 5, 12, and 13 for more on styles.

box in the Save As dialog box. Type a name for the document, and then click on the Save button. Word gives the HTML file the extension .htm, so you don't necessarily have to use a different name for it (different from the original Word document filename, that is). Still, a one-word name for your HTML document will work best, because the various systems on the Internet handle spaces in filenames differently.

Formatting the Document for the Web

Now you can apply Web formatting, which usually amounts to nothing more than headings, horizontal lines, and hyperlinks (though you can look through the style list to see what's available). Conversion of things such as numbered lists and bold and italic will be handled automatically.

Web documents generally start with an H1 heading, so select the title of your document and assign the Heading 1,H1 style. Make subordinate headings H2, and so on. The easiest way to apply styles to selections is to choose the styles from the Style drop-down list box in the Formatting toolbar.

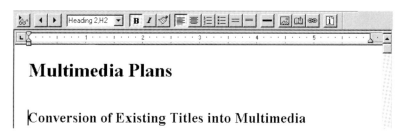

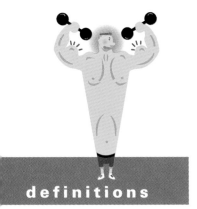

Hyperlink: Also known as a link, or hypertext link, a highlighted portion of a document that, when clicked on or otherwise activated, connects the reader to another document, another portion of the document, or another site on the Internet.

Anchor: A mark that can indicate either end of a hyperlink—either the "hot" word or the destination to which it is linked.

Adding Hyperlinks

Web documents can stand alone, but a prominent feature of the World Wide Web is the fact that so many of the documents on it are interlinked, with hypertext links embedded within them pointing to other documents. Adding hyperlinks to documents is a breeze with IA.

First, select the word (or graphic) you want to use as the launching point to the linked destination. Then choose Insert | HyperLink or click on the Hyperlink button.

This brings up the HyperLink <A> dialog box, shown in Figure 15.2. (<A> is the HTML tag for links; it stands for *anchor*.) From this box you will choose to link to a document on your computer, an address on the Web, or a bookmark within a document.

If you want to link to a local document, choose it from the to Local Document tab of the HyperLink dialog box. (The box lists both .doc and .htm files. If you link to a regular Word file, only people using Word as a Web browser will be able to read it.) To link to an address on the Web, click on the to URL tab. Then type the URL in the box or choose one

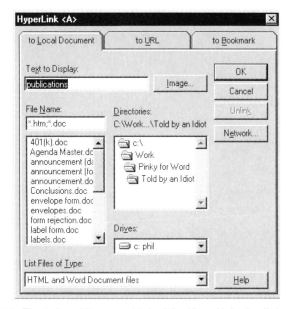

Figure 15.2 The to Local Document tab of the HyperLink <A> dialog box

habits & strategies

If you plan to link to a bookmark within a document, make sure that the bookmark exists (or create it), before you try to link to it. (There's a Bookmark button on the HTML toolbar.) Bookmarks are explained in Chapter 13.

Web browsers typically display the title of a document in the title bar of the main window of the browser.

from a list of URLs you've used in the past. (Internet Assistant will remember all the URLs you type and allow you to reuse them.) To link to a specific section of a document, choose the to Bookmark tab in the dialog box and choose a document and bookmark name.

When you have chosen the link, click on OK. The text that activates the link will appear underlined and in blue type (as is typical of links when they are displayed in Web browsers).

Not all of the publications in Told by an Idiot's backlist are suitable for multimedia adaptation. Some can be converted simply in the sense of making the text and illustrations available in an online format and perhaps with hyperlinked tables of contents, indices, and

Giving Your Web Document a Title

Each Web document needs a title that is distinct from the filename and from the H1 text, although it can be identical to either in content. To assign a title, choose File | HTML Document Info, or just click on the Title button on the toolbar. In the HTML Document Head Information dialog box that appears, type a title for the document (spaces are allowed here) and click on OK. Then save the document again. (It's OK this time to use the regular Save command as opposed to Save As.)

WORD AS A WEB BROWSER

Most programs that help users create a Web document require users to open the document within a separate program—a Web browser—in order to test it. Internet Assistant lets you turn Word into a reasonably functional Web browser so that you can test documents immediately without launching a separate program. You do, however, need direct Internet access to use Word to browse the Web. With Internet Assistant, you can also browse the Internet at large from within Word.

Switching to Web Browse View

To browse the Web from within Word, choose View | Web Browse or click on the Switch to Web Browse View button. Internet Assistant puts the Switch to Web Browse View button on *every* Formatting toolbar, no matter what template is attached to the current document. This changes even the customized toolbars you created in Chapter 2.

The toolbars change once again. Now they feature Web navigation shortcuts, as shown here.

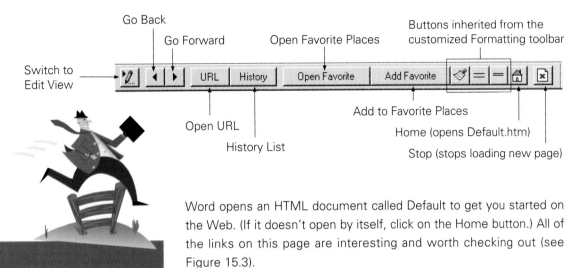

Word opens an HTML document called Default to get you started on the Web. (If it doesn't open by itself, click on the Home button.) All of the links on this page are interesting and worth checking out (see Figure 15.3).

Figure 15.3 Default.htm, the Internet Assistant home page

Following Links

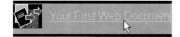

Click on Your First Web Document. The link is highlighted. Then Word opens another local document, which is called creating.htm. At any point you can retrace your steps by clicking on the Go Back button.

You can jump directly to a Web address without clicking on a premade link. The following step by step shows you how.

ENTERING WEB ADDRESSES DIRECTLY step by step

1. Click on the Open URL button on the toolbar. This brings up the Open URL dialog box.

2. Type the URL (carefully, letter-for-letter) into the box.

3. Click on OK. IA keeps you abreast of its progress on the Internet by displaying the typical Windows progress indicator. When the new document appears, you can continue browsing by clicking on links.

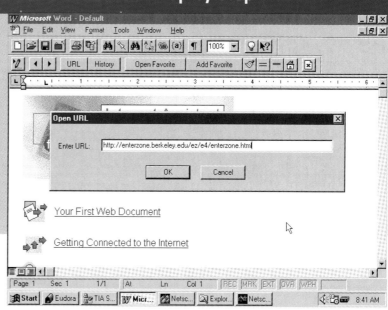

SHORTCUT

Until the list gets too long, you can jump to earlier pages by choosing them from the bottom of the Window menu.

Figure 15.4 shows a Web page you could reach by typing http://enterzone.berkeley.edu/ez/e4/enterzone.html into the Open URL dialog box.

Revisiting the Path You've Followed

Aside from being able to return along the path you followed with the Go Back command or retrace your steps with Go Forward, you can also see an entire history list of the documents you've visited. To do so, click on the History button or choose Window | History List.

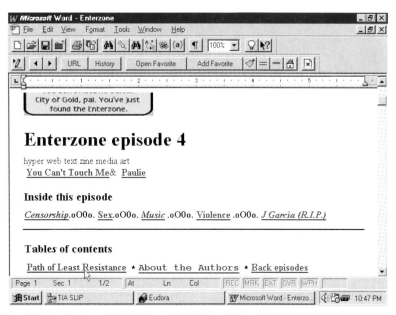

Figure 15.4 A Web page sporting several hyperlinks

The History List dialog box appears (see Figure 15.5). To jump to a document in the history list, choose it and click on the Go To button. To copy its address so that you can paste it into a Web document, click on the Copy HyperLink button.

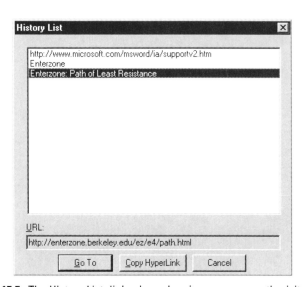

Figure 15.5 The History List dialog box, showing pages recently visited

Adding a Page to Your Favorites

To save the location of a Web page for later perusal, add it to your list of favorites. Click on the Add Favorite button on the toolbar. IA adds the current page to your Favorite Places document and opens the Favorite Places page (it's called favorite.htm). To see your Favorite Places at any time, click on the Open Favorite button. There you'll see that Microsoft has already seeded your Favorite Places list with a link to "cool places" (see Figure 15.6). The Web is too big and chaotic to explore without being able to save useful links in a central location such as this.

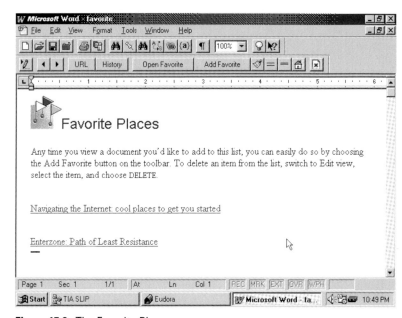

Figure 15.6 The Favorite Places page

Done Browsing?

Close all your windows when you're done browsing. (Don't save documents from the Internet unless you specifically want to keep your own local copies.)

CREATING A WEB DOCUMENT FROM SCRATCH

In addition to converting existing documents to HTML format, you may also be called upon to create new Web documents from scratch.

CAUTION

Don't start your new document by clicking on the New button on the Standard toolbar—if you do, you'll just be creating a normal Word document.

To learn what all the HTML- related styles in the template do, look for the HTML Tags and Equivalent Word Commands topic in Internet Assistant for Word Help (on the Help menu).

Wow your boss and colleagues with your mastery of this esoteric science without letting them know that all you did was format a document almost exactly as you normally would in Word.

To create a Web document, start by choosing File | New (or pressing CTRL-N). In the General tab of the New dialog box that appears, choose the HTML template and then click on OK. (The WEBVIEW template you also see in the dialog box is the one Word uses to turn itself into a Web browser.)

Before you start typing your document, save it first. (This is necessary because if you create any local links, Word will need to understand the relative locations of various documents.) Choose File | Save As, make sure HTML Document is chosen in the Save as Type list box, type a one-word filename, and click on the Save button.

Making Headings

Start with a first-level heading for your document. Type it and then assign the H1 style to it. Outline the rest of your document with lower-level headings, if you wish. Format as you go, adding enhancements such as bold and italics in the normal way, and use the toolbar buttons, styles, and menu options to insert special Web elements such as horizontal rules. You have to use just the styles provided, though. Any new styles you create will vanish when the document is saved.

Creating Hyperlinks

To create a hyperlink, select the text you want to use to activate the link, and then click on the Hyperlink button on the Formatting toolbar (or choose Insert | HyperLink). In the to URL tab of the HyperLink <A> dialog box that appears, choose a previously used link (and edit it if you want) or type a new link from scratch (see Figure 15.7). Choose one of the other tabs to link to a local document or a bookmark within a document.

Assigning a Title

Assign a title to your document by clicking on the Title button on the Formatting toolbar or by choosing File | HTML Document Info. In

Figure 15.7 The to URL tab of the HyperLink <A> dialog box

the HTML Document Head Information dialog box that appears, replace the dummy text with an informative title. When you're done, save the document again. Try switching to Browse view to test out the new document's links.

See my book, The Internet for Busy People *(Osborne/McGraw-Hill, 1996) for more about the Web and the Internet in general.*

GETTING HELP

The scope of this book doesn't allow me to do much more than give you the quick overview of Web documents you have just read. The Internet and the World Wide Web constitute entire universes of information, and we've only scratched the surface. If at any point you run into terminology you don't understand, or strange behavior from any of the special IA templates or other features, check out the help information that comes with Internet Assistant. To do so, choose Help | Internet Assistant for Word Help. This brings up the Help Topics dialog box, which offers useful definitions, explanations, and hands-on advice. Choose a topic for a step-by-step explanation.

habits & strategies

You can also move the WIAHTM32.WLL file from the Winword\Startup folder and place it in the Templates folder, either within the Winword folder or within the MSOffice folder, to prevent it from adding itself into every Normal document.)

REMOVING THE INTERNET ASSISTANT ADD-IN

If you don't want the Switch to Browse View button to appear on your toolbar (or the few other special IA commands to appear on the menus) while you are working with a non-Web document, choose File | Templates, uncheck the WIAHTM32.WLL add-in in the lower box, and then click on OK.

To remove the Internet Assistant completely, from the Windows Start button choose Settings | Control Panel, double-click on the Add/Remove Programs icon, choose Microsoft Internet Assistant, and click on the Remove button. IA will be uninstalled. Then click on Close.

THE WORLD OF MICROSOFT WORD

Now that you've learned how to convert Word documents to make them available on the Web, you've reached a pinnacle of sorts. Your mastery of Word (in a very short time, I might add) enables you to share information, not just with the people down the hall, but with people all over the world.

If you've been paying attention, you've probably jumped around in this book, picking the plums you need right now and saving time by skipping extraneous information. Now it's time to put this book on the shelf and use it as a reference. The next time something doesn't work the way it should, or the next time you need to try something new, take this book down again and head directly for the answer you need. Now get back to work!

A

Installing Word

It's easy to install Word yourself, though of course it's easier to have someone else install it for you. However, if you're the one who gets stuck with the job, this appendix will help you over any bumps you might encounter. For the most part, you click on OK a lot until the process is done. I'll walk you through your options in this appendix.

STARTING THE SETUP PROGRAM

To install Word, start by going to the folder or disk drive in which the Setup program is located and double-clicking on the Setup icon, shown here. The Setup program will start. Alternatively, you can choose Start | Settings | Control Panel, double-click on Add/Remove Programs icon in the Control Panel window, click on the Install button in the top part of the Install/Uninstall tab, insert the Word installation disk into your computer, and then click on Next. When you click on the Finish button, the Setup program will start.

VERBOSE FEEDBACK

Word's setup spends a lot of time telling you what it's doing. (This is actually helpful if something goes wrong, because you'll be able to describe to a technical support person fairly accurately how far you got.) First it will tell you, "Starting Word [or Office] for Windows 95 Setup, please wait...." Then the Setup window and dialog box will appear. Click on Continue.

The Name and Organization Information dialog box will appear. Type your name, press TAB, and type the name of your organization (if any). Then click on OK. Click on OK again to confirm (or click on Change and retype if you catch an error).

The next screen shows your Product ID, a long serial number. Write it down on your registration card. (You might want to keep it somewhere else as well—although you can always find it by choosing Help | About. Keep this number handy in case a tech support person requests it.) Then click on OK.

If Setup finds an earlier version of Microsoft Word or Office already installed on your computer, it will ask you whether you want to overwrite the older version or put the new one in a different folder. It should be OK to overwrite the old one, but that's not my decision to make.

CHOOSING THE TYPE OF INSTALLATION

Next, Setup will ask you to choose whether you want a Typical, Custom, Full, or Compact installation. If you're not sure what you want, try the Typical choice. (You can always return to the Setup program later to install components that aren't part of the Typical installation. For example, not all the templates and Wizards come with that choice.)

If you choose a Typical, Full, or Compact installation, jump ahead in this appendix to the section titled "The Actual Installation."

ASSEMBLING A CUSTOM INSTALLATION

If you choose a Custom installation, Word will show you the Typical choices, but it will let you overrule them if you want. Figure A.1 shows the first set of choices. When you first view this box, it shows you what would be installed in a Typical installation. Checked components are installed in full, unchecked components are not installed, and grayed components are partially installed. The Setup program shows you how much space you have available on your drive, so you can add and subtract components to make everything fit. The following sections review this first set of choices.

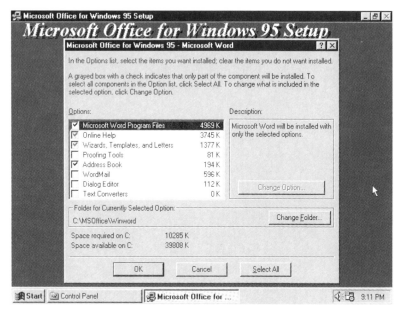

Figure A.1 The first list of options in a Custom installation

Microsoft Word Program Files

Leave this checked. You need them all.

Online Help

To choose among Online Help options, highlight this choice and click on the Change Option button. The components of Online Help (and their default settings) are

- Online Help for Microsoft Word (checked)
- WordBasic Help (unchecked)
- Help for WordPerfect Users (unchecked)

Check WordBasic Help if you plan to write complicated macros. Check Help for WordPerfect Users if you are more familiar with WordPerfect than with Word and would appreciate some pointed advice about the differences. (These help options will all be available from the Help menu.) Click on OK when you're done.

Wizards, Templates, and Letters

To choose among Wizards, Templates, and Letters options, highlight that choice and click on the Change Option button. The components of Wizards, Templates, and Letters (and their default settings) are

- Faxes (checked)
- Letters (checked)
- Memos (checked)
- Reports (checked)
- Forms (unchecked)

- More Wizards (unchecked)
- Newsletters (unchecked
- Press Releases (unchecked)
- Publications (unchecked)
- Resumes (unchecked)

- Table Wizard (unchecked)
- Sample Letters (unchecked)
- Macro Templates (unchecked)

The obvious trade-off here is between automation and disk storage. More Wizards is especially big. If you want all these elements, click on the Select All button at the bottom right. Click on OK when you're done.

Proofing Tools

Leave this as is. You definitely want all the proofing tools suggested for a Typical installation.

Address Book

Leave this checked. The address book is a handy tool not just for Word but for any program that can send e-mail or faxes.

WordMail

Check this if you'd prefer to use Word as your e-mail editor. Word will replace Microsoft Exchange's normal e-mail message window.

Dialog Editor

Leave this unchecked unless you're writing complicated applications from within Word.

Text Converters

If you can afford the space, I recommend that you install as many text converters as possible if you have to share documents with people using many different systems and word processing programs. Click on Text Converters and then click on the Change Option button. Then check as many of the options as you can fit. If your space is limited, skip Works for Windows (both versions) first, and then skip WordStar. (They are the least common alternatives these days.) When you're done, click on OK.

Done Choosing Custom Options?

Once you've explored all your options and suboptions, when you return to the original version of the dialog box, there will be a Continue button available. Click on the Continue button to proceed with the installation.

THE ACTUAL INSTALLATION

Setup will search for installed components and then let you know that it's checking for necessary disk space. If there's not enough room on your disk for the installation you've requested, Setup will tell you so. Click on the Change Options button to deselect some components of Word. (Go back to the section "Assembling a Custom Installation" for instructions on how to do this.)

Setup will then begin installing the program. While it copies files to your disk, it displays its progress and flashes informational and marketing blurbs on the screen (see Figure A.2).

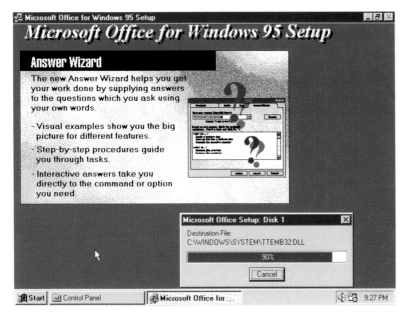

Figure A.2 Setup at work

Setup then tells you "Setup is updating your system." And finally you see "Microsoft Office for Windows 95 Setup was completed successfully."

RUNNING WORD FOR THE FIRST TIME

The first time you run Word, it automatically displays a What's New message (see Figure A.3). Click on the little gray squares to get more information about these new features.

IF SOMETHING GOES WRONG

If something goes wrong or if you interrupt the installation, Setup will display this dialog box:

Click on OK and then try to install the program again.

If the installation is stopped while Setup is copying files, it will display this dialog box:

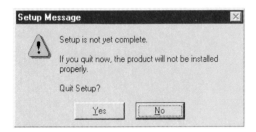

Click on No to continue with Setup as usual, or click on Yes to end the installation (for now). If you choose to halt the installation at this point, you'll have to repeat part of the installation the next time you try to install Word.

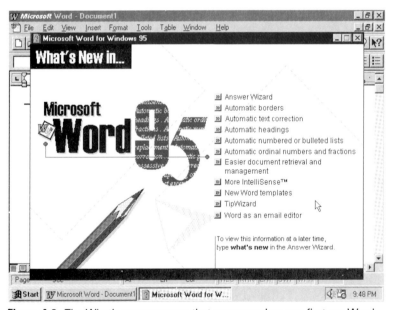

Figure A.3 The What's new message that appears when you first run Word

UNINSTALLING WORD

If at some point you want to take Word off your computer, choose Start | Settings | Control Panel and double-click on the Add/Remove Programs icon. Then choose Microsoft Word in the lower half of the dialog box that appears, and click on the Add/Remove button (see Figure A.4).

Alternatively, you can just open the Winword folder and double-click on the Setup icon. Either method will start the Setup program.

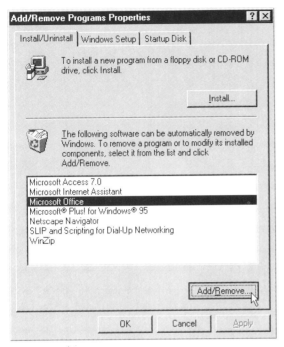

Figure A.4 The Add/Remove Programs Properties dialog box

Click on the Remove All button. (If you just want to change some components of the installation, click on the Add/Remove button and then follow the instructions in the "Assembling a Custom Installation" section earlier.) Setup asks you if you're sure you want to do this. Click on Yes. Setup mysteriously tells you that it is once again checking for necessary disk space. (It needs disk space to *remove* files?) A dialog box reports on Setup's progress as it removes files.

Setup then tells you that it is "updating your system," and finally it announces that Word was successfully uninstalled.

MAIL

CA

The Basics of Windows 95

This book assumes that you've already learned the basics of Windows 95, and have perhaps read *Windows 95 for Busy People* (Osborne/McGraw-Hill, 1996). But if you haven't, this appendix should help you get started.

All of Microsoft's Office 95 programs (Word, Excel, PowerPoint, Schedule +, and Access) were especially designed to take advantage of the new Windows 95 operating system. If you know your way around Windows 95, you have a leg up on getting the most out of these and many other programs.

THE DESKTOP

Windows 95 starts when you turn on your computer. You don't need to type anything first, but you might be asked for a password once or twice. If you don't know one of the passwords, try pressing the ESC key (you should be able to use Windows but you might not have access to your network or to e-mail; so if passwords are required, you should contact your network administrator to set one up). When Windows 95 starts, it displays a screen called the *desktop*. Figure B.1 shows a typical Windows 95 desktop. Yours might look different. That's perfectly OK.

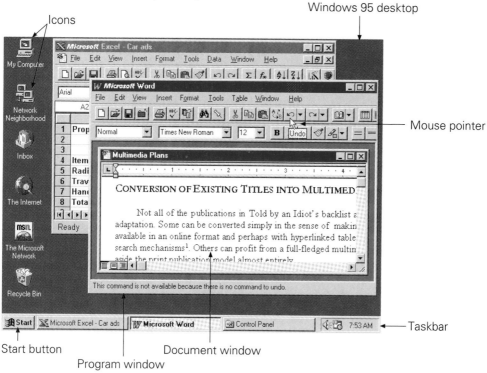

Figure B.1 A typical Windows 95 desktop

The desktop contains small pictures of items like disk drives, a recycle bin, and so on. These little pictures are called *icons*. At the bottom of the Windows 95 desktop you'll probably see the Taskbar, which will be discussed later in this appendix. Windows 95 also displays *windows*. These windows are the spaces in which you do your work. *Program windows* contain programs (like Word, or Excel, or whatever) and can also contain other windows, often called *document windows* or *child windows*. So, for example, you might have a Word window on your desktop with one or more word processing document windows inside it. Any time you double-click a folder icon (or an icon representing a disk drive), it will open up as a window on the screen (and a button on the Taskbar), showing the contents of the folder (or drive).

MOUSE BASICS

You use the mouse to point to objects on the desktop. (Incidentally, some computers have trackballs or other pointing devices, but all of these devices share some common characteristics: each has at least two buttons, and each lets you point to things.) As you move the mouse or other pointing device, a corresponding *pointer* moves on the desktop. Sometimes the shape of the pointer changes to give you a clue about what you can do next, because what you can do depends on what you're pointing to.

You can also make choices with the mouse (such as choosing a menu option), and you can use it to move and resize objects. You do this by pointing to something and clicking on it, which usually selects the object or causes something to happen. *Clicking* is accomplished by pressing and releasing a mouse button. *Double-clicking* is the act of pressing and releasing a mouse button twice in rapid succession. *Dragging* is the act of clicking on an object (a window, an icon, or whatever) and moving your mouse while holding down the button.

Most computer pointing devices (mice, trackballs, and so on) have two buttons. If the buttons are side by side, and if you have not modified Windows 95's default mouse settings, you will use the left button for clicking to select things and initiate most actions. You will also use the left button to drag objects around on the desktop and to change the size and shape of things. (Lefties who like to customize their environments—I'm a lefty myself, but more of the coping-with-a-righty-world type—can switch the functions of the right and left mouse buttons.)

Windows 95 makes extensive use of the right button as well. Clicking the right button (also called *right-clicking*) on almost any screen element will pop up a *shortcut menu* full of useful options. For example, you can change the appearance of your desktop by right-clicking just about anywhere on the desktop and choosing Properties from the menu that pops up. Many programs, including Word, will display shortcut menus when you use the right mouse button. Examples of right-clicking appear throughout this book.

There is one more mouse technique worth mentioning. It is called *hovering*. Frequently, if you slide the mouse pointer over an object and leave it there for a second, a little message called a *tool tip* will pop up that will tell you something about the object. In Figure B.1, for example, Word is telling you that the button under the mouse pointer is for activating the Undo feature.

THE TASKBAR

The Taskbar lets you easily run programs and switch from window to window. (If you don't see the Taskbar at the bottom of the desktop, slide your mouse pointer down to the bottom of the screen. The Taskbar should appear.) On the left end of the Taskbar you will always see the Start button. If you have opened windows or started programs (or if Windows has started them for you), your Taskbar will also contain other buttons. See "Taskbar Tips," later, for an explanation of how these buttons work.

The Start Menu

Let's begin with a look at the Start button and the Start menu that is displayed when you click on it. This is the menu from which you start programs, change Windows settings, retrieve recently used documents, find "lost" files, and get Windows 95 help. You point to items in the Start menu to choose them.

Everyone's Start menu looks a little different, particularly when you scratch the surface. (You can also add shortcuts to programs to the Start menu, such as the Winword item at the top of my menu, just shown.) The Start menu often reveals additional levels of menus called *submenus*. Let's look at the primary Start menu choices.

Programs

Roughly equivalent to the old Program Manager program groups in earlier versions of Windows, the Programs item on the Start menu pops up a submenu of programs and special Start menu folders. The folders themselves open sub-submenus, and so on. You can run any properly installed program in Windows 95 by clicking on the Start button, then clicking on the Programs choice in the Start menu, and then clicking on the desired program (or perhaps on a folder and then on a program in the folder).

Documents

The Start menu remembers the last 15 documents you've opened and displays their names in the Documents menu. (However, be forewarned that programs designed prior to Windows 95 often fail to add documents to the Documents menu.) When you want to work with a recently used document again, click on its name in the Documents menu. The document will appear on your screen in the program in which it was created. If the program is not already running, Windows 95 will launch it for you automatically.

Settings

To change the various settings for your computer, such as the way the Start menu looks or how your screen saver works, choose Settings from the Start menu and then choose Control Panel from the Settings submenu. From the resulting Control Panel window, a part of which is shown here, you can exercise centralized control over all of your computer's settings.

You'll need to consult online help and perhaps read a book like *Windows 95 for Busy People* to learn more about the thousands of possible setting changes.

Find

Windows 95's Find feature can be an invaluable aid for digging up files that seem to be lost in the system. To search for a file, choose Find from the Start menu and then choose Files or Folders. In the dialog box that appears, type a filename or part of one in the Named box and press ENTER or click on Find Now.

Help

Stuck? Not sure what to do? You can always consult Windows Help. To do so, choose Help from the Start menu. (If you're doing this for the first time, Windows will tell you that it's setting up Help.) In the Help Topics dialog box that appears (see Figure B.2), click on a topic from the expandable Contents list or click on the Index tab, type a key word in the first box, and choose a topic from the index list in the second box.

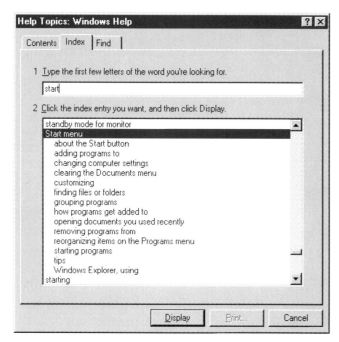

Figure B.2 Choose a topic or subtopic from the Help Topics dialog box

In most programs, if you're not sure what a button or other screen element does, you can hover the mouse pointer over it for a moment and a tool tip will appear, naming or explaining the object.

Also, in a dialog box, you can click on the What's This? button (a question mark) in the top-right corner and then click on the item in the dialog box that you want more information on. A brief explanation should pop up.

Run

Any time you know the name of a program file (although sometimes you also have to know the "path" of the folders on the hard disk that leads to the program), you can choose Run from the Start menu, type the name (or path and name) in the box, and press ENTER to run the program. It's usually easier, though, to start the program from the Start menu or one of its submenus.

Shut Down

When you want to turn off your computer, first shut down Windows 95. To do so, choose Shut Down from the Start menu. Click on Yes when asked if you want to shut down the computer. Wait until Windows tells you it's OK to turn off the computer, and then turn it off.

Taskbar Tips

Every time you start a program or open or minimize some types of windows, the program or window gets its own button on the Taskbar.

This makes it easy to switch to a program that is already running, to make a particular window active, or to maximize a window. All you have to do is click on the appropriate button on the Taskbar. When a button looks depressed (pushed in), it means that the task represented by the button is the active one, and its window will appear "in front of" the other windows.

If the Taskbar gets too crowded, you can point to its top edge and drag it so that it gets taller. You can also move the Taskbar to any side of the screen (top, bottom, left, or right) by clicking on any part of the Taskbar that is not a button and dragging. When the Taskbar is on the left or right side, you can drag its inner edge to set it to any width, up to half the width of the screen.

THE MY COMPUTER ICON

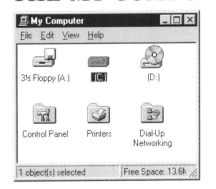

One way to explore the files and programs on your computer is to double-click on the My Computer icon. In general, double-clicking on an icon opens it, runs the program it represents, or runs the program in which the document it represents was created. If the icon is a folder or a special icon such as My Computer, it will open into a window and display its contents, which will also appear as icons. Some of these icons might represent programs, and others might represent folders or other special icons.

The My Computer window contains icons that represent your hard disk drive, floppy disk drives, and CD-ROM drive (if applicable), as well as icons for your printers, for dial-up networking, and for the Control Panel.

Double-click on the hard disk drive icon to see the contents of the hard disk. The icon opens into a window that shows folders and other icons. Double-click on any folder to see its contents. Repeat as often as necessary. You can go back up a folder level by pressing Backspace.

THE NETWORK NEIGHBORHOOD ICON

If your computer is connected to a network, you will see a Network Neighborhood icon on the desktop. Double-clicking on it will show you a list of the remote computers, disk drives, and folders that you can access.

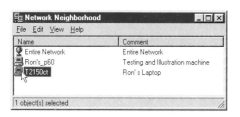

You might need to know the appropriate passwords to access some of the information on the network, and you might be limited in what you can do with files and folders on the network. For example, the owners of some files might let you read the files but not change them. When you have questions, contact your network administrator or help desk.

THE RECYCLE BIN

When you delete files in Windows 95, they are not immediately erased from the disk. They are moved to the Recycle Bin. To recover an accidentally deleted file, double-click on the Recycle Bin icon and choose the item or items you wish to restore. Then choose Restore from the File menu in the Recycle Bin window (see Figure B.3).

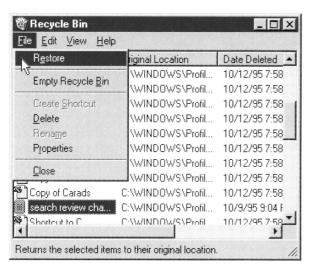

Figure B.3 The Recycle Bin gives you one more chance to "undelete" your files after trashing them

As you add new files to the Recycle Bin, Windows will eventually start discarding the earliest files left. If you want to free up space, right-click on the Recycle Bin and choose Empty Recycle Bin on the File menu.

FOLDERS

You and Windows 95 can organize your files into *folders,* which are the equivalent of directories in oldspeak. You can place folders within folders, thereby creating what used to be called subdirectories. You can create a new folder at any point by right-clicking on the desktop or in a folder (or disk drive) window and choosing New | Folder. You can put a document or program in a folder by dragging its icon onto a folder icon or into an open folder window.

NEW RULES FOR FILENAMES

Windows 95 allows you to use long filenames (up to 255 characters) that include spaces, if you want, so you can give your documents natural sounding names, instead of the pinched, cryptic filenames that DOS used to force on you. Now you can call that document Amortization Projections for 1997 instead of AMTPRJ97.

You might also notice that filename extensions seem to have pretty much disappeared. They're still there at the ends of filenames, but Windows hides all the extensions it recognizes. If you want to see the extensions associated with all filenames, choose Options from the View menu in the My Computer window, the Windows Explorer window, or any folder (or disk drive) window. Click on the View tab. Then uncheck Hide MS-DOS file extensions for file types that are registered. Click on OK. All extensions will appear. To hide most extensions again, repeat the same steps and check the box.

When you are sharing files with non-Windows 95 users, and with programs that were sold prior to the release of Windows 95, filenames get shortened automatically. This can cause some confusion. Again, consult online help and Windows 95 books for details.

WINDOWS EXPLORER

Windows 95 allows you to look through the folders on your computer in a single window, with the entire folder tree in a pane on the left side (sort of like the old File Manager). To do this, choose Programs from the Start menu and Windows Explorer from the Programs menu (or right-click on any folder and choose Explore from the menu that pops up). The Windows Explorer window will appear (see Figure B.4), with its folder tree in the left pane and the contents of the selected folder in the right pane.

To see the contents of a folder, click on it in the left pane. To expand or collapse a folder's contents, double-click on the folder in the left pane (or click the little plus or minus icon in a box to the left of the folder). You can go up a folder level by pressing Backspace, as you can in any such window.

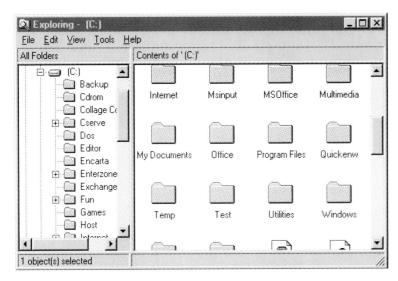

Figure B.4 The Explorer window shows a hierarchical view of the computer in its left pane. There you can thumb through your tree of folders without having to plow through separate folder windows

SHORTCUT ICONS

Windows 95 allows you to create *shortcut icons* that "point to" a program, document, folder, or other Windows 95 resource that you use regularly. This is particularly useful when something you use every day is "buried" in a folder within a folder. A popular place to keep shortcuts is on the desktop. That way, when you want to open your favorite folder, you just double-click on the shortcut icon on the desktop. Another place you can create a shortcut is on the Start menu, where it will look like a normal menu choice, not like a shortcut icon.

In general, the easiest way to create a shortcut is to right-click and drag a copy of the program's icon to the place where you want the shortcut. To do this, open the window that contains the program's original icon. Right-click on the icon and drag to a new location, such as another folder or the desktop. When you release the mouse button, a menu will pop up. Choose Create Shortcut(s) Here to make the shortcut. You'll probably want to rename the new shortcut icon. (Press F2, type a new name, and press ENTER.) If you drag an icon onto the Start button, even without first *right*-clicking, a shortcut to that icon will be placed on the Start menu.

THAT'S THE SHORT COURSE

Well, there you have a taste of Windows 95. Obviously, there's a lot more worth knowing. And the more you learn, the more productive you will become, so I encourage you to do some independent study, either by using Windows 95's online help or by cracking a good book or two.

Index

The Books to Use When There's No Time to Lose

Computer Fundamentals for Complicated Lives

Whether you set aside an *evening*, a *lunch hour*, or reach for a **Busy People** guide as you need it, you're guaranteed to save time with Windows 95 and its associated productivity applications. Organized for a quick orientation to Windows 95, Word, Excel, Access, and the Internet, each **Busy People** title offers exceptional time-saving features and has the right blend of vital skills and handy shortcuts that you must know to get a job done quickly and accurately. Full-color text make the going easy and fun.

　　Written by a busy person (like you!) with a skeptic's view of computing, these opinionated, well-organized, and authoritative books are all you'll need to master the important ins and outs of Windows 95 and other best-selling software releases—without wasting your precious hours!

To Order, Call Toll Free **1-800-822-8158**

OSBORNE

Leaders of the Pack

The Internet
Health, Fitness & Medicine
Yellow Pages
by Matthew Naythons, M.D. with Anthony Catsimatides
$22.95 U.S.A.
ISBN: 0-07-882188-6

The Internet Yellow Pages
Third Edition
by Harley Hahn
$29.95 U.S.A.
ISBN: 0-07-882182-7

The Internet Science,
Research & Technology
Yellow Pages
by Rick Stout and Morgan Davis
$22.95 U.S.A.
ISBN: 0-07-882187-8

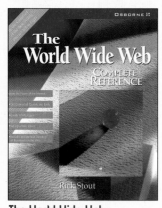

The World Wide Web
Complete Reference
by Rick Stout
$29.95 U.S.A.
ISBN: 0-07-882142-8

NetLaw:
Your Rights in the Online World
by Lance Rose
$19.95 U.S.A.
ISBN: 0-07-882077-4

The Internet
Complete Reference
Second Edition
by Harley Hahn
$32.95 U.S.A.
ISBN: 0-07-882138-X

To Order, Call Toll Free **1-800-822-8158**
By Mail: Osborne/McGraw-Hill Order Services, P.O. Box 545, Blacklick, OH 43004-0546, FAX 1-614-755-5654

OSBORNE
McGRAW-HILL

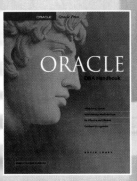